ORIGINS
Volume 2
The Word Families

ORIGINS
Volume 2
The Word Families

by Sandra R. Robinson
with Lindsay McAuliffe

Teachers & Writers Collaborative
New York

Origins: Volume 2

Copyright © 1989 by Sandra R. Robinson and Lindsay McAuliffe. All rights reserved. Printed in the United States of America. No part of this publication may be reproduced, stored in a retrieval system, or transmitted, in any form or by any means, electronic, mechanical, photocopying, recording, or otherwise, without prior written permission of the publisher.

Teachers & Writers is grateful to the following foundations and corporations for their support of our program: American Stock Exchange, Mr. Bingham's Trust for Charity, Columbia Committee for Community Service, Consolidated Edison, Aaron Diamond Foundation, Manufacturers Hanover Trust Company, Mobil Foundation, Morgan Stanley Foundation, New York Telephone, New York Times Company Foundation, Henry Nias Foundation, Helena Rubinstein Foundation, the Scherman Foundation, and the Steele-Reese Foundation. T&W also receives funds from the New York State Council on the Arts, the National Endowment for the Arts, and the New York Foundation for the Arts Artists-in-Residence Program, administered by the Foundation on behalf of the New York State Council on the Arts and in cooperation with the New York State Education Department with funds provided by the National Endowment for the Arts and the Council.

Teachers & Writers Collaborative
5 Union Square West
New York, N.Y. 10003

Library of Congress Cataloging-in-Publication Data

Robinson, Sandra R. (Sandra Rockwell), 1944-
    Origins: bringing words to life / by Sandra R. Robinson
  with Lindsay McAuliffe
        p.   c.m.
        Bibliography: p.
        ISBN 0-915924-90-0 (set) — ISBN 0-915924-91-9 (v. 1). —0-915924-92-7 (v. 2).
    1. English language—Etymology—Studying and teaching. 2.
English language—Studying and teaching. 3. Vocabulary—
Studying and teaching.
I. McAuliffe, Lindsay. II. Title.
PE 1576.R6 1989
422´.071´073—dc20   89-31355
                                                                           CIP

Photographs: Sally Halvorson
Word trees: Trevor Winkfield

Printed by Philmark Lithographics, New York, N.Y.

Permissions

"Legend" from *The Gateway* by Judith Wright reprinted by permission of Angus & Robertson, Ltd. • "The Flattered Flying Fish" from *The Flattered Flying Fish & Other Poems* by E.V. Rieu reprinted by permission of Associated Book Publishers PLC. • "Hymn to the Sun" and "Song for the Sun That Disappeared behind the Rainclouds" from *African Poetry* edited by Ulli Beier. Reprinted by permission of Cambridge University Press and Professor Beier. • "The Extraordinary Adventure that Happened to Me, Vladimir Maiakovsky, at the Rumiantsev Dacha, Pushkino, Akulovo Mountain, on the Iaroslavl' Rail Line" by Vladimir Maiakovsky and "Twilight" by Fyodor Tiutchev translated by Christopher Edgar. Reprinted by permission of the translator. • "Fireworks" and "Marbles" from *More Small Poems* by Valerie Worth. Copyright © 1976 by Valerie Worth. Reprinted by permission of Farrar, Straus and Giroux, Inc. • "Prairie Waters by Night" from *Cornhuskers* by Carl Sandburg, copyright 1918 by Holt, Rinehart and Winston, Inc. and renewed 1946 by Carl Sandburg, reprinted by permission of Harcourt Brace Jovanovich, Inc. • "Listening to grownups quarreling" from *The Marriage Wig and Other Poems*, copyright © 1968 by Ruth Whitman, reprinted by permission of Harcourt Brace Jovanovich, Inc. • "Number 5—December" by David Henderson from *Black Out Loud* edited by Arnold Adoff used by permission of the author. • "The Dream Keeper" by Langston Hughes. Copyright 1932 and renewed 1960 by Langston Hughes. Reprinted from *The Dream Keeper and Other Poems* by Langston Hughes, by permission of Alfred A. Knopf, Inc. "The Negro Speaks of Rivers" copyright 1926 by Alfred A. Knopf, Inc. and renewed 1954 by Langston Hughes. Reprinted from *The Selected Poems of Langston Hughes* by permission of Alfred A. Knopf, Inc. • "l)a" is reprinted from *Complete Poems, 1913-1962* by e.e. cummings, by permission of Liveright Publishing Corporation. Copyright © 1923, 1925, 1931, 1935, 1938, 1939, 1940, 1944, 1945, 1946, 1947, 1948, 1949, 1950, 1951, 1952, 1953, 1954, 1955, 1956, 1957, 1958, 1959, 1960, 1961, 1962 by the Trustees for the E.E. Cummings Trust. Copyright © 1961, 1963, 1968 by Marion Morehouse Cummings. • "Those Winter Sundays" and excerpt from "Runagate, Runagate" by Robert Hayden. Reprinted from *Angle of Ascent: New & Selected Poems*, by Robert Hayden, by permission of Liveright Publishing Corporation. Copyright © 1975, 1972, 1970, 1966 by Robert Hayden. • "The Cat and the Moon" by W.B. Yeats. Reprinted with permission of Macmillan Publishing Company from *The Poems of W.B. Yeats: A New Edition*, edited by Richard J. Finneran. Copyright 1919 by Macmillan Publishing Company, renewed 1947 by Bertha Georgie Yeats. • "Learn to Be a Rock" by Matthew Barzun and "Wings" by Elizabeth McKim from *Beyond Words* published by Wampeter Press, Green Harbor, Massachusetts, 1983. Reprinted by permission of Elizabeth McKim. • "The Giraffe" from *Tulsa Kid* by Ron Padgett, published by Z Press, Calais, Vermont, 1979. Used by permission of the author. • "The Invisible Beast" and "The Poltergeist" from *The Headless Horseman Rides Tonight: More Poems to Trouble Your Sleep* by Jack Prelutsky. Copyright © by Jack Prelutsky and Greenwillow Books (a division of William Morrow and Co., Inc.) Reprinted by permission of Greenwillow Books. • "Life Doesn't Frighten Me" from *And Still I Rise* by Maya Angelou. Copyright © 1978 by Maya Angelou. Reprinted by permission of Random House, Inc. • "When the Shadows Meet the Stars" and "The Idea" by Veronica Schanoes reprinted by permission of David and Veronica Schanoes. • "Riding at Daybreak" by Sun Yung Feng from *Poems of the Hundred Names* edited and translated by Henry H. Hart. Reprinted by permission of Stanford University Press. • "In the Mountains on a Summer Day" by Li Po from *Chinese Poems* translated by Arthur Waley and published by George Allen & Unwin, Ltd. Reprinted by permission of Unwin Hyman, Ltd. We regret that we were unable to locate Barbara Mahone to request permission to reprint her poem "sugarfields," and Alden Nowlan to request permission to reprint his poem "I, Icarus."

Table of Contents

The BHEL Family 1
The DHREU Family 19
The GHEIS Family 31
The KER Family 43
The GHEL Family 61
The FLEU Family 83
The MEDHYO Famiy 105
The KEL Family 115
The WER Family 127
The DWO Family 145
The DERU Family 165
The OINO Family 177
Student Word Tree 194

The BHEL chapter begins with a plunge into familiar words that reveal the pattern and imagery of the word family and takes an informal look at "extensions" of their meanings. It includes a pantomime that gets students to their feet for some high-spirited dramatic play that can both illuminate the word *bold* and introduce the poetry that accompanies the family. If you use the BHEL chapter first, be sure to review the "Using *Origins*" chapter in Volume 1 for ideas teachers have used to introduce the concept of word families and for the ideas underlying the materials of all the word family chapters.

Materials useful for introducing the family are: a balloon, a ball, two grocery bags, and a bulky sweater or parka.

Introduction to the BHEL Word Family

BHEL—*to swell*		
balloon	bowl	bulky
ball	bulge	billow
belly	boulder	bold

BALLOON, BALL, BELLY, BOWL

These familiar words can readily introduce the look of the family and provide graphic examples of the image of *swelling* that lies at its root. Here are possible starting points:

> Inflate a balloon. What happens?
> What part of you swells outward after you eat a huge meal? Try a group pantomime.
> How are a ball and a balloon related? What happens if a ball is deflated? What might you do to restore its shape?
> What do we eat from that resembles the "swelled" shape of a ball or balloon?

Elicit the words, record them on the board and ask students to detect what spelling pattern they all share. What letters do they all have in common? What comes between the *b* and the *l*?

The *b*-vowel-*l* pattern is typical of the spelling patterns of *Origins* families. You may want to discuss why the vowels—and not the consonants—are likely to change over time. (*Ow* is considered a vowel combination.) See the "Linguistic Background" chapter in Volume 1.

Be sure you have elicited and recorded the root meaning of the family, *to swell*.

> *Belly* is used to refer to part of an airplane or ship. Which part? Why?
>
> Why do you think the word *bowl* came to be used in the names Super Bowl, Rose Bowl, etc.?
>
> What are *balloon* tires? *Balloon* sleeves? What picture comes to your mind if you hear a description of "sails *ballooning* outward in the wind"? What else might balloon outward? What does "Membership in the club has really *ballooned* this year" mean? Did membership shrink or swell?

BULGE

Start with a group demonstration.

> Use your arm to show you've got the strongest muscles in the world. We could describe those muscles as swelling or...
>
> *bulging.*
>
> When something swells out from a surface, we describe it as "bulging." Muscles can bulge; bellies can bulge with food or a baby. What are some other examples of bulging?
>
> A squirrel with nuts in its cheeks.
> A plug of tobacco or wad of gum in someone's cheek.
> The eyes of a frog, which bulge to allow the frog to see in all directions.
> Pockets that are overstuffed.

Algy

> Algy met a bear,
> The bear met Algy,
> The bear was bulgy,
> The bulge was Algy.
>
> —*Anonymous*

Here are ways you might use "Algy" during or after exploring the word family:

• Have students pantomime the poem. You might supply the bear with an improvised cloak for "swallowing" Algy.

• If you like, use a pantomime of "Algy" as a possible alternative introduction to the BHEL family or an introduction to a second session of exploring the family.

• Hand out copies of the poem and ask students to illustrate the scene it describes. Let them draw without preliminary discussion.

In some parts of the South, the expression "to get the bulge" on someone means to take advantage of them or get ahead of them. How does "getting the bulge" on someone relate to images of things bulging outward?

BOULDER

You are in the countryside or the woods, and you see a large, rounded rock. That kind of large and rounded rock—that looks swelled up—is called a...

> *boulder.*

The swollen appearance of a boulder has to do only with how it looks. Rather than having swelled up, the boulder has in fact been worn into a rounded shape by thousands of years of water, ice, and wind-blown dirt. The people who named the boulder hundreds of years ago didn't know this history, however. To them the boulder *looked* swelled up, and they named it for its appearance.

BULKY

Stuffed grocery bags are good for introducing *bulky*. Have a volunteer hold one bag in each arm, then set a scene that will bring out the meaning of *bulky* as "awkwardly large."

> You have just done some shopping, and now you have to take the bus home. Is it going to be easy for you to get on the bus with those two large packages? What kinds of problems might you have?
>
> Who knows a word we could use to describe things like these packages that are awkwardly or inconveniently large? Remember, we are looking for a word that is a member of today's family, so it will share the *b-vowel-l* pattern.
>
>> *Bulky.*
>
> What connection can you see between our bulky packages and the root idea "to swell"?
>
>> The packages "swell up" to a large size because they are stuffed full.

A bulky parka or a bulky knit sweater can also show how the word is used. Have a volunteer put on a bulky parka or sweater.

> Why might we describe the parka/sweater as bulky?
>
>> It is large in a "puffed up" kind of way.
>
> Would it be easy to play an active game like tag in a bulky parka/sweater?
>
>> Bulky clothes are too large and awkward for quick games.

BILLOW

Swelling waves; curtains, banners or flags bellying outward in the breeze; smoke rising in swelling clouds from a fire—all of these can be described by another of the BHEL words, one that is lighter in spirit than the others...

billow.

Or here's a poem you can use to introduce the word.

Fireworks

First
A far thud,
Then the rocket
Climbs the air,
A dull red flare,
To hang, a moment,
Invisible, before
Its shut black shell cracks
And claps against the ears,
Breaks and billows into bloom,
Spilling down clear green sparks, gold spears,
Silent sliding silver waterfalls and stars.

—Valery Worth

BOLD

A pantomime that emphasizes the contrast between how we hold our bodies when feeling scared and how we hold them when feeling brave can provide a lively introduction to *bold*. Have all students stand and participate. Encourage exaggeration.

A huge monster is approaching and you are terrified. Show with your body that you are feeling very scared. Now freeze in that pose.

But suddenly you feel a burst of courage. The monster doesn't look so threatening after all. You're going to fight back and kill it. Show how you feel now. Show how brave you're feeling by the way you stand.

As you shifted from showing how scared you were to showing how brave you were, did you make yourself look bigger or smaller?

Does anyone know a word that means "brave" and might be part of today's family? Remember, we're looking for a *b-vowel-l* pattern.

If no one volunteers *bold*, supply the word.

The word *bold* had its origins in the battle tactics of warriors, who plunged into battle with a terrifying war cry to make themselves look and feel larger. The lungs of a bold warrior would indeed swell as he gathered force for that cry.

We still tend to draw up to our fullest size when feeling bold. The same connection between a bold appearance and swelling in size can be observed in many animals. What animals make themselves look bigger in order to scare an enemy?

> Cats, lions, and tigers make their hair stand on end before a fight.
> Some fish inflate themselves to scare an enemy.
> Owls and swans ruffle their feathers to intimidate intruders.

Which is going to grab your attention more—a person or animal who is taking a bold stand to scare off the enemy or one who is trying to shrink out of sight in fright? What is *bold* print? How does it grab your attention?

In Appalachia, a *bold* running stream is a *swift* running stream. How does this meaning connect with the root image of swelling? Does a stream run more swiftly before or after a rain? We also refer to it as a "swollen" stream.

The Root: Meaning and Spelling

Review the spelling pattern shared by all the words by having a volunteer underline the *b*-vowel-*l* pattern in each of the words on the board.

What spelling pattern is our root likely to have?

> *b*-vowel-*l*

The root from which all of the words in today's family grew is BHEL.

And what is the meaning of BHEL?

> *To swell.*

What letter in BHEL is no longer part of the spelling pattern shared by the words of the BHEL family?

> The letter *h*.

What happened to the letter *h*? Originally, it represented a breathy sound following the *b* of BHEL. Gradually, however, people stopped pronouncing that breathy sound.

Are there any letters in today's words that people don't pronounce? Some people don't pronounce the final *d* of bold.

(See the "Linguistic Background" chapter for further information.)

A Note on "Sound Cousins"

The word *bellow* means "to make a loud, deep noise; roar; shout loudly," and is often proposed as a member of the BHEL family. Although *bellow* does not happen to come from the same root as the other words of the family, it can legitimately be considered a "sound cousin" of the family and listed to the side of the word tree. Linguists recognize that words that share a spelling pattern and some area of meaning do bear a relationship to each other. *Bellow* not only shares a spelling pattern with the BHEL words, it also shares in the imagery of "swelling"—lungs have to swell to produce a roar or shout. Three other words, *bell, belch,* and *bawl,* come from the same root as *bellow* (a root meaning "to roar, shout") and can also be considered sound cousins. See the section on sound cousins in the "Using *Origins*" chapter for further discussion.

The Word Trees

As soon as you have completed the introduction to the BHEL family, hand out some 3 x 5 cards (or other suitable slips of paper) and ask for volunteers to record the root and words of the family for the class word tree. Then hand out the individual word trees (a tree to copy is found at the end of each volume of *Origins*) and ask students to fill in the root and the words of the family for their own notebooks.

Student Illustrations

Brainstorm ideas with the entire class for a "picture that tells a story" and include as many words of the BHEL family as possible. When introducing the idea of integrating the words of the family into one illustration, it is sometimes useful to share a sample of how other students have done this. A sample student illustration is included in the "Using *Origins*" chapter.

Definitions to Record

bulge: to swell outward
bulky: awkwardly large
boulder: a large, rounded rock
bold: brave and daring
billow: 1. to surge or swell
2. a great, swelling wave or surge of water, smoke, cloth, etc.

Story Puzzle

When you introduce the story puzzle "Bold Jack, the Giant Killer," let students know that in some cases they will need to add endings (*-ed, -s, -ing*) to make words of the BHEL family fit the blanks. Because words of a family occasionally have some overlap in meaning, a given word may fit logically in more than one space. Using the same word twice is not wrong, but the challenge of the puzzle is to use all the words of the family instead of repeating any of them. Some students might like to experiment with intentionally putting the wrong words in the blanks, an exercise that can illuminate the words in offbeat ways.

Additional Related Words

BOLSTER: 1. a long pillow or cushion for a bed or couch
2. to prop up

The second meaning is rooted in the image of propping up with pillows or cushions and is used both literally and figuratively.

Nina always props herself up with one of the bolsters from the couch while she watches Monday night football.

Tony's praise bolstered my confidence.

BLOAT: to swell up; puff up

Their stomachs were bloated after they stuffed themselves with cake and ice cream.

BOLE: the stem or trunk of a tree

To early observers the trunk of a tree might indeed have seemed to swell with life and energy as, each year, it grew wider and taller.

BOLL: the rounded seed pod of a plant, especially cotton or flax

The boll weevil is a small beetle whose larva lives in and causes damage to cotton bolls.

BELLOWS

The bellows used for blowing the sparks of a fire into flames is a member of the family.

BALE: a large bundle wrapped or bound for shipping or storage; to wrap in bundles

If students are familiar with bales of cotton or bales of hay, they might be interested to know this word is a member of the family.

Life Doesn't Frighten Me at All

Shadows on the wall
Noises down the hall
Life doesn't frighten me at all
Bad dogs barking loud
Big ghosts in a cloud
Life doesn't frighten me at all.

Mean old Mother Goose
Lions on the loose
They don't frighten me at all
Dragons breathing flame
On my counterpane
That doesn't
frighten me at all.

I go boo
Make them shoo
I make fun
Way they run
I won't cry
So they fly
I just smile
They go wild
Life doesn't frighten me at all.

Tough guys in a fight
All alone at night
Life doesn't frighten me at all.
Panthers in the park
Strangers in the dark
No, they don't frighten me at all.

That new classroom where
Boys all pull my hair
(Kissy little girls
with their hair in curls)
They don't frighten me at all.

Don't show me frogs and snakes
And listen for my scream,
If I'm afraid at all
It's only in my dreams.

I've got a magic charm
That I keep up my sleeve,
I can walk the ocean floor
And never have to breathe.

Life doesn't frighten me at all
Not at all
Not at all.
Life doesn't frighten me at all.

—*Maya Angelou*

Legend

The blacksmith's boy went out with a rifle
and a black dog running behind.
Cobwebs snatched at his feet,
rivers hindered him,
thorn branches caught at his eyes to make him blind
and the sky turned into an unlucky opal,
but he didn't mind,
I can break branches, I can swim rivers, I can stare out any spider I meet,
said he to his dog and his rifle.

The blacksmith's boy went over the paddocks
with his old black hat on his head.
Mountains jumped in his way, rocks rolled down on him,
and the old crow cried, You'll soon be dead.

And the rain came down like mattocks.
But he only said
I can climb mountains, I can dodge rocks, I can shoot any old crow any day,
and he went over the paddocks.

When he came to the end of the day the sun began falling.
Up came the night ready to swallow him,
like the barrel of a gun, like an old black hat,
like a black dog hungry to follow him.
Then the pigeon, the magpie and the dove began wailing
and the grass lay down to billow him.
His rifle broke, his hat flew away and his dog was gone
and the sun was falling.

But in front of the night the rainbow stood on a mountain
just as his heart foretold. He ran like a hare
he climbed like a fox;
he caught it in his hands, the colour and the cold—
like a bar of ice, like the column of a fountain,
like a ring of gold.
The pigeon, the magpie and the dove flew up to stare,
and the grass stood up again on the mountain.

The blacksmith's boy hung the rainbow on his shoulder
instead of his broken gun.
Lizards ran out to see,
snakes made way for him,
and the rainbow shone as brightly as the sun.
All the world said, Nobody is braver, nobody is bolder
nobody else has done
anything to equal it. He went home as bold as he could be
with the swinging rainbow on his shoulder.

—Judith Wright

Discussion and Writing Ideas

The write-ups below include pantomimes for introducing and exploring the poems as well as writing ideas.

• Life Doesn't Frighten Me at All

Has life got you down? Feel like a weakling? Up on your feet for a little practice in being bold. We'll begin with the body. Shake off the shivers and begin to think bold. Plant yourself firmly on your feet and imagine your strongest, most invincible self. How would you hold your head? Chin down or thrust out to meet the world head-on? Eyes downcast or wide open? How would you express determination with your mouth? Now find your shoulders and arms. What is your most powerful pose? Find it and hold it all the way down to your fingertips. Now consider your legs and torso. How can you make yourself look bigger and more fierce?

Now that your body is warmed up, stay on your feet and read "Life Doesn't Frighten Me" by Maya Angelou. Try for your boldest voice. How many scary or intimidating things does she mention? How does repetition add force to her bold stance? With classmates, brainstorm for a list of as many frightening things as you can think of, both imaginary and real. Does your list "frighten (you) at all"?

• Legend

Read "Legend" by Judith Wright. What challenges and difficulties confront the blacksmith's boy on his journey? Which lines describing these obstacles are your favorite? What bold boasts does the boy make in response? At the end of the poem, how is the boy's boldness different from the boldness he expresses in his boasts? (Why do you think the poem is called "Legend" and not, say, "Journey" or "Adventure"?) Which boldness is more joyful? Which is tougher? Which appeals to you the most?

Now invent your own bold boasts. Your claims can be as extravagant as you wish. You can be tough or you can claim magical powers that will help you overcome any challenge. With classmates, brainstorm bold boasts and, in addition, obstacles to be overcome. Select your favorite boasts and obstacles and include them in a poem of your own.

❧

Pantomime can help students understand this poem better. Push back all the tables and chairs. Read "Legend" aloud, making a list of all the characters, both animate and inanimate. Read it a second time, searching out the action for each character. Begin with the obvious action, such as the thorn branches that "caught at his eyes to make him blind" or the cobwebs that "snatched at his feet." Have one person play the role of the blacksmith's boy and others act out the obstacles he encountered. Next try some harder lines. How might the sky turn into "an unlucky opal"? How might rivers hinder him? How might the rain come down like mattocks? How can you use your body to interpret the action? When everybody has had enough practice, choose parts for a group dramatization of the poem. Tables and chairs might be used as "tree" perches for the magpie, crow, pigeon, and dove. You also might suggest that the rainbow and the mountain work together, since one needs to appear on top of the other. When everybody feels set, you're ready to roll. Read the poem aloud and let the action unfold.

Story Puzzle for Students

Read the story to yourself before filling in the blanks with words from your BHEL word tree. In some cases the same word will fit in more than one place. However, the challenge is to see if you can find a way to use *all* the words of the BHEL family.

Bold Jack, the Giant Killer

I'm going to tell you a story just the way I heard it from my granddaddy in the Tennessee mountains. It's a story about a boy named Jack. Jack is awful lazy sometimes, but very clever. He gets himself into all sorts of trouble, like that time he met a giant. Here's what happened.

Jack was walking down a dirt road about noon and wishing his empty _____ would stop rumbling. He sure was hungry. He sure was tired. He put down the _____ sack of coal he was carrying to market. Just then he looked up and saw a fine big stone house sitting on a hill. He figured that some rich folks must live there and wondered if he might ask them for a _____ of soup and a glass of milk. Jack stepped up to the door and hollered, "Hello!" A tall man wearing an old tin crown greeted him. "Hello, stranger. What'll you have?"

"I'm awful hungry and looking for a meal," said Jack. "I'll do a job of work for you in return."

"Well now," said the man, "I'm king of these parts and I could use a strong worker. Can you clear my land of all the rocks and trees?"

"Sure enough," replied Jack. "Won't take me but a day."

"Can you kill giants?" asked the king.

"Well, I reckon I could try," said Jack.

"Good," said the king, "because an old giant lives up in that field yonder and he won't let anybody near enough to clear and plow the land. If you can and he won't let anybody near enough to clear and plow the land. If you can get rid of the giant, I'll pay you a thousand dollars. Now you come in and have some dinner with me."

After Jack had eaten his fill, he started off with an ax to clear the field. He'd just begun to cut down a tree when a fearful sight appeared over the ridge. A two-headed giant was stomping and crashing toward him. Muscles _____ beneath his shirt. One pair of eyes were as big as basket_____ and one pair of ears were as big as inflated _____.

"Law me!" exclaimed Jack. "I can't stand the sight of that. I'll hide."

Quickly, he bounded into a hollow tree log and crouched low. The giant's two heads looked all around, trying to find the tree-cutter. Jack picked up a rock and hurled it toward one of the giant's heads.

"Ouch! Why'd you hit me?" said one head to the other.

"I didn't," said the second head. Jack leaped behind a bush and fired off another rock. "Now stop hitting me," warned the first head, "or I'll put a mark on you that won't rub off."

"I didn't touch you," complained the second head. Jack climbed a tree, ran behind a stump, and hid behind a _____, throwing rocks every time. Finally, the two heads of the giant got so angry at each other that the body started fighting with itself. The giant rushed this way and that, tumbling on the ground, knocking down trees, kicking up rocks and dirt. His tunic _____ out behind him, flapping in the wind like the wings of an old crow. He made such a racket that the earth shook—and everything in his path was cleared flat as a board. The giant took off from the king's land, never to be seen in those parts again.

Now, Jack watched all of this and felt quite satisfied with himself. "I reckon it's time to collect my reward money," he said and he set off for the king's house. The king was very surprised to see Jack at his door.

"Law me!" said the king. "I didn't think I'd see you here alive. You must be a brave and _____ young man."

"There wasn't nothing to it," smiled Jack.

Last I heard, Jack was living happily with his folks down in the holler and they had more than enough food on their table.

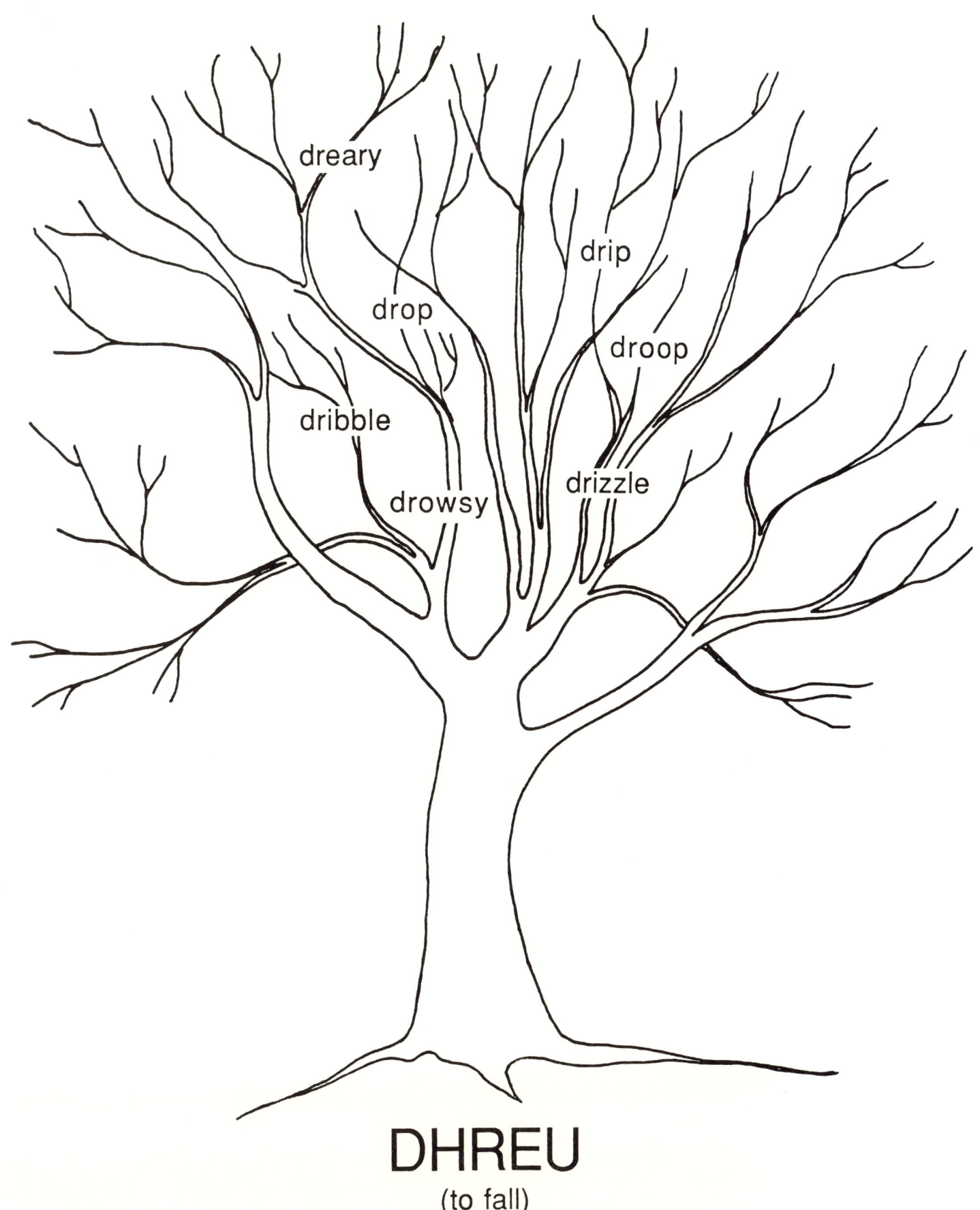

The DHREU chapter introduces a soggy, droopy, drowsy vocabulary and poetry that evokes and extends the imagery of the family. A rainy day is ideal for immersing yourself in it. As counterpoint to the "falling" imagery of the DHREU family, you may want to brainstorm words and phrases that reflect connections between images of "up" and feelings of happiness. Both the DHREU and GHEL chapters can alert students to how our language and literature often suggest connections between inner and outer weather.

Materials useful for introducing the family are: a non-breakable object to drop on the floor, a rag, a pan of water, and a basketball.

Introduction to the DHREU Word Family

> **DHREU**—*to fall*
>
> | | | |
> |---|---|---|
> | drip | drizzle | droop |
> | drop | dreary | drowsy |
> | | dribble | |

DRIP, DROP, DRIBBLE

Ask for three volunteers. Give one volunteer (we'll call him Eric) a pan of water and a rag. Ask him to soak the rag in the water, then hold it, dripping wet, high enough so the rest of the class can see the water dripping from the rag into the pan. Have him dip the rag in the pan as often as necessary to keep it dripping wet while you are asking questions about the scene.

Give the second volunteer (we'll call her Nichole) an object—an eraser, a pencil, anything handy—and ask her to drop the object repeatedly on the floor. Humorous dramatic play in this scene helps focus attention on the idea of dropping rather than on the idea of releasing, the idea students tend to focus on when a volunteer merely holds an object, then deliberately lets go of it. Nichole might pretend she is trying to hold onto the object, but fumble with it as though it were a hot potato and drop it "accidentally" each time she picks it up.

Give the third volunteer (we'll call her Shelley) a basketball and ask her to dribble it. Have the three volunteers stand side by side so the class can compare the *dripping* water, the *dropping* object, and the *dribbling* of the basketball.

> We've got quite a lot of movement in these three scenes. Let's see if we can find some words to describe what's going on. What's happening to the water in Eric's rag?
>
> > It's *dripping/falling/dropping* into the basin.
>
> What's happening to Nichole's object? What is she doing with it?
>
> > She keeps *dropping* it, letting it *fall*.
>
> And what is Shelley doing with the basketball?
>
> > *Dribbling* it.
>
> What is the same about the movement in each of these three scenes? What do they all have in common?
>
> > They all involve *dropping* or *falling*.

Record *drop, drip* and *dribble* on the board as the first three words of the family. Explain that *fall* is the root meaning of today's family as you record it on the board. Be sure you pantomime how *drip, drop,* and *dribble* might have grown from the root idea of falling.

> What do you think the spelling pattern for today's family is going to be?
>
> *d-r-*vowel
>
> What's another example of *dribbling*? What happens to babies when they're drinking something?
>
> What they're drinking *dribbles* down their chin.
>
> What are some other examples of *dripping* and *dropping*?
>
> Icicles, ice cream cones, and popsicles melting.
> Faucets or noses dripping.
> Hot faces dripping with perspiration.
> Rainy day drips and drops: raindrops falling; raindrops clinging to leaves, windowpanes, cars; water dripping from umbrellas, leaky gutters, tree branches.

DRIZZLE

> The next word in our family is a rainy day word. This word describes a light, misty kind of rain. Who can think of a word that shares a spelling pattern with the other words of our family and describes a gentle, misty rain?
>
> *Drizzle.*

DREARY

> Our next word often is associated with grey, rainy days. Let's explore the word with a pantomime.
>
> It is a dull, grey, rainy day and you have just heard that there will be no outdoor recess. Pantomime how you would feel. To show disappointment, are you going to sit up straight and tall with a big smile on your face?

For contrast, you might ask students to pantomime how they would feel if the sun suddenly burst through and recess was moved outside, then have them return to the gloomy day pantomime. The contrast helps some students see each posture more clearly.

> Does anybody know a word for the kind of dull, grey day that might make our spirits—and sometimes our posture—fall?
>
> *Dreary.*

Dreary means "dull and grey, cheerless." How did our pantomime show us the connection between *dreary* and its root meaning?

Other things besides grey, rainy days can be dreary—and make our spirits fall:

> We might describe a room that has nothing interesting or cheerful in it as dreary. When you walk into that room, your spirits might fall.
>
> We might describe a job that is dull and boring as dreary—it's a job that gets you down.

Elicit other examples from your students' own experiences.

DROOP

> There's a word that belongs to today's family that we could use to describe the way loose socks sometimes drop down around your ankles, or the way baggy pants hang loosely from your belt, or the way a plant needing water bends over and hangs limply. We could say they are...
>
> > *drooping.*
>
> When a plant droops from lack of water, it loses strength. What does "The players were drooping after a game in the hot sun" mean?
>
> > Their energy and perhaps their bodies are beginning to sag.
>
> Pine branches may droop under the weight of a heavy snow. Sometimes people's spirits droop under the weight of things. What kinds of things might "weigh you down" and make your spirits droop?
>
> > Sad news, problems that seem too big to handle, losing something you care about....

Kithara Hakushu's poem "Rain on Castle Island," found in the poetry selections below, connects the idea of dripping rain with drooping spirits.

DROWSY

Here's a scene to pantomime:

> It's a hot, quiet afternoon and you're not feeling too lively. You're trying to finish your assignments before school ends, but every once in a while your head nods with sleepiness. When your head begins to fall toward your shoulder, the movement wakes you. You work for a while, then your head begins to nod again.

> Does anybody know a *d-r*-vowel word that describes feeling sleepy or half asleep?
>
> > *Drowsy.*

Drowsy describes that in-between state of sleepiness when you are almost ready to fall asleep, but manage to stay awake.

Have you ever seen a drowsy person dropping off to sleep, then waking up, then dropping off and waking again?

Let students give examples from their own experiences.

Carl Sandburg's poem "Prairie Waters by Night" (near the end of this chapter) brings the image embedded in *drowsy* to life. The poem can be used as an alternative way to introduce the word or can be read aloud at any appropriate point.

The Root: Meaning and Spelling

Review the spelling pattern shared by all the words of the family by having a volunteer underline the *d-r*-vowel pattern in each of the words on the board.

What spelling pattern is our root likely to have?

d-r-vowel

The root from which all of the words in today's family grew is DHREU.

What consonant in DHREU is no longer part of the spelling pattern shared by the words of the DHREU family?

The letter *h*.

H represented a breathy sound following the *d*. People stopped pronouncing that breathy sound, however, and therefore the sound is not represented in today's words.

(See the "Linguistic Background" chapter in Volume 1 for further information.)

What is the root meaning of DHREU?

To fall.

Be sure the root meaning "to fall" is recorded next to DHREU.

Note on "Sound Cousins"

Drink, drench, drown, and *drag* are often proposed as members of this family. All of them happen to come from another root, DRAGH, which means "to pull." The first three arise from an image of pulling in or absorbing water. All of them can be seen, however, to share in some fashion in the general imagery of downward movement central to the DHREU family and can be considered "sound cousins." *Drink, drench,* and *drown,* of course, also partake of the imagery of falling rain suggested by some of the DHREU words. They should be welcomed as part of the writing vocabulary.

The Word Trees

As soon as you have completed the introduction to the DHREU family, hand out 3 x 5 cards (or similar slips of paper) and ask for volunteers to record the root and words of the family for the class word tree. Then hand out the individual word trees (a tree to copy is found at the end of both volumes of *Origins*) and ask students to fill in the root and the words of the family for inclusion in their own notebooks.

Student Illustrations

Brainstorm ideas with the entire class for a "picture that tells a story" and include as many words of the DHREU family as possible. For a sample student illustration and a discussion of using the illustrations, see the "Using *Origins*" chapter.

Definitions to Record

dreary: cheerless; dull and gloomy
drizzle: a light rain
droop: 1. hang down, bend down
       2. to lose strength or energy
       3. to become sad or gloomy
drowsy: half asleep; sleepy

Story Puzzle

When you introduce the Story Puzzle "The Big Game," let students know that in some cases they will need to add endings (*-ed, -s, -ing*) to make words of the DHREU family fit the blanks. Because words of a family occasionally have some overlap in meaning, a given word may fit logically in more than one space. Using the same word twice is not wrong, but the challenge is to use all the words of the family instead of repeating any of them. Students may enjoy experimenting with deliberately putting words in the wrong blanks.

Review Pantomimes

Students often enjoy inventing their own pantomimes using the words of a given word family. Such pantomimes often inspire lively, inventive thinking about the by-now-familiar words. Sometimes the teacher has difficulty figuring out which word is being dramatized, but fellow students usually are quick to identify it.

Images of Up and Down and the Feelings They Reflect

Many of the words in the DHREU family reflect the way we use the images of up and down and of high and low to express feelings. Kate Rushin's "Blues Song" (below) provides a good example of the connection between images of downward motion and the feeling of being down. Here are some other expressions using images of up and down to express feelings.

down in the dumps	on top of the world
feeling down	on cloud nine
feeling low	feeling up
downcast	upbeat
downhearted	in high spirits
my heart sank	my spirits rose
crestfallen	cheered up

Blues Song

I'm so tired of struggling
My life just dribbles away,
I'm so tired of struggling
My life just dribbles away,
Work my fingers to the bone
The money's spent before pay day.

Everything is so dreary
Seems like the sun has dropped out o' sight
Everything is so dreary
Seems like the sun has dropped out o' sight,
My heart is drooping so low
Just want to drowse and dream all day and night.

Oh, it's a gray day
It drizzles all day long
Oh, it's a gray day
It drizzles all day long,
I'm so lonely and so blue
Can't do nothin' but sing this song.

Standing at this bus stop
Rain dripping down my neck
Standing at this bus stop
Rain dripping down my neck,
All alone with my little wet dog
Seems like my whole life is a wreck.

—*Kate Rushin*

Prairie Waters by Night

Chatter of birds two by two
raises a night song
joining a litany of running water—sheer waters showing the
russet of old stones
remembering many rains.

And the long willows drowse on the shoulders of the running
water,
and sleep from much music;
joined songs of day-end,
feathery throats and stony waters,
in a choir chanting new psalms.

It is too much for the long willows
when low laughter of a red moon comes down;
and the willows drowse and sleep
on the shoulders of the running water.

—Carl Sandburg

Rain on Castle Island

Rain:
Grey, rat-grey rain
On Castle Island shore;

Rain:
Is it pearls or
Evening mist, or my tears?

A boat
Puts out—my man's
Boat, sail and mast dripping.

Boats
Moved by oars; oars
By songs; songs by the bos'n's mood.

Rain
From cloud-grey sky.
Boat bobbing, sail distant, dim.

—Kithara Hakushu

Discussion and Writing Ideas

- **Blues Song**

Students enjoy simply reading "Blues Song" aloud. Try orchestrating various combinations of voices. Which lines sound best with solo voices? Which with choral voices?

- **Prairie Waters by Night**

Feeling sleepy? Can't stay awake? Read "Prairie Waters by Night," and you'll discover unexpected company. "Feathery throats and stony waters" sing a nighttime lullaby to Sandburg's "long willows" as they "drowse on the shoulders of the running water." What other things might be secretly sleeping? Do stones nap in the heat of the day? Have you ever seen horses nap standing up? Does oil sleep in silent pools beneath the earth's crust? Who sings lullabies to ships drifting at anchor? Save your ideas and imagine them instead of sheep when you can't get to sleep. Or use your ideas to write a lullaby of your own.

- **Rain on Castle Island**

In "Rain on Castle Island" by Kithara Hakushu, the rain is falling and so are the woman's tears. Why is she so sad? How does the presence of rain in her poem add force to what she is feeling?

We all have dreary days of our own, when a light rain seems to be falling inside us somewhere. We don't have to be cold to feel bored, out-of-sorts, disappointed, or grief-stricken. What seems dreary to you? When are you "down in the dumps"? Close your eyes for a moment and let dreary, drizzly images come to mind. Now choose a partner and find a private workspace with one piece of paper. Without showing your partner, write down one specific image (word or picture) that comes to mind when you think of drizzle or dreary. Fold the paper over so that your writing is barely covered up and pass it to your partner. Have your partner do the same. Keep trading the paper back and forth, folding over the writing each time until both of you run out of ideas.

Now unfold the paper and compare your images. Were any of them the same? Did they have any common threads running through them? Which ones best capture the mood you want to express? Compare your teamwork with classmates'. Which images seem to fall under the category "the human condition" and which are more particular to you? Choose one that speaks more particularly to you as an individual and try to capture its feeling.

Story Puzzle for Students

Read the story to yourself before filling in the blanks with words from your DHREU word tree. In some cases the same word will fit in more than one place. However, the challenge is to see if you can find a way to use *all* the words of the DHREU family.

The Big Game

It's the day of the big game, and the fans cheer loudly as their teams come out on the basketball court. The Friday afternoon sky is gray and _____ and a light _____ is falling from the clouds, but now, inside the gym, excitement buzzes through the air. The home team, the Falcons, need to win this game to go on to the semi-finals. The pressure is on the star shooter, Nathan Brown, who hopes someday to be the next Michael Jordan. The score is close going into the fourth quarter. Beads of sweat _____ down the hot, tired bodies of the players, and one or two of them are beginning to _____ with exhaustion. But the fans are wide awake; there's not a _____ face in the audience. The lead goes back and forth in the final minute. Now it's tied. Nathan _____ the ball toward the basket, trying desperately to find an opening and make the winning two points. He fakes out his man, leaps, and sends the ball soaring toward the basket. For a moment, fans and players hold their breath—then scream wildly as the ball neatly _____ into the hoop. Nathan's face breaks into a big smile.

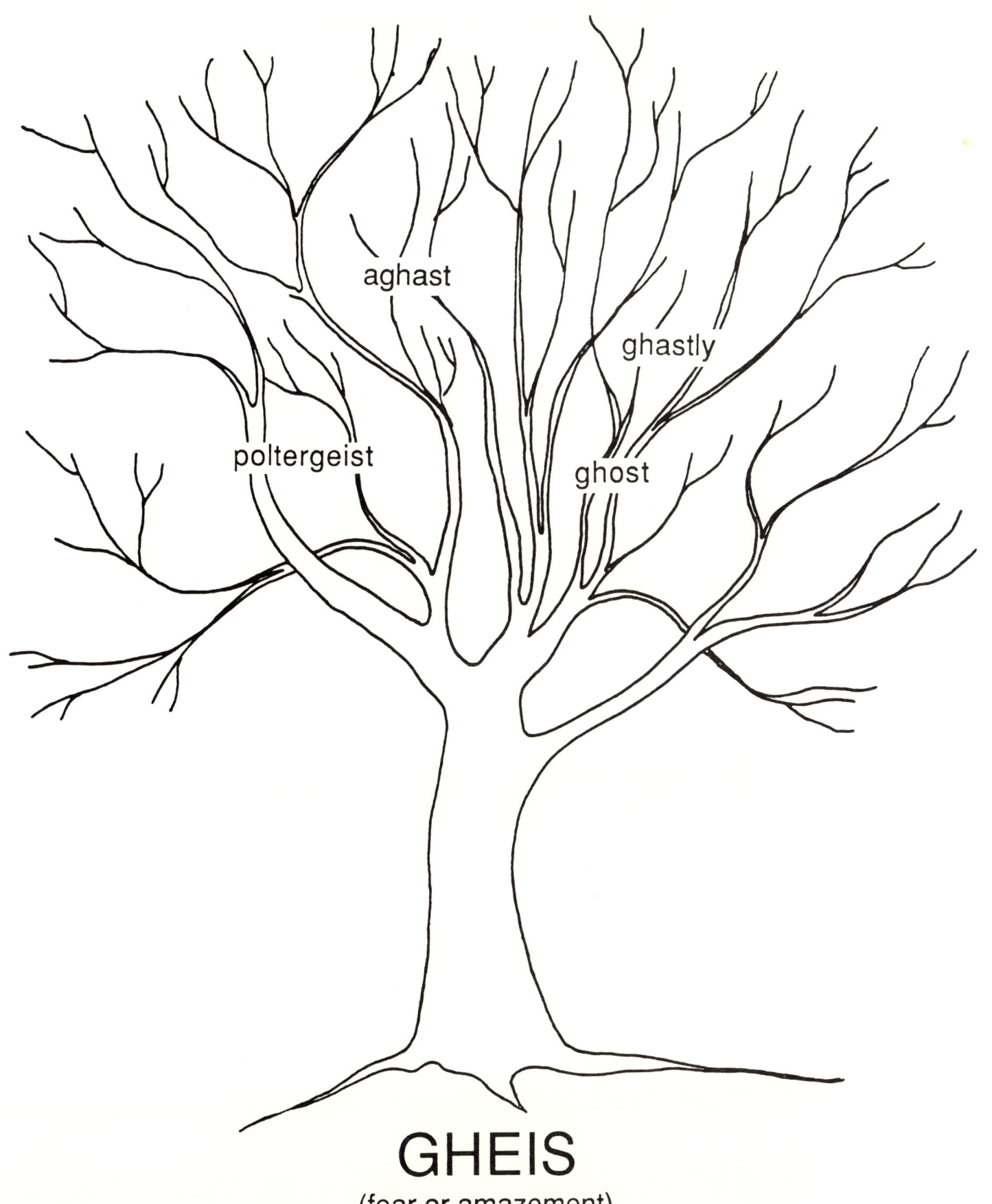

The GHEIS family is a small family that we have included because of its appeal for young students, especially around Halloween. The format of the "Introduction to the Word Family" differs somewhat from the format of other families. One opening skit, which includes a poem to be read aloud, is the basis for discovering all the words of the family. The chapter includes examples of how the literal meaning of *ghost* has been extended to figurative uses in the language, as well as poetry related to the word family.

Materials needed for the lesson are: some kind of improvised ghost costumes and objects the poltergeist can use for making noises.

Introduction to the GHEIS Word Family

> **GHEIS**—*fear or amazement*
>
> ghost   aghast
> ghastly poltergeist

GHOST, POLTERGEIST, GHASTLY, AGHAST

One skit, especially appropriate if staged near Halloween, can introduce the GHEIS family. The important props are two improvised ghost costumes (white sheets or white tissue paper taped together). Out of sight of the class, drape two volunteers with the costumes. One ghost should carry pots, pans, or some noisemaker.

Ask for other volunteers to play the part of listeners in a ghost storytelling scene. Help the volunteer listeners prepare for how they will react when the ghost and poltergeist appear. (See below.) Storyteller and listeners then seat themselves in a circle to begin the skit. The storyteller reads "The Invisible Beast," or another ghost tale, to the listeners.

The Invisible Beast

The beast that is invisible
is stalking through the park,
but you cannot see it coming
though it isn't very dark.
Oh you know it's out there somewhere
though just why you cannot tell,
but although you cannot see it
it can see you very well.

You sense its frightful features
and its great ungainly form,
and you wish that you were home now
where it's cozy, safe, and warm.
And you know it's coming closer
for you smell its awful smell,
and although you cannot see it
it can see you very well.

> Oh your heart is beating faster,
> beating louder than a drum,
> for you hear its footsteps falling
> and your body's frozen numb.
> And you cannot scream for terror
> and your fear you cannot quell,
> for although you cannot see it
> it can see you very well.
>
> *—Jack Prelutsky*

At an appropriate moment near the end of the reading, the first ghost appears to the listeners, who react with fear and surprise, but who remain seated. Then the poltergeist, the noisy ghost, appears, rattling and clanking and knocking over a few things on her way across the room. The actors become terrified and call out appropriate comments, such as:

> "Help! Help! A ghost and a poltergeist!"
> "Help! I'm scared!"
> "Oh no, the story's coming true!"
> "Get me out of here. This is horrible!"

The actors and actresses all run out; the ghost and poltergeist linger for a moment, then disappear.

Direct discussion of the skit along these lines:

> What kind of poem were our actors listening to?
>
>> A scary poem, a ghost poem.
>
> Who appeared to the listeners at the end of the poem?
>
>> Two *ghosts*.
>
> What was the difference between the two ghosts?
>
>> One was silent; the other was noisy and knocked things over.
>
> There's a special name for a noisy ghost. Does anyone know it?
>
>> A *poltergeist*.

Poltergeist comes from the German words *poltern* ("to make noises") and *geist* ("ghost"). The combination of the two conjured up a noisy, rattling, knocking ghost—a ghost that also causes objects to fly around the room and knock into things.

Here's a description of an evening with a poltergeist:

The Poltergeist

Something strange is flitting through your hair,
but when you try to find it, nothing's there.
You know, though, when it gives your cheek a bite,
a poltergeist is in your house tonight.

Your rocking chair is rocking by itself,
and all your books have tumbled from the shelf,
and something keeps on flicking out the light—
a poltergeist is in your house tonight.

The chandelier has shattered on the floor,
and things unseen are rapping on the door,
and when you look, no creature meets your sight—
a poltergeist is in your house tonight.

Within the kitchen cups and saucers shake,
and there before your eyes the windows break,
and when it laughs, you scream with all your might—
a poltergeist is in your house tonight.

—*Jack Prelutsky*

If you were a poltergeist, what would be your favorite activities?

Here are some questions for discovering the root meaning of *ghost* or *poltergeist*:

In our skit, how did the storyteller and listeners react when the ghost and poltergeist appeared?

Fearful, afraid, scared...

Did they seem to be expecting someone or did they appear surprised by the visit?

They were surprised, shocked, amazed...

You may want to ask the class to pantomime the reactions before describing them in words.

The root meaning of *ghost* and *poltergeist* describes these reactions; the root meaning of today's family is "fear or amazement."

The family includes two more words. Have you ever heard the expression "I turned white as a ghost" to describe a feeling of terror or shock at a horrible sight? There is a *gh*-vowel-*st* word that can be used to describe a horrible or shocking event. You might say that a scene was a horrible sight or that it was a _____ sight.

Ghastly.

You might say: *"The ghastly sight of the shrouded ghost sent them running for home."*

Ghastly describes the fearful or dreadful nature of a sight or event. The last word of our family, which is very similar to ghastly, describes the feelings of a person encountering a ghastly sight or event. When our actors saw the ghastly sight of the ghost and poltergeist, they were...

aghast.

You might say: *"Scrooge was aghast when the Ghost of Christmas Past appeared and dragged him forth into the night."* Or: *"The searchers were aghast when they first saw the terrible wreckage of the plane."*

The Root: Meaning and Spelling

The words of today's family all share the root meaning of "fear or amazement," and three of them share the same spelling pattern, which is

gh-vowel-*st*.

Which word is missing a letter of the pattern?

Over time the *h* of the spelling pattern became silent, and was dropped from the spelling of *poltergeist*. *Ghost, ghastly*, and *aghast* kept the *h* as a silent letter.

The root of today's word family is **GHEIS**, which means "fear or amazement."

Wrap-up

Hand out 3 x 5 cards and ask for volunteers to record the root and words of the family for the class word tree. Then hand out the individual word trees and ask students to fill in the root and the words of the family for their own notebooks.

The illustration can be an opportunity for students to get a good hold on understanding *ghastly* and *aghast*, the words least familiar to students. Comments in cartoon balloons ("What a ghastly sight"; "The children were aghast when they saw the ghostly figures float by") provide a good way to include the words in illustrations.

Definitions to Record

ghastly: something that causes terror; something horrible or shocking
aghast: struck with surprise or horror; filled with terror
poltergeist: a noisy ghost that throws objects about

Additional Meanings

ghastly: 1. like a dead person or ghost; deathly pale, as in *"The sick man looked ghastly."*
2. very bad, as in *"I made a ghastly mistake in not telling the truth the first time."*

Ghostly Words and Expressions

What are some words you might use to describe the appearance of a ghost?

Pale, dim, shadowy, misty, faint, wispy, fleeting...

Several expressions have the meaning of ghost as something pale and shadowy, something with no substance, something that can't be seen clearly. Here are three such expressions.

GHOST TOWN

Have any of you ever visited or read about a ghost town? Close your eyes for a moment and picture it in your minds. What does it look like?

Deserted, empty, falling down, dusty, lifeless...

How do you think ghost towns got that name? Do ghosts actually have to be living in a deserted town for it to be called a ghost town?

No, the old town itself is like a ghost, a ghost or shadow of its former self. All that's left is the memory of what it once was.

Ghost towns exist primarily in the United States. Do you know what kind of town most ghost towns were before they were abandoned?

Gold Rush towns in the West, where people used to mine for gold or silver. Once the gold, silver, or other valuable minerals ran out, people left the town. There was no more work to keep them there.

GHOST WRITER

Is a ghost writer a talented ghost who writes books and stories? What kind of a writer is a ghost writer?

> A person who writes a book for someone else and lets the other person, who often is famous, get credit for writing the book.

Why do you think the term ghost writer is used to describe this kind of writer?

> Because when you buy the book, its real author can't be clearly seen. The ghost writer is in the shadows, in the background.

Why do you suppose some people hire ghost writers to write books for them?

> Famous people are often interested in putting the story of their life in a book, but they may not be writers. Instead of writing the story themselves, they hire a professional ghost writer to help them.

GHOST OF A...

Several expressions begin with "a ghost of a..." to mean "faint," "very little" or "a small amount." If you saw "a ghost of a smile" pass across your friend's face, would she be giving you a broad, happy smile or a small, faint smile? What things might cause you to respond with a ghost of a smile?

Do you know any other expressions that use "a ghost of a..."? How are they used?

> The team doesn't have a *ghost of a chance* of winning the tournament.

> The detectives hadn't begun to solve the case; they didn't have a *ghost of an idea* where to start.

The Invisible Beast

The beast that is invisible
is stalking through the park,
but you cannot see it coming
though it isn't very dark.
Oh you know it's out there somewhere
though just why you cannot tell,
but although you cannot see it
it can see you very well.

You sense its frightful features
and its great ungainly form,
and you wish that you were home now
where it's cozy, safe and warm.
And you know it's coming closer
for you smell its awful smell,
and although you cannot see it
it can see you very well.

Oh your heart is beating faster,
beating louder than a drum,
for you hear its footsteps falling
and your body's frozen numb.
And you cannot scream for terror
and your fear you cannot quell,
for although you cannot see it
it can see you very well.

—*Jack Prelutsky*

The Suspended Ghost

Once there was a boy named Robert Rodriguez
He was a 4th grader in P.S. 2
His teacher was Mrs. Bertha Kubinsky
He was smarter than me or you

He could add and subtract, multiply and divide
Reading and writing was easy to do
He studied science and history
He had a 160 IQ

Robert was a little Spanish kid
With witchblack hair and grass-green eyes
He liked to play football and build sandcastles
And eat coconut, cherry, and pineapple pies

One day in the school cafeteria
A kid named Angel Cordoba
Threw greasy french fries at Robert's head
The furious principal came running over

He took both kids into the office
And accused Robert of starting the fight
"I'm calling your mother," he told the child
Robert felt the icy tremble of fright

Angel was excused and went back to his class
Mrs. Rodriguez could not understand
Her son was suspended for seven weeks
She took him tightly by the hand

He said, "But mother, it wasn't my fault."
"I don't want to hear about it," she angrily replied.
"Go to your room now for seven weeks."
That night little Robert lay down and cried

In the morning it was time for school
Robert looked out the window and saw his friends go
He couldn't resist, so he picked up his books
And sneaked out the back door, quiet, and slow...

For, you see, Robert just loved to be
In the classrooms and playgrounds of public school
So he made himself invisible
And floated down the street so cool!

The halls were crowded with noisy pupils
Robert peeked into his class
He saw Mrs. Kubinsky writing an assignment
His body was as clear as glass

Angel Cordoba walked down the hall
Robert Rodriguez floated by his side
He whispered into Angel's ear,
"It's all your fault!" Cordoba cried,

"Help! A ghost! It's all my fault!
Suspend me forever! Let Robert come back!"
Cordoba's conscience grabbed at his heart
His heart began to have an attack...

—3rd-6th grade collaboration

Discussion and Writing Ideas

• **The Invisible Beast**

Jack Prelutsky writes spine-tingling Halloween poetry. How does he create this atmosphere of dread? What ghostly happenings cause you to glance over your shoulder in fear and anticipation? Make a list. Find sounds that make your ears go on red alert—rustlings, ghostly laughs, unseen rappings—as well as sights that make your eyes shrink from shadowy corners—flickering lights, a chair rocking by itself, ghostly tendrils writhing in the mist. With classmates, take five minutes to brainstorm a list of your own scary sounds and shivery sights.

Poets send shivers up our spines not only with words that suggest scary sounds, but also with the thumping rhythms. What lines in this poem build suspense by echoing over and over again through the poem?

Now try your hand at your own ghostly poem. Frighten your readers by selecting your scariest, most dreadful sounds and images. Repeat words or phrases if they help to build the suspense. Use rhyme if you want to. Read your poem to a friend in your most bewitching voice. Does the poem pass the "shiver" test?

• **The Suspended Ghost**

Why does Robert glide back into school as a ghost? Can you think of times when you would like to float invisible among your friends? Brainstorm to make a list of situations in which it would be handy to turn yourself into a ghost. Choose your favorite and write your own ghost story.

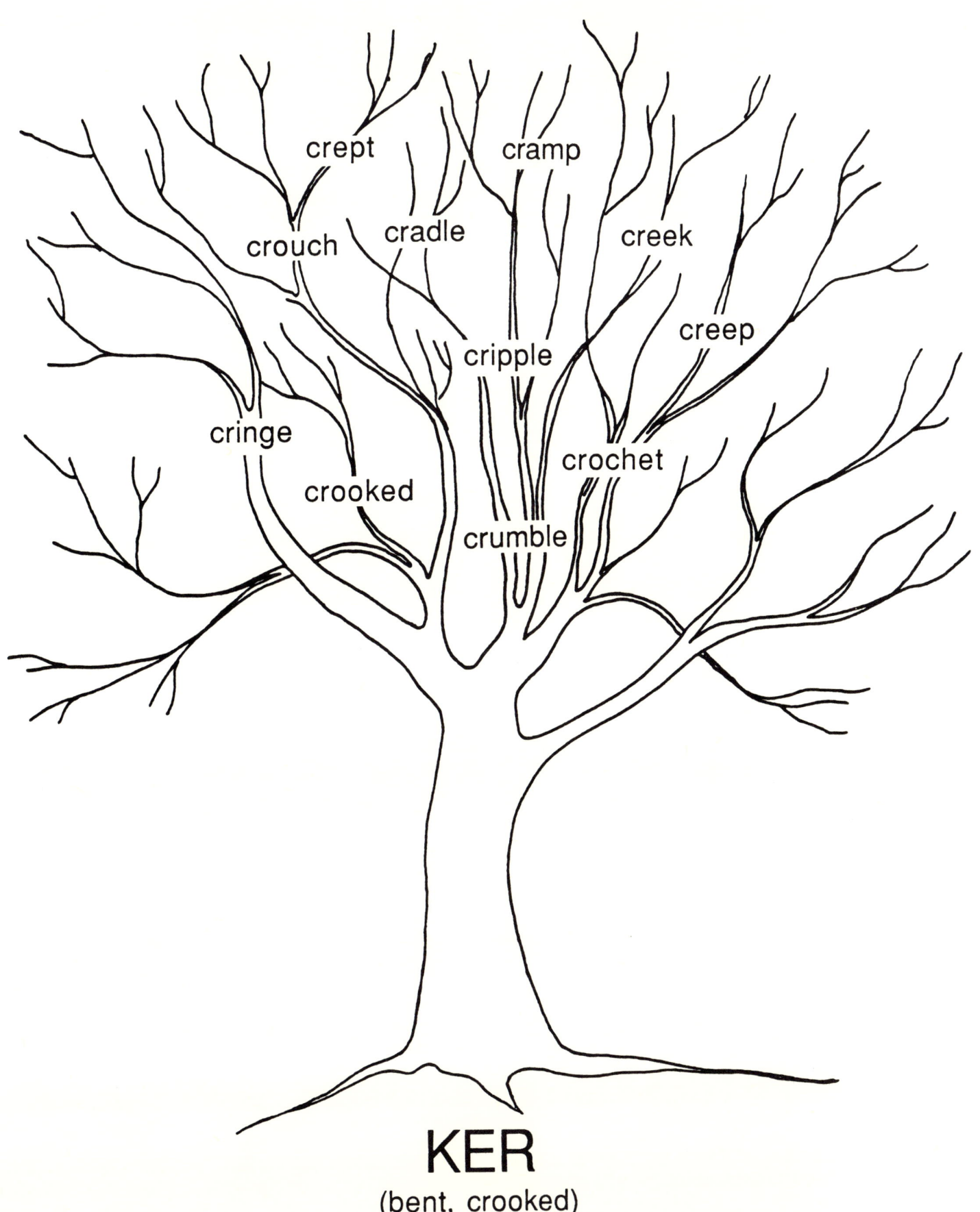

Since students are by now familiar with generating the words of a family, the introductory pantomimes for *cramp, crouch, creep*, and *crooked* are often all they need to unlock the whole KER family. Move ahead quickly if you like, but at some point, remember to discuss the connection between the meaning of each word and the root image of the family. If the pace set by the students becomes too fast and their proposals for members of the family too random, stopping for such a discussion can get things back on track.

The KER chapter introduces "Exploring Extended Meanings," a section that provides examples of how concrete and literal meanings of words are extended to abstract and figurative uses. This section, which is included in many subsequent chapters, can help students develop a general understanding of abstract and figurative meaning.

This chapter also includes poetry related to the word family.

Materials useful for introducing the family are: a crochet hook or picture of a crochet hook, a picture of a cradle, and a scrap of paper.

Introduction to the KER Word Family

> **KER**—*bent, crooked*
>
> crooked   creek
> cramp   crochet
> crouch   crumple
> creep, crept cripple
> cradle   cringe

Cramp, crouch, and *creep* can provide lively pantomimes for discovering the root meaning of the family, then the individual words. Have volunteers hold poses for all three of the following pantomimes:

- A person doubling over in pain caused by a cramp in the side.
- A runner crouched for the start of a race.
- One person creeping up on another to scare him (emphasizing the bent, somewhat crouched posture that helps you sneak up on someone without being seen).

Ask questions to help students discover the root meaning as it is brought to life in these poses. Identify the three actors who are bent over (the person being crept up on is not bending) as the target of your questions.

> How can we describe the posture of these three actors?
> Are they standing straight and tall? What are words that describe the opposite of straight?

> *Bent, crooked.*

"*Bent* or *crooked*" is the root meaning of the words of the KER family.

CROOKED

> *Crooked* is not only part of the root meaning, but is also one of the words in the KER family.

CRAMP

> Why is one of our actors bending over and clutching his side? What might be the matter?

> A *cramp* —from running, swimming, etc.

What other kinds of cramp might you get?

45

A leg cramp—from any sports activity.
A writer's cramp—from writing a long time.

Cramp can also refer to being shut up in a small space, not having enough room to move around, perhaps even bending over to make room. You might say:

Thirty-five children felt cramped in their small classroom.
My toes were cramped in my old boots.

≥●

Around the turn of the century, *cramp* was used regionally to mean "to turn or curve sharply." In all likelihood the meaning derived from familiarity with a *cramp* iron, a metal tool with a hook at the end. Here's an example from Mark Twain: "A boat hates shoal water—now cramp her down, snatch her." And from New Hampshire comes "The road cramps around a building."

CROUCH

What is (identify the runner) doing?

Getting ready to run.

What word describes the runner's bent position as she prepares for the start of the race?

A *crouch*.

What other athletes crouch?

Swimmers.
Football players.
The catcher in a baseball game.

Students enjoy demonstrating the various crouches used in their favorite sports.

What animals crouch as they get ready to pounce?

The cat family:	house cats	lions
	wildcats	leopards
	bobcats	tigers

What is the spelling pattern shared by the words of today's family?

c-r-vowel

CREEP, CREPT

What is (identify the actor who is creeping up on someone) doing? When you sneak up on someone do you usually walk upright, or do you crouch low to avoid being seen? What is a *c-r*-vowel word that describes this kind of sneaking up on someone?

> *Creep.*

When might people or animals creep?

> A cat stalks a bird by creeping after it.
> A child playing hide and seek might creep from one hiding place to another.
> If you get home later than you were supposed to, you might creep into the house, hoping no one will notice your lateness.
> Soldiers creep cautiously to spy on the enemy.

Creep can also refer to the movement of a snake, an alligator, or any other reptile that moves along close to the ground by wiggling back and forth. Vines that snake along the surface of the ground or up the surface of a wall are called *creepers*.

Creep is used, as well, to describe the pre-crawling movement of babies—the use of hands and knees to wiggle across the floor on their tummies.

Although *crawl* looks as though it should belong to the KER word family, it in fact comes from the root GERBH, which means "to scratch." Two relatives in the GERBH family are *crab* and *crayfish*. Many of these creatures either scratch on the sea bottom for food or scratch in the sand to make burrows. Today *crawl* is often used interchangeably with *creep* and, because it shares both imagery and a sound pattern with *creep*, it can be considered a "sound cousin" and listed to the side of the "family tree." It should be welcomed as part of the writing vocabulary.

CRADLE

A picture or blackboard drawing of a cradle will help students guess this word.

> What piece of furniture would you put a baby in to rock her to sleep?

> A *cradle*.

How is a cradle connected to the idea of bending or curving?

> The rockers are curved.

For a group pantomime:

> Show how you might cradle a baby in your arms. Are your arms straight or bending?

Show how you would hold yourself if you wanted to cradle the telephone on your shoulder to free your hands for writing a message. Is your shoulder straight or curved toward your ear?

CREEK

When water flows across land, it always moves in a bending, curving pattern. Although you may not be able to see the bends and curves when you walk along the banks of a large river, you can see them if you get a view of the river from an airplane. If you walk along the banks of a stream, however, you can easily see the bends and curves as you follow its path. What's another name for a small stream?

Creek.

Originally creeks were arms of the sea that extended into the land following the same winding path as the streams that flowed into them. Later the word was extended to include the streams.

A regional variant of the word *creek* is *crick*.

CROCHET

Take out a crochet hook or draw a picture of one:

Do you know the name of this needlework tool? Why do you think *crochet* is a member of today's word family?

Because of its shape—with a bent hook at the end—and its *c-r*-vowel spelling pattern.

CRUMPLE

Hold up a piece of scrap paper for students to see. Then crumple it in your hand.

If you're trying to write a letter or story and feel you need to start over, what might you do with the paper?

Crumple it up.

"The accident crumpled the car fender." What happened?

The fender got bent out of shape, squashed.

"When the boxer took a knockout punch, he crumpled and fell to the floor." What happened?

The boxer "folded up."

Crumple can also mean to fold up and fall in a heap the way you do when your legs suddenly won't hold you up any longer.

CRIPPLE

Some people's fingers become more bent and crooked than normal because of arthritis or other disease. At times they may describe their fingers as _____ by the disease.

Crippled.

"The boxer dealt his opponent a crippling blow." What happened to his opponent?

He would probably be bent over with pain.

CRINGE

A group pantomime can help embody this word.

Show me how you would react if someone dropped an ice cube down your back.

There is a word that describes how people sometimes pull or shrink away from danger or pain—the way you arched your back to pull away from the pain or discomfort of the imaginary ice cube. Does anybody know a *c-r*-vowel word that describes this body movement—bending or pulling the body away from danger of some kind?

Cringe.

When else might people cringe?

In a scary movie.
From embarrassment.

You might have seen a dog cringe when threatened with being hit or attacked.

The Root: Meaning and Spelling

What sound do all the words of today's family begin with? And how is that sound represented in these words?

c-r

What other letters could we use to represent that sound?

k-r

The root for today's family has a *k* and an *r* instead of a *c* and an *r*. The root is KER. You will notice that the *r* and the vowel switched places over time.

And what does KER mean? What is the root meaning of all our words?

Bent or crooked.

(For further background on the *r*-vowel inversion, see the "Linguistic Background" chapter.)

Other "Sound Cousins"

In addition to *crawl*, the following words are frequently proposed as members of the KER family, though they happen to come from other roots: *crash, crease, cross, crush, cruel,* and *crime*. Because the words share a sound pattern with the words of the KER family and can be seen as sharing the imagery of being bent and crooked, they can be considered "sound cousins," listed to the side of the family tree, and welcomed as part of the writing vocabulary.

The Word Trees

As soon as you have completed the introduction to the KER family, hand out 3 x 5 cards and ask for volunteers to record the root and words of the family for the class word tree. Then hand out individual word trees and ask students to fill in the root and the words of the family for their own notebooks.

Student Illustrations

You may want to brainstorm ideas for a "picture that tells a story" as you have done for other word families. For the KER family a good alternative is to have students complete the "How Spider Got Eight Legs" story puzzle and then illustrate the story.

Definitions to Record

crouch: to stoop low with bent legs, as though ready to jump
creep: to move slowly with the body close to the ground; to sneak up on someone; to move slowly
creek: a small stream
crumple: to crush or bend out of shape, to wrinkle
cringe: to pull or shrink away from danger or pain

Story Puzzle

When you introduce the "How Spider Got Eight Legs" story puzzle, let students know that in some cases they will need to add endings (-ed, -s, -ing) to make words fit the blanks. Because words of a family occasionally have some overlap in meaning, a given word may fit logically in more than one space. Using the same word twice is not wrong, but you will want to encourage students to meet the challenge of the puzzle—using all the words of the family instead of repeating any of them.

Additional Related Words

CRINKLE

CRUTCH

A crutch was originally a bent stick, like a shepherd's crook.

CRIB, CRECHE

Crib and *creche* are closely related to *cradle*—all originally being woven baskets used both for holding animal feed and infants. In the Biblical story, the cradle of Jesus was an animal feed box—or creche—so creche has come to mean the representation of the Nativity scene.

CURL

CRUMB, CRUMBLE

Crumble comes from *crumb,* and though the word is easily confused with *crumple,* the two words are used quite differently. The connection between *crumb* and the root meaning is the curved or "bent" shape of the crumb.

CROQUET

The name *croquet* probably comes from *crochet,* meaning hook—the shape of the wire arches or wickets used in the game.

LACROSSE: a ball game in which team members use long-handled racquets with loose nets on the end for catching, carrying or throwing the ball

Lacrosse is an American Indian game. The French were the first Europeans to see the game played and adopt it as their own. They called the game *lacrosse* because the shape of the racquet head reminded them of a bishop's crosier, which resembles a shepherd's crook.

CROCK

The curving form of the early handmade clay pot gave the crock its name.

CRANK: the handle of a machine connected to a shaft to set it in motion

The definition of a crank is of limited usefulness unless you have a picture of it in mind. An example of a crank familiar to students might be the handle of a hand-driven wall pencil sharpener.

How do you think the "bent" shape of a crank might have led someone to coin the word *cranky* as a way to describe someone who is cross or irritable? Might a cranky person feel "bent out of shape"?

ENCROACH: 1. to trespass or intrude upon the property or rights of another
2. to go beyond proper or usual limits

This word comes from the French *encrochier*, "to catch in a hook." The picture springs to mind of "encroachers" reaching over onto their neighbor's property with a long, hooked pole to pull a branch of apples or a vine of grapes—perhaps even a baby pig or lamb—over the boundary line and onto their own turf. The spirit of such a scene still clings to the use of the word today.

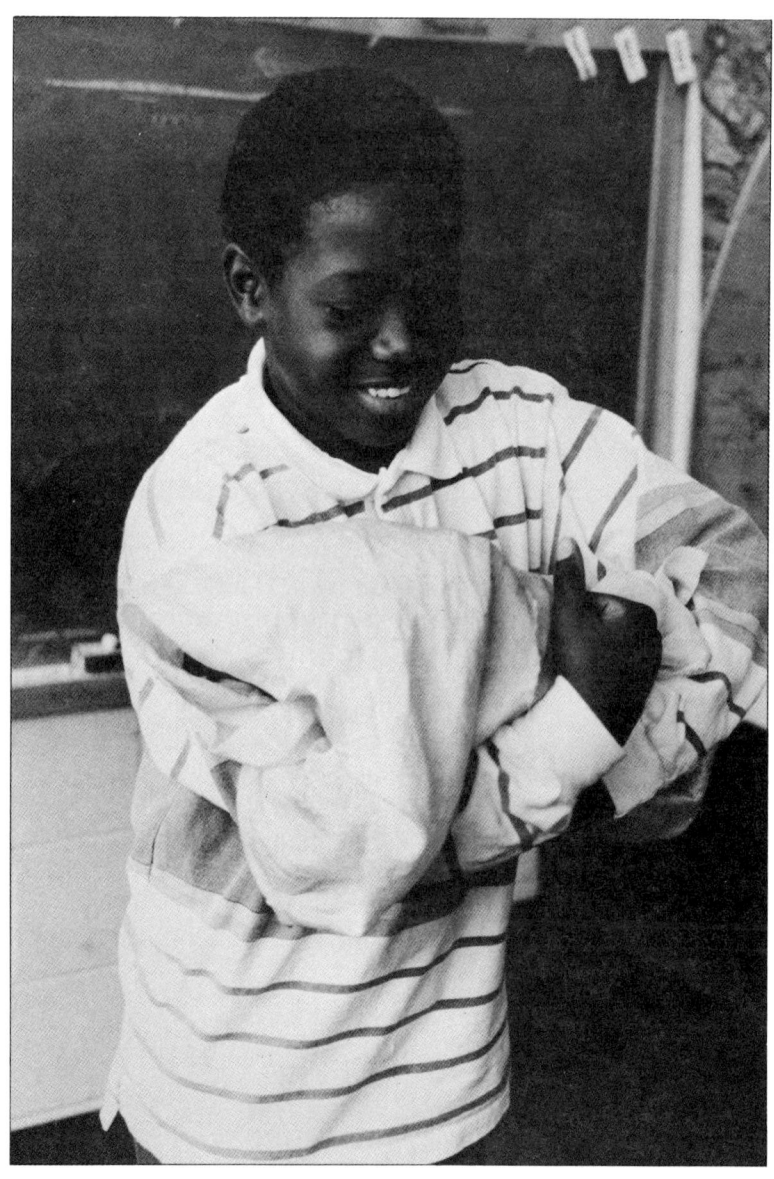

Exploring Extended Meanings

The following sentences help students discover how word meanings are extended. For further background, please see the "Exploring Extended Meanings" section of the "Using *Origins*" chapter. The discussion sentences are reproduced for students on a separate page at the end of this section under the heading, "Stretch the Meaning."

1. *As I sat reading on the couch my sister crept up behind me and startled me.*
   The day for handing in the report crept up on me before I knew it.

    Can a day crouch low to creep up on you the way an animal or a person can? How is time creeping up on you like a person creeping up on you and startling you?

    They both can sneak up on you and take you by surprise.

    Can a person creep up on you if you are watching him? If the day for a report creeps up on you, have you been paying attention to the deadline?

2. *The man's fingers were crippled by arthritis.*
   The automobile factory was crippled by the strike and had to close down.

    Was the factory really twisted and bent out of shape? How is a factory crippled by a strike like fingers crippled by arthritis?

    Both are weakened in their ability to work normally. The factory is disabled because it can't produce cars.

3. *When the boxer took a knockout punch, he crumpled and fell to the floor.*
   When the Bullets got a twenty-five point lead, the opposition began to crumple.

    Did the opposition fall down in a heap the way a boxer might after a knock-out punch? How is the opposition crumpling like a boxer falling to the floor?

    The opposing team's spirits fell, or crumpled, when they realized they couldn't win. When their spirits fell, it was hard for them to feel "up" enough to put up a good fight.

4. *The family of six was cramped in only three rooms.*
   I had to be home by ten. That really cramped my style.

    Can style be squeezed into a small space the way a family can? How is cramping one's style like a person being cramped into a small space?

    If you feel someone is cramping your style, you feel limited; you're unable to move freely, to do what you want.

The Cat and the Moon

The cat went here and there
And the moon spun round like a top,
And the nearest kin of the moon,
The creeping cat looked up.
Black Minaloushe stared at the moon,
For, wander and wail as he would,
The pure cold light in the sky
Troubled his animal blood.
Minaloushe runs in the grass
Lifting his delicate feet.
Do you dance, Minaloushe, do you dance?
When two close kindred meet
What better than call a dance?
Maybe the moon may learn,
Tired of that courtly fashion,
A new dance turn.
Minaloushe creeps through the grass
From moonlit place to place,
The sacred moon overhead has taken a new phase.
Does Minaloushe know that his pupils
Will pass from change to change,
And that from round to crescent,
From crescent to round they range?
Minaloushe creeps through the grass
Alone, important and wise,
And lifts to the changing moon
His changing eyes.

—William Butler Yeats

Where the Shadows Meet the Stars

Where daylight cringes
is where
the shadows meet the stars.
Where creatures of day
are never to venture
is where
the shadows meet the stars.
Where reality
crumbles into Nothingness
is where
the shadows meet the stars.
Where light
will not rule but
two strides over the threshold
is where
the shadows meet the stars.
Where beyond one door
is a single black candle
and around it
dance twenty three-old hags
is where
the shadows meet the stars.
Where around another
is yourself held captive by a troll
is where
the shadows meet the stars.
As I tremble with my head
under the covers
I know
I am where
the shadows meet the stars.

—*Veronica Schanoes, grade 6*

Discussion and Writing Ideas

• The Cat and the Moon

Some poems illuminate a scene from a new angle, allowing us to see connections and contrasts we never noticed before. In "The Cat and the Moon" Yeats sees a kinship between the moon that creeps across the arc of the sky and the cat Minaloushe who creeps through the grass by the light of the moon. You can have fun discovering what Yeats sees as links between these two strange partners, but, even better, you can close your eyes and listen to the music of Yeats' lines. Could you call the poem "Dance Music for a Creeping Cat"? Can you feel Minaloushe creeping through the lines? If you were Minaloushe, which lines would be your favorite for a delicate, creeping dance?

Some of you may want to pair off to invent your own cat and moon dance, while another reads the poem aloud. Or you may want to draw images from the poem. How will you "light" the scene? How will you bring to the page the "pure cold light in the sky"? The moonlit places? The eyes of Minaloushe?

• Where the Shadows Meet the Stars

Veronica Schanoes' poem lists creepy things that happen in a dark and mysterious place "where the shadows meet the stars." Each creepy thing is set between *where* and the title refrain, and a sense of mystery builds as the pattern repeats itself. The poem concludes as the writer varies the pattern and speaks directly about herself.

Imagine a mysterious place where creepy, crooked, crouchy things happen. How can you describe them? Experiment with using patterns of repetition to deepen the sense of mystery as you introduce one creepy, crouchy thing after another.

Story Puzzle for Students

Read the story to yourself before filling in the blanks with words from your KER word tree. In some cases the same word will fit in more than one place. However, the challenge is to see if you can find a way to use *all* the words of the KER family.

How Spider Got Eight Legs

I am the storyteller, and here is my story. Do not believe it, for it never really happened. It is only a story. I am the storyteller, and here is my story.

Many seasons ago, when the world was still young, Spider was a big man in his village. He did not look as he looks today, for he had ten long, graceful legs. Today, as all of you know, he has only eight legs. This is how it came to pass.

Spider was walking along the little _____ that flowed by his village, hoping to find someone cooking dinner. He came upon his wife Aso who was using a _____ hook to make yarn caps for their children. She was keeping an eye on the ten baby spiders in their ten tiny _____ . "Good day, Aso," Spider said politely. "I'm glad to see you working so hard. I'm off to gather food for our supper." Now you know that Spider is very lazy, and what he really hoped for was a free meal.

Soon he came upon Antelope, who was finishing his meal of sweet-smelling rice, yams, and beans. But Antelope was looking very unhappy. "Good day, Antelope," said Spider politely. "Why are you looking so unhappy when you've just eaten that big pot of sweet-smelling stew?"

"Oh hello, Spider," said Antelope sadly. "I'm unhappy because Leopard attacked me yesterday and he _____ my hind leg. I was lucky to get away."

Now Spider may be lazy, but he is kind-hearted. "Let me help you, Antelope," he said. Spider _____ up an old rag, soaked it in the creek, and gently bathed Antelope's wound.

"Thank you, Spider," said Antelope. "Now let me give you some advice. Leopard is resting in the next clearing. If you want to avoid him, don't go the direct way but take the _____ path. It's longer but you won't meet Leopard."

"Thank you for the warning, Antelope," said Spider. "I'll be careful."

But lazy Spider was never one to take good advice. By now he was very hungry and had no time to waste. Foolishly he headed straight toward the clearing. When Leopard heard Spider coming, he _____ down low in the bushes. His silent eyes followed Spider. As Spider passed him, Leopard _____ quietly behind. Now Spider would not make a big meal for Leopard, but he would be a tasty appetizer. Leopard pounced! Quick as a flash, Spider jumped aside and headed for the nearest tree. But Spider was not quick enough. Hanging from Leopard's jaws were two of Spider's long, graceful hind legs. Frightened, Spider _____ in the tree. In a shaking voice he said, "Good day, Leopard. You certainly gave me a scare." Leopard only scowled.

It was not until daybreak that Spider dared crawl back home. His eight remaining legs were _____ from clinging to the tree all night and his hungry belly rumbled.

To this day Spider has eight long, graceful legs instead of ten, but he hardly ever misses the other two.

Stretch the Meaning

1. As I sat reading on the couch my sister crept up behind me and startled me.
   The day for handing in the report crept up on me before I knew it.

2. The man's fingers were crippled by arthritis.
   The automobile factory was crippled by the strike and had to close down.

3. When the boxer took a knockout punch, he crumpled and fell to the floor.
   When the Bullets got a twenty-five point lead, the opposition began to crumple.

4. The family of six was cramped in only three rooms.
   I had to be home by ten. That really cramped my style.

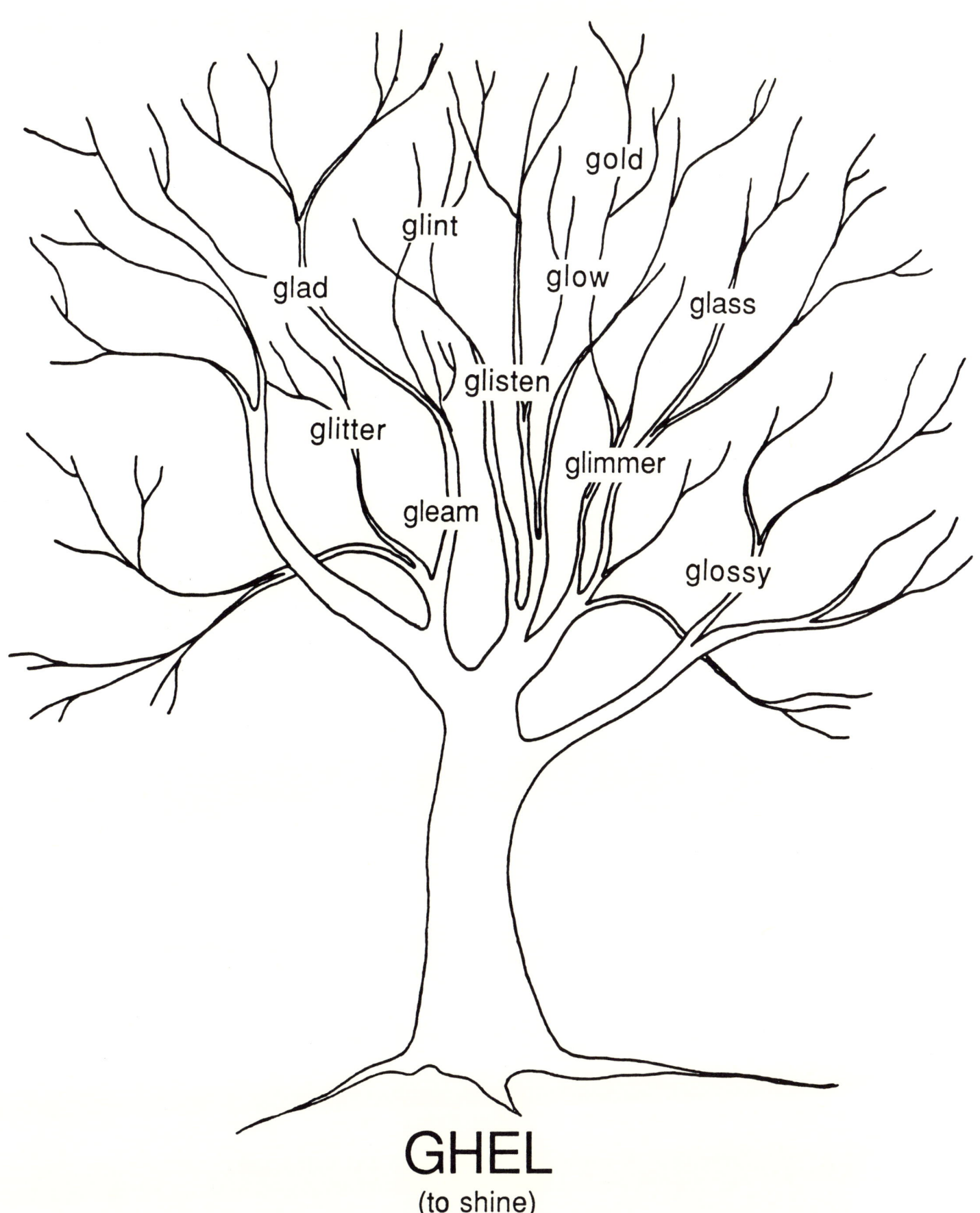

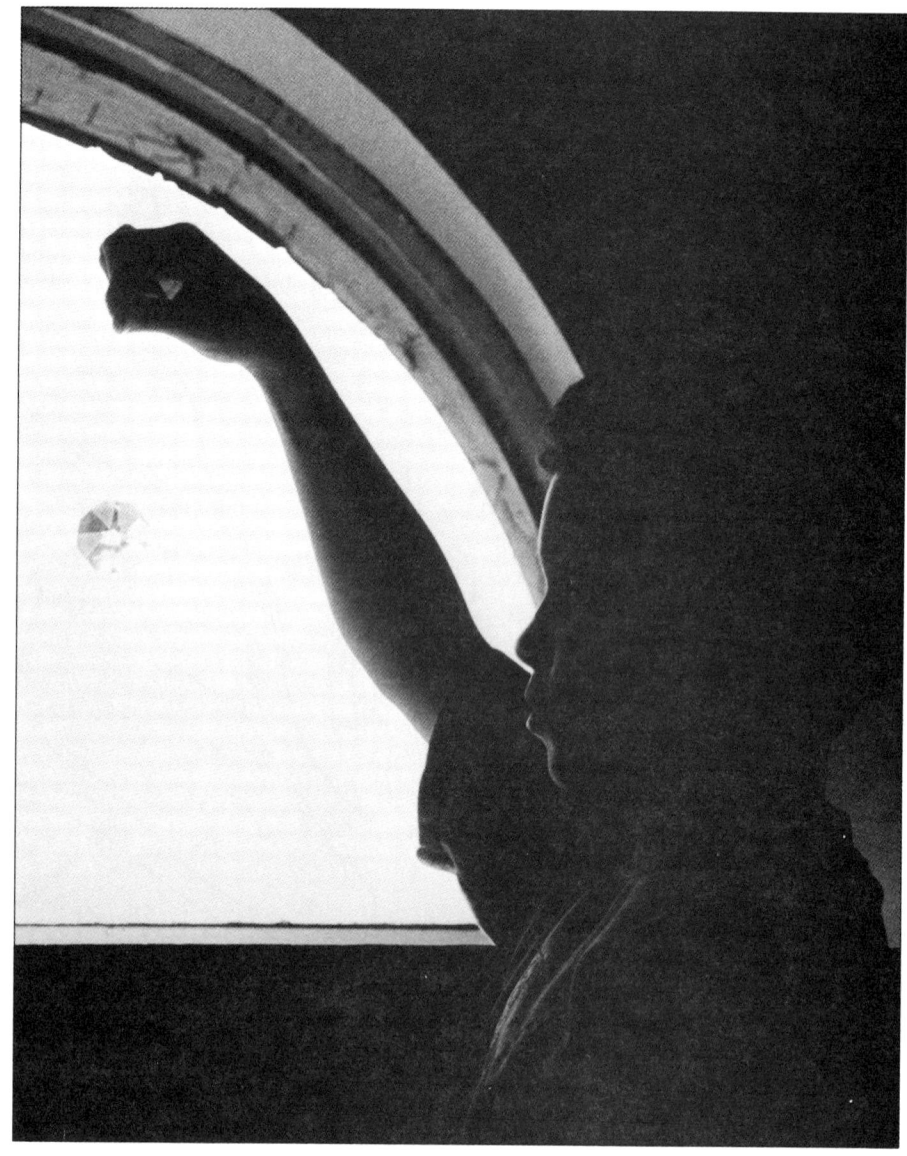

We have often introduced the GHEL family in conjunction with the December holidays, but it is a family that sparkles in any season, and can be connected with celebrations of light found in many cultures.

The poetry that accompanies the family ranges from traditional African and Native American poetry to a rap song and a translation of a Russian poet's conversation with the sun. The chapter includes an "Exploring Extended Meanings" section.

Imagination can substitute for any of the following props, but having them can enliven the lesson: a string of Christmas tree lights, gold glitter, glittery jewelry, glass and metal tree ornaments, tinsel, ornaments decorated with glitter and sparkle; glossy and flat wrapping paper, glossy and matte photographs or magazine illustrations.

Introduction to the GHEL Word Family

> **GHEL**—*to shine*
>
> | | |
> |---|---|
> | glow | glint |
> | gleam | glossy |
> | glimmer | glass, glassy |
> | glitter | gold |
> | glisten | glad |

For thousands of years people in the northern latitudes have celebrated the winter solstice—the seasonal turn that comes during the darkest days of the year and promises a return of light and warmth to the land. The Eskimo poem "There is Joy" reflects yearnings for spring. Lights (candles) in trees, the blaze of the Yule log, and the wreath of candles worn for the feast of Santa Lucia all originally celebrated (and magically invited) the rebirth of light that begins after the solstice. With the coming of Christianity, such lights were used to symbolize a rebirth of spiritual light. The candles of the Hanukkah menorah and the candles launched in tiny boats for the Buddhist Festival of Lights celebrate the rebirth of inner light, as well. The Native American "Song of the Sky Loom" expresses longing for the light of the spirit in a somewhat different mode.

In all cultures that live close to nature, the power and importance of sun and light have been celebrated. "Hymn to the Sun," "Song for the Sun That Disappeared behind the Rainclouds," and "Darkness Song" (all found toward the end of this chapter) celebrate the return of the sun after night or cloudy weather. Flooded with artificial light as we are in our culture, we do not sense the power of light as readily as our ancestors or people in other parts of the world—though we may still remember being afraid of the dark when we were young. Reading the African and Native American poetry can remind us of how fiercely light is treasured when sun and firelight are its only source. Imagine depending on being able to grow food only in a season of light and warmth. How would you feel as you watched the days grow shorter and colder?

You can introduce this family during December celebrations of light, or begin with some of the poetry.

GLOW, GLEAM, GLIMMER, GLITTER, GLISTEN

Responses to the following scenes and questions may overlap, but each new question should elicit some new "shine" words. There are no wrong answers here. The point is to generate as many words as possible that describe shining. List all of them on the board—but list the *gl-* words in a central space and the others in a separate space somewhat to the side of the *gl-* list.

Ask students to close their eyes and imagine the lit candles of a menorah or a Christmas tree as the only light in a dark room. Or ask them to picture tiny boats carrying lit candles and floating on a pond or lake in the dark of night, as in the ceremony of the Buddhist Festival of Lights.

> What words come to mind from these images?
>
> They shine, they *glow,* they *gleam.*

Light a string of clear tree lights in a darkened room, and ask students to describe the lights they use to decorate their homes during the December holidays. Remind students of *why* we use lights to decorate.

> Can you think of other things that glow with a soft light, such as candles in the dark?
>
> > Coals in the fireplace.
> > A campfire seen at a distance.
> > The lights of a city seen from afar.
> > The headlights of a car on a foggy night.
> > A cat's eyes in the dark.
> > The sky at sunset.

In contrast to the moon, stars are described as "twinkling." As you watch a star, its light often seems to grow bright, then dim, bright, then dim—the way a candle might burn unsteadily in a drafty room. What words besides *twinkle* could you use to describe such unsteady light?

> Flicker, *glimmer.*

Close your eyes and imagine the following scene: snow has fallen most of the night. Then, toward morning, the snow turned to sleet, coating tree branches with ice and leaving a glaze of ice over the snow. At dawn the clouds blew away and the sun rose in a clear sky. You awoke to see the sun shining on an icy world. What words come to mind as you try to describe this scene?

> Sparkle, *glitter, glisten.*

The *gl-* words you've discovered all describe some sort of shining, but each one slightly different. The words with smooth-sounding *m*'s and *w*'s describe soft lights—*glow, gleam, glimmer.* The words with the sharper *s* and *t* sounds tend to describe a livelier light that sparkles and dances. *Glisten* and *glitter* are just right for describing the light of the sun on an ice-covered scene. Can you think of other examples of glittering, dancing light?

> Diamonds glitter.
> Broken glass can glitter and glisten in the sun.
> The water of an ocean, a lake or a brook can glitter and glisten in the sun.

If you can, supply props such as gold glitter, glittery jewelry and glittery holiday ornaments: glass and metal ornaments, tinsel, ornaments decorated with glitter and sparkle. Let students experience the glittery nature of these props firsthand.

GLINT

There is another *gl-* word that, like *glitter*, has a sharp *t* sound and, like *glitter,* tends to describe a light that flashes off a shiny surface—especially a moving surface that throws light off in many different directions. Christmas tree lights might flash off mirrored and metallic ornaments as they dangle on a tree. You could describe the light as _____ off the ornaments.

Glinting.

We might see light glinting off many different smooth, shiny surfaces. Can you think of some examples?

Light might glint off: a polished car.
a sword.
the metal armor of a medieval knight.
diamonds.
water.

GLOSSY, GLASS, GLASSY

Use the poem "Marbles" to introduce *glossy* and *glassy*, or ask students to imagine handfuls of marbles catching the light, and fashion your own introduction based on that image.

Think about marbles' shiny surfaces—about light bouncing off them and shining through them. Listen to one poet's thoughts on marbles and see if you can discover the *gl-* words in her description of these shining objects.

Marbles

Marbles picked up
Heavy by the handful
And held, weighed
Hard, glossy,
Glassy, cold,
Then poured clicking,
Water-smooth, back
To their bag, seem
Treasure: round jewels,
Slithering gold.

—*Valerie Worth*

Why do you think the words *glass* and *glassy* might have come from a root that means "to shine"?

Light shines through glass; light bounces off its smooth surface and can create a shiny, sparkling surface.

Glossy is a word used to describe a smooth, shiny surface.

Supply contrasting props such as glossy wrapping paper and paper with a flat finish, a glossy and a matte photograph, a magazine with glossy pages and a magazine or book with pages that have a flat finish, perhaps some glossy material such as satin. Let students get a feel for the meaning of *glossy* as they examine the props.

We often think of things that shine as attractive, and the words *gloss* and *glossy* often show up in commercials to advertise positive qualities of a product. For example...

Lip *gloss*.
A shampoo or conditioner to make your hair *glossy*.
A floor wax to give a high-*gloss* shine to your floor.
Dog food that claims it will make your dog's coat healthy and *glossy*.

GOLD

Archaeologists sometimes unearth treasures from ancient civilizations that have been buried for thousands of years. Some of their more famous "digs" have been Tutankhamen's tomb and ancient palaces at Troy, Mycenae, and Knossos. Many things at these sites had disintegrated after lying in the earth for thousands of years, but things made of a certain metal had kept their shine, and, on the day they were dug from the earth, they looked as bright as the day they were buried. The metal of these objects—jewelry, masks and goblets—is a metal that has always been treasured for its ability to keep its shine and never grow dull—and its name is one of our "shine" words. Its spelling pattern is *g*-vowel-*l* instead of *g*-*l*-vowel and it is...

gold.

GLAD

We often feel more cheerful on a bright day than we do on a dark, grey day. One of the GHEL words reflects this connection between light and happiness and actually *means* happy. A *g*-*l*-vowel word that means happy is...

glad.

When we talk about a "glow of happiness" or somebody's face "shining with happiness" we are connecting light and happiness. Here are some other examples:

He has a sunny disposition.
There is a song that begins: "You *light* up my life."
And another that begins: "You are the sunshine of my life."

The Root: Meaning and Spelling

Ask a volunteer to underline the spelling pattern shared by all but one of the words.

> What is the spelling pattern of the one word that is left over?
>
> *g*-vowel-*l*

Sometimes, over time, a vowel switches places with a consonant. This happens particularly often with *r* and *l*. It so happens that our root today has the same *g*-vowel-*l* pattern as *gold*.

The root of today's family is GHEL. (It was really all the other words in the family that changed pattern slightly and *gold* which kept the pattern of the root.) What is the meaning of GHEL?

> *To shine.*

What happened to the *h* of GHEL? As in BHEL and DHREU, people stopped pronouncing the breathy sound represented by the *h*, and it fell out of use.

Note on *Glory* and *Glorious* as "Sound Cousins"

Glory and *glorious* do not come from GHEL. They can be traced back only as far as the Latin *gloria*, which means "glory"—not much added illumination there. But they can legitimately be considered "sound cousins" of the GHEL words. Glory is defined as "great honor, praise, or fame" or "great magnificence"—and we readily associate such highly positive attributes with images of light. Medieval paintings present religious glory in golden and glowing hues, and with haloes and aureoles. A glorious day is likely to be one full of sunshine. A person who has "great honor, praise, or fame" is likely to be considered a "shining example to others."

Include *glory* and *glorious* as "sound cousins," if they come up, and record them off to the side of the GHEL word tree.

Wrap-up

Have students fill in the root and the words of the family on the class word tree and on their individual word trees. Possibilities for GHEL illustrations are many. Encourage students to brainstorm for ideas for a variety of scenes. Alternatively, use the poetry as a source of inspiration.

Definitions to Record

gleam: to shine with a soft light, sometimes steadily, sometimes in a brief flash of light; a soft light
glimmer: to shine with a soft, flickering light; a dim, flickering light
glow: to shine brightly and warmly, as glowing coals shine; a warm light
glitter: to shine with bright, sparkling light; a bright, sparkling light
glint: to flash off a shiny surface; a brief flash of light
glossy: smooth and shiny
glisten: to shine with reflected light

Additional Related Words

GLEE

Have you ever heard of a *glee* club? In the Middle Ages, gleemen were wandering singers and entertainers who sang, played musical instruments, and recited stories and poetry. Their entertainment brightened people's lives. Today, a glee club is a singing group.

GLAZE

The potter put a bright red glaze on his pots.
Marie's eyes were glazed with fever.

With older students you may want to point out that *glaze* is a variant of *glass* in which the *s* is "voiced" (see the "Linguistic Background" chapter in Volume 1 of *Origins*). *Bath/bathe* and *house/house* are similar noun/verb pairs.

GILT: a thin layer of real or fake gold applied to a surface to make it look golden

Most of the museum's Renaissance paintings were hung in gilt frames.

GLARE: 1. a strong, bright light
2. to shine so brightly that it hurts the eyes
3. to stare fiercely and angrily

As the actors delivered their lines, they had to pretend they could see the people in the audience, but the glare of the footlights made it impossible for them to see any faces beyond the edge of the stage.

The strike breaker carefully avoided looking at the glaring faces of the men and women who walked the picket line.

GLIN: a certain glint of light on the horizon, usually seen in cold weather, a portent of storm

You're not likely to find this word in the dictionary, but it is found in regional speech in Maine. It even has its own saying, "See a sea glin, catch a wet skin."

Exploring Extended Meanings

The following sentences provide a resource for helping students discover how word meanings are extended. See the section on "Exploring Extended Meanings" in the "Using *Origins*" chapter for further background. The sentences are repeated for students at the end of this section under the heading, "Stretch the Meaning."

1. *During the Gold Rush thousands of people traveled west to try to make their fortunes digging for gold.*
   Darron has a heart of gold; he's always helping other people.

   Is Darron's heart really made out of the mineral gold? How is Darron's heart of gold similar to gold mined from the earth?

   Both are valuable. Darron's friends value his generous spirit the way a miner values his gold.

2. *The king said, "Bring me my sword with the golden handle."*
   The queen said, "This is our golden opportunity to slay the dragon."

   Is a once-in-a-lifetime opportunity really made of gold? How is the king's golden sword similar to a golden opportunity?

   They are both special. The golden sword shines, and the golden opportunity stands out or shines above all others.

3. *The jewels and treasure which had been buried for centuries now lay glittering in the sunlight.*
   The flute player gave a glittering performance.

   In what way is a glittering performance like jewels glittering in the sunlight? Is the performer actually sparkling and shining in the sunlight?

   No, but the feeling you get from listening to the performance is similar to the feeling you might get from looking at the beauty of something sparkling in the sun.

4. *Flickering candles glimmered in the windows.*
   As Tania started the sketch for her paintings, she had only a glimmer of an idea of what she wanted to do. As she worked, however, the idea grew stronger and she began to feel excited about what she was doing.

   Did Tania's idea really flicker like a candle? How is a glimmer of an idea similar to a flickering candle?

> A glimmer of an idea is an idea that comes to you in a faint, unsteady way. The idea flickers in the back of your mind. Sometimes the idea will just flicker and die out. Sometimes, however, a glimmer of an idea will catch fire and become a good strong idea.

What happened to Tania's glimmer of an idea?

5. *Chris put a high-gloss coat of wax on the floor.*
   The publicity office tried to gloss over the bad news.

   Did someone put wax over the bad news?
   How is a high-gloss coat of wax similar to glossing over bad news?

   > A coat of wax looks shiny and slippery. You slip and slide on a waxed floor more than you do on a rough surface. When you gloss over bad news you try to slide by it and ignore it.

Hymn to the Sun

The fearful night sinks
Trembling into the depth
Before your lightning eye
And the rapid arrows
From your fiery quiver.
With sparkling blows of light
You tear her cloak
The black cloak lined with fire
And studded with gleaming stars—
With sparkling blows of light
You tear the black cloak.

*—Fang poem
(African)*

**Song for the Sun That Disappeared
Behind the Rainclouds**

The fire darkens, the wood turns black.
The flame extinguishes, misfortune is upon us.
God sets out in search of the sun.
The rainbow sparkles in his hand,
The bow of the divine hunter.
He has heard the lamentations of his children.
He walks along the milky way, he collects the stars.
With quick arms he piles them into a basket...
Until the basket overflows with light.

*—Hottentot poem
(African)*

There is joy in
Feeling the warmth
Come to the great world
And seeing the sun
Follow its old footprints
In the summer night.

There is fear in
Feeling the cold
Come to the great world
And seeing the moon
—Now new moon, now full moon—
Follow its old footprints
In the winter night.

—Eskimo poem

Darkness Song

We wait in the darkness!
Come, all you who listen,
Help in our night journey:
Now no sun is shining;
Now no star is glowing;
Come show us the pathway:
The night is not friendly;
She closes her eyelids;
The moon has forgot us,
We wait in the darkness!

*—Iroquois poem
(North America)*

The Rapper As Light

I am Bad and Tough Enough,
Super Cool and Super Jive.
Just listen to my Rap,
I don't tell no lies.

My lips are all honey,
And my heart is pure gold.
My clothes are all fine,
You know my Rap is bold.

My rings are all rubies.
I don't deal with glass.
If you can't cut it,
Better get lost fast.

I glitter like diamonds,
I glisten like dew.
I gleam like gold,
I glow through and through.

My eyes shine yellow,
My hair is glossy black.
You can't play with me,
I don't cut no slack.

When the sun sees me coming,
He just steps aside.
When the sun sees me coming,
He just tries to hide.

When I talk my stuff,
Just listen to me.
I can make you glad.
I fill your heart with glee.

So, listen to my Rap,
See the glint in my eye.
You'll feel a glimmer of hope.
I electrify.

I outshine the sun,
I'm quick as a cat.
I am the Light,
And you know that!

—*Kate Rushin*

**The Extraordinary Adventure
That Happened to Me,
Vladimir Maiakovsky,
at the Rumiantsev Dacha,
Pushkino, Akulovo Mountain,
on the Iaroslavl' Rail Line**

Sunset glowed in one hundred forty suns,
Summer slid into July.
It was hot,
And the heat made waves.
So it was, in the country.
The hill of Pushkino humped by
Akulovo Mountain,
The bottom of the mountain
A village:
Bent bark roofs.
Beyond the town was a hole
And through that hole, most likely
The sun descended each time
Slowly and surely.
Then in the morning
The sun rose up anew
To pour scarlet over the world,
And day after day
It bugged me
Something awful—
That's how this all
Came to pass.
At last one day I got so mad,
That in anger all else faded,
I shouted in the sun's face:
"Get down!
Rather than drifting 'round inferno—"
I shouted at the sun:
"Freeloader!
You're spoiled up there in the clouds,
But down here
I don't know what winter is, or summer.
Sitting around
Painting posters."
I barked at the sun:
"Hold on!
Listen here, goldilocks—
Instead of wandering about aimlessly
Drop by my place
For some tea."
What'd I done?
Now I'd had it!
Straight towards me
In good will
The sun himself
Spread his beam-steps
And stepped out into the field.

I don't want to show my fear
And retreat a few paces.
Soon the beams of his eyes were in the yard
Already he'd squeezed in through the garden.
In the little windows
Through the doors
Each crack and cranny
The sun's mass barged in.
Barged in.
Taking a breath
He pronounced *in basso*:
"I'm holding in my fires
For the first time since Creation.
You know me, brother?
Serve up the tea, poet!
And some jam, too."
Tears ran from my eyes
The heat was driving me insane
But I
Pointed him
To the samovar.
"What the heck—
Have a seat, you big fireball!"
The Devil'd given me the gall
To yell at him like that.
Confused
I sat on the corner of the bench.
I was afraid
Things would come to worse.
But then a strange
Brightness
From the sun
Streamed out.
Having forgotten
My station
I sat chatting
Idly with the fireball.
Gradually
Before long
We got chummy,
I slapped him on the back
The sun did the same to me, and said:
"You
And I,
Comrade, are two peas in a pod.
Let's go, poet,
Let's go light it up,
Really let 'er rip
In this gray and trashy world.
Me, the sun, I'll pour my own
And you
Your own
With verses."

Walls of shadows
The prison of nights
Felled by double-barrelled suns.
Crescendo of rays and light—
Shine out
At whatever's in your way!
The sun began to tire out
And night wished to lie down.
Go lie down—
Sleepyhead.
Then suddenly
I
Lit up with all my might
And again the day pealed forth.
To shine always
To shine everywhere.
To the days of the last dregs.
To shine
No matter what!
That's my slogan
And the sun's.

—*Vladimir Maiakovsky*
Translated by Christopher Edgar

Song of the Sky Loom

O our Mother the Earth, O our Father the Sky,
Your children are we, and with tired backs
We bring you the gifts you love.
Then weave for us a garment of brightness;
May the warp be the white light of morning,
May the weft be the red light of evening,
May the fringes be the falling rain,
May the border be the standing rainbow.
Thus weave for us a garment of brightness,
That we may walk fittingly where birds sing,
That we may walk fittingly where grass is green,
O our Mother the Earth, O our Father the Sky.

—Tewa
(North America)

Gold

Gold,
    its reflection bends
  the earth
      with awe.
It tempts
    the gangsters
  and
      touches the
  heart.
It speaks coldly
       and
    answers softly
    while whistling
  a tune of
the sun's rays.
Kissing the galaxy
    and warming the
      seas
        it opens
    all feeling
    and greed.
It tackles the
  mind
and touches
the bones.

—*Amy DuRoss, grade 4*

Discussion and Writing Ideas

The GHEL family lends itself to the playful use of the whole "shine" vocabulary as a resource for writing as described in the "Writing" section of the "Using *Origins*" chapter. Individual words of the family can also be the starting point for a poem, as in the following writing idea for students.

Brainstorm with classmates all the words that come to mind when you think of the word *glitter*. You don't need to restrict yourself to words that suggest glittery surfaces. Words that simply *sound* glittery are fine as well. Why might sharp, staccato-sounding words sound more glittery than smooth, drawn-out syllables? Try a few on your own tongue and test the difference. When the list is complete, write a *glitter* poem of your own, incorporating any of the words on the class list that lend themselves to your particular image. Decorate your paper with glitter and exchange your quick flashes with your classmates.

- **Hymn to the Sun**
- **Song for the Sun that Disappeared behind the Rainclouds**
- **Darkness Song**

The disappearance of light can evoke powerful feelings. Read "Hymn to the Sun," "Song for the Sun that Disappeared behind the Rainclouds" and "Darkness Song." Which meditation on darkness speaks most eloquently to you? In "Song for the Sun" the divine hunter collects stars to set against the darkness. Where else might the divine hunter gather light? Where would *you* gather light to set against the dark? From fireflies? The gleam in the eyes of panthers? The yellow of buttercups? The phosphorescent shine of jellyfish? The sparkle in the eyes of a friend? Make a list of places where you might seek light. Use your list as inspiration for a poem.

- **The Rapper As Light**

Can you tap your foot and roll glints and gleams and glimmers off your tongue at the same time? Can you shimmy and shine and stay with the beat? Try it. Try chanting the rap in small groups, with the whole class, or alone. Which performance outshines the sun?

- **The Extraordinary Adventure...**
- **Song of the Sky Loom**

Light is not only for the eyes. The dazzling sun chats with Maiakovsky and inspires him to bring light into the world through his poems. The poet is encouraged to "shine/No matter what." When do you "light up"? When dancing? Running? Arcing a ball into a basket? Singing? Writing? Thinking up a new adventure? When tending your dog? Helping a friend? Sitting by a lake? Take a few minutes to make your own private list. Show your list to friends if you like and brainstorm further examples. Do you share your light with others? How? Next time you feel yourself light up, take a minute to think about how such moments help you to "walk fittingly" in the world.

- **Gold**

Read Amy DuRoss' poem for one writer's meditation on the wonder of gold. Which images are your favorites? When *you* think of gold, which comes more quickly to mind—the lure of finding it or the glow of a sunrise?

Explore your own rich deposits of *gold* imagery by setting a few minutes aside for reflection. Close your eyes and focus on gold—gold as a color or gold nestled under the earth or golden treasure glittering in the sun. Let your imagination make its own connections and quickly jot down the pictures that come to your mind. Let your thoughts steer their own course and try not to discard any ideas that pop in. Next, use the strongest of your images in your own poem.

Stretch the Meaning

1. During the California gold rush thousands of people traveled west to try to make their fortunes digging for gold.
   Darron has a heart of gold; he's always helping other people.

2. The king said, "Bring me my sword with the golden handle."
   The queen said, "This is our golden opportunity to slay the dragon."

3. The jewels and treasure which had been buried for centuries now lay glittering in the sunlight.
   The flute player gave a glittering performance.

4. Flickering candles glimmered in the windows.
   As Tania started the sketch for her paintings, she had only a glimmer of an idea of what she wanted to do. As she worked, however, the idea grew stronger and she began to feel excited about what she was doing.

5. Chris put a high-gloss coat of wax on the floor.
   The publicity office tried to gloss over the bad news.

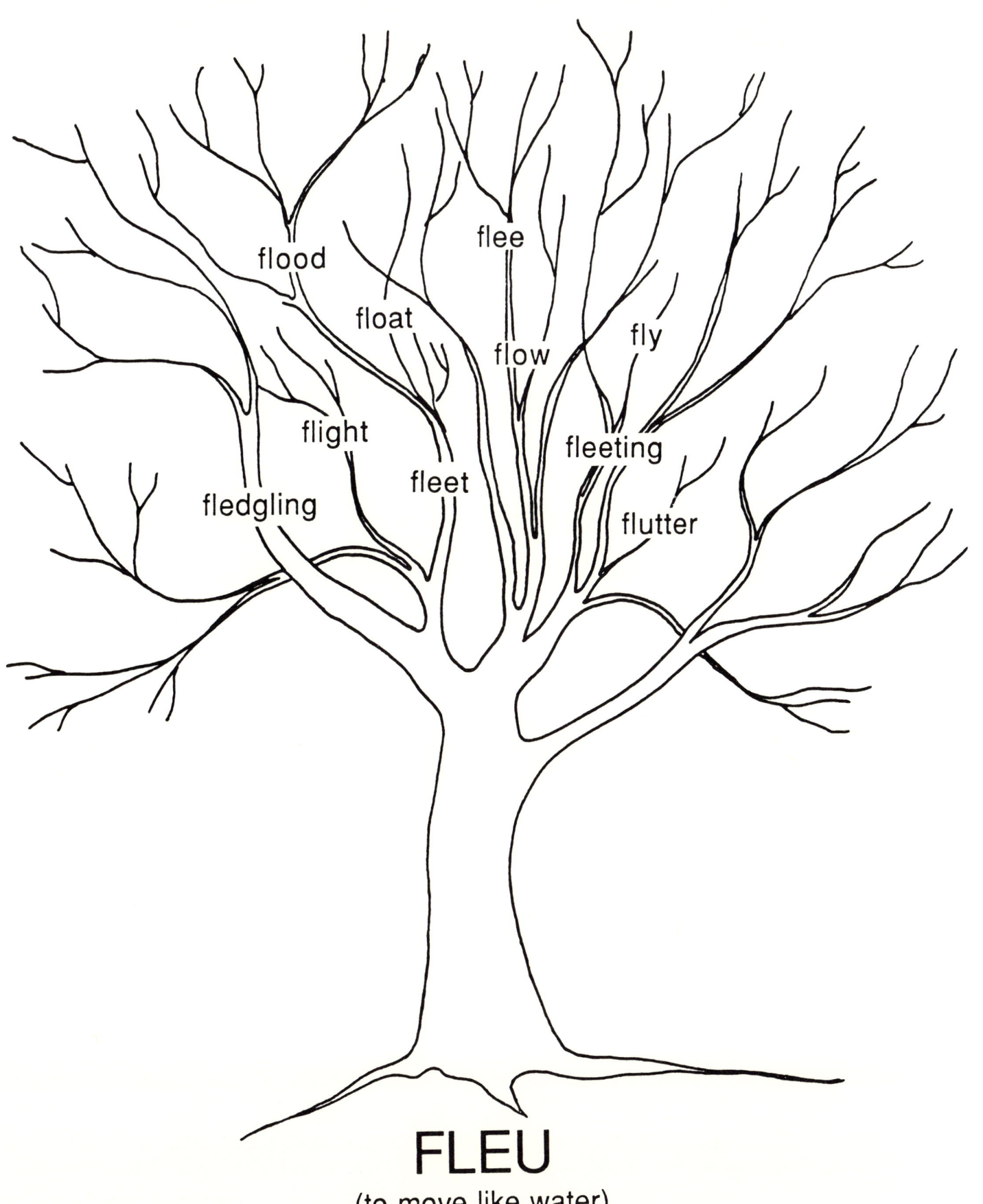

Images of moving water underlie the words of the FLEU family, but in some words the images have shifted from water to air: a boat *floats* on currents of water, a bird *floats* on currents of air. If students quickly generate many words of the family on their own, use the introduction to trace with them how each word moved from its original image to its current meaning. For students interested in such word journeys, we have, at the end of the lesson, suggested several independent projects for exploring FLEU word histories further. "Exploring Extended Meanings" tracks the words of the family as they evolve toward metaphor.

The chapter includes two poems about flight, a version of the Daedalus myth, two poems about the African-American heritage, a seventeenth-century poem by Robert Herrick, and two student poems. *I, Icarus* provides a glimpse of the kinship between flying and moving through water and might be used to introduce the family.

We have labeled the two separate meanings of *flight* and *fleet* with numbers, but you do not need to use these numbers as you discuss the words with students. You can simply say, "Another meaning of *flight* is...."

Introduction to the FLEU Word Family

> **FLEU**—*to move like water*
>
> | | | |
> |---|---|---|
> | fly, flew | flood | fleet[2] |
> | flight[1] | flutter | fleeting |
> | float | fledgling | flee |
> | flow | fleet[1] | flight[2] |

FLY, FLIGHT[1], FLOAT, FLOW

The words of today's family have to do with water and wings—and with that sense of free and easy movement that can come when you leave solid ground and take to the water or the sky. If you take to the water and drift with the currents or on a raft or on your back, you are...

floating.

If you take to the sky on wings of some sort, you are...

flying.

And once you are in the air we might say you are...

in *flight.*

If currents of air or currents of water move along without bumping into any major obstacles, they move freely and smoothly, they...

flow.

What is the spelling pattern for today's word family?

*f-l-*vowel

Today's family comes from the root FLEU, which means "to move like water."

FLOOD

After heavy rains, streams and rivers may become so full they overflow their banks. The overflowing water can cause a...

flood.

FLUTTER

Demonstrate (or have a student demonstrate) the contrast between an object fluttering in air and one that falls straight to the ground. Handy props are two sheets of paper, one flat and one crumpled into a ball. Hold both aloft and release them.

> How did the two pieces of paper fall?
>
>> The crumpled one fell straight to the ground and the open one floated slowly down, moving back and forth.

You may want to drop the sheet of paper once or twice more to help students focus on its back-and-forth movement as it floats to the ground.

> The quick, light, back-and-forth movement you see as the open sheet of paper rides currents of air to the ground is at the heart of the idea of fluttering. What things in nature might we see fluttering to the ground?
>
>> Leaves, especially in the fall; tree seeds, such as maple seeds; a bird's feather.

Originally, *flutter* described the movement of things that were floating and being tossed back and forth by waves and currents of water. This meaning has receded, and now the word is most often used to describe things fluttering in the air. What creatures move through the air with a fluttering movement?

>> Butterflies, moths, some birds.

You might see things made of cloth and hung outside (or by a window) fluttering in the breeze, such as...

>> flags, banners, clothes drying on a line, curtains in an open window.

FLEDGLING

> Often a young bird's first attempts at flight involve fluttery movements—a lot of rapid flapping of wings as the bird tries out its wings for the first time. The name used to describe young birds whose feathers have just grown in (at first baby birds are covered only with fluffy down) and who are just learning to fly is...
>
>> *fledgling.*

A fledgling has the same feathers as an adult bird, but it doesn't have the strength or experience of an adult. The fledgling needs a lot of practice in order to become a full-fledged adult.

FLEET[1]

What do we call a group of ships that sail together under one command?

A fleet.

The use of *fleet* to describe a group of ships reminds us of what ships do: they float. Hundreds of years ago the word was used to mean floating or sailing as well as to describe a particular group of ships. What are some examples, besides the U.S. Navy, of ships or boats or barges operating together as a fleet?

Fishing boats are often organized into a fleet; fleets of coal barges and grain barges float down the Mississippi; fleets of tugboats operate in harbors and help large ships to dock.

When airplanes were developed and began to fill the skies, the word *fleet* was extended to describe planes that operate together as a group. What are some examples?

A fleet of air force or navy jets, such as the Blue Angels.
A fleet of airplanes owned by one airline.

The word *fleet* has, in fact, been extended to describe any group of vehicles that operate together under one command, such as a fleet of buses, a fleet of taxis, or a fleet of trucks.

FLEET[2]

We have discussed one meaning of the word *fleet*—a meaning that is connected to the root meaning of "to move like water" through the image of floating. There is a second meaning of *fleet* that comes from a different image of water—an image of water flowing swiftly. To be fleet is to move swiftly.

The word has often been used to describe the Greek god Hermes (known in Roman mythology as Mercury), who served as messenger for the other gods. Hermes had wings on his cap and on his shoes, and could move from place to place in a flash. Because of his speed, Hermes was often described as...

fleet-footed.

Who might we describe as fleet-footed?

Runners, deer, cheetahs, greyhounds, race horses...

Fleet is usually used to describe living creatures, not objects.

FLEETING

If you watch a toy boat being carried along by a swift-moving stream, will you be able to watch that boat for a long time? Another form of the word *fleet* is used to describe things that pass by swiftly—as a small boat carried by a rushing stream will pass by swiftly. If you catch a brief glimpse of something as it passes by quickly, we might say you caught...

> a *fleeting* glimpse of it.

You might catch a fleeting glimpse of something because *it* is moving swiftly past *you* or because *you* are moving swiftly past *it*. Can you think of examples in both categories?

> You might catch a fleeting glimpse of something if you are moving past it in a car or a train or a boat.

> You might catch a fleeting glimpse of...a rat disappearing around the corner of an alley, a car flashing by on a crossroad, a deer running through the woods, a fish that darts into hiding under a rock, a bird disappearing into the branches of a tree, a shooting star.

FLEE

Close your eyes and imagine something very scary. You want to escape from it as fast as possible. You want to move like swift-flowing water, you want to glide around obstacles, you want to be a fleet-footed runner. Who knows a word that fits the spelling pattern of our family and describes this swift-moving kind of escaping?

> *Flee.*

Gliding easily around obstacles in your path can be an important part of fleeing—and water provides a wonderful example of doing that. What happens when water runs up against a rock or a fallen tree blocking its path? Does it stop?

> As anyone who has ever tried to fix a leak knows, water will flow around (or over or under) most things in its path. A tree falling across a stream might slow its flow temporarily, but the water will quickly build up until it is deep enough to flow over the barrier.

Fleeing successfully often requires this ability to "flow" past barriers as skillfully as possible.

You may want to let students get into the spirit of the word by making their own attempts at fleeing across the room. Who glides around objects with the greatest ease?

FLIGHT[2]

The noun form of the word *flee* is the same word—with a different meaning—as one of the words we have already listed as a member of the FLEU family. We don't talk about people running "in flee" from a fire-breathing dragon or an avalanche or a burning building. We talk about them running in...

flight.

Like the word *fleet*, the word *flight* has two entirely separate meanings. The first meaning of *flight* comes from the same source as the word *fly*. The second meaning comes from the same source as the word *flee*.

Note on "Sound Cousins"

Fluid, fluent, and *flush* are often proposed as members of the FLEU family. *Fluid* and *fluent* both come from a separate root that means "to overflow." *Flush* was originally an onomatopoeic word suggesting a sudden burst of movement—as was the word *flash* originally (as in *flashflood*). All of these words can be considered "sound cousins" of the family since they share both the imagery and the sound pattern. They can be listed to the side of the word tree and they should certainly be welcomed as part of the writing vocabulary.

Wrap-up

Do a brief review of the root, its meaning, and the words of the family. Have students record these on the class word tree and on their individual word trees. Brainstorm ideas for a "picture that tells a story" to launch students on their illustrations for the family.

Definitions to Record

The following definitions should be recorded *after* doing the "Extended Meanings" section because they include meanings from that section.

flight[1]:
1. the act of flying
2. a scheduled airplane trip
3. soaring beyond ordinary limits, as in a flight of imagination

flight[2]: the act of fleeing; escape

flutter:
1. to wave back and forth lightly
2. to wave, flap or toss about in the air

fledgling:
1. a young bird that is learning to fly
2. an inexperienced person

fleet[1]:
1. a group of ships that operate under the command of one person
2. a group of vehicles that operate as a unit

fleet[2]: swift-moving

fleeting: passing swiftly; brief

flee: to run away; to move away swiftly

Independent Projects

Here is a quick bit of speculation a student could do and present to the class. How do you think the word *flight* came to be applied to stairs, as in *flight of stairs*? How does climbing a flight of stairs compare to climbing a ladder? Which is quicker? Which came first in the history of building—ladders or stairs?

A brief project for students interested in doing some further exploration of the FLEU family is to check a dictionary for additional meanings of the word *flutter*. How do these meanings relate to the original meaning of the word, "tossed back and forth on currents of water"?

A somewhat weightier project is to explore the full history of the word *fleet* in *The Oxford English Dictionary* (or *The Compact Edition of the Oxford English Dictionary*). In general, *Origins* has students look at word meanings that are current in the language. It is interesting, however, to find what additional meanings have been part of a word's history. *The Oxford English Dictionary* includes word meanings that go back to the time of the Norman Conquest—supplemented by dated quotations from texts of the time. The quotations are often difficult to read (many are in Middle English), but one can get a sense of the history of a word simply by reading the numbered list of meanings and by noting the dates of the quotations that illustrate each meaning. Past meanings of the word *fleet* include:

> A place where water flows; an arm of the sea.
> A drain or sewer.
> To skim off what is floating on the surface—used to describe skimming milk or cheese.
> To float; to sail.
> To drift or be carried by the current or tide.
> To swim—used to describe fish.
> To float in air—used to describe clouds or mists or scents.

Additional Related Words

FLOTSAM: 1. wreckage that remains afloat after a ship has sunk
2. discarded odds and ends

FLOTILLA: a small fleet

FLETCHER: a person who makes arrows

In the Middle Ages, when hunting was done with bows and arrows, a good fletcher was highly valued. A skillful fletcher knew how to choose the right feathers and attach them at the proper angle to the shaft of the arrow. A well-fletched arrow would fly straight and true to its mark.

The word *fletcher* is derived from the word *fledge,* which means to grow feathers. Do you know anybody by the name of Fletcher? They may well have had a fletcher somewhere in their ancestry.

FULL-FLEDGED: having attained full rank or status

A bird that is *fledged* (see above) has grown all the feathers it needs in order to fly. The term *full-fledged* never seems to have been applied directly to birds, but sprang up as a way of describing people who have gained all the training and credentials that are required in order to "fly" in their particular profession. By contrast, if people are described as "fledglings," they may have all their "feathers," but they still need lots of practice in order to become experienced pros.

Exploring Extended Meanings

The discussion sentences are reproduced for students on a separate page at the end of the FLEU chapter under the heading, "Stretch the Meaning."

1. *The hawk flew across the fields looking for mice.*
   The batter flew into a rage when he was called out on strikes.

   Did the batter literally fly? Did he flap his wings and take to the air? How might flying into a rage be like flapping your wings and taking to the air in flight?

   > It causes a commotion. It happens quickly. People who fly into a rage "take off" emotionally, and it is hard for others to bring them down to earth.

2. *A flood of water gushed from the hydrant.*
   The newspaper ad brought a flood of mail.

   Did the ad draw a little mail or a lot?

   > A lot; the flow of mail was overwhelming.

3. *When hawks are hunting for food they soar in flight, catching a current of air and riding it in their search for prey on the ground below.*
   As Kim waited for the bus, her thoughts took off in a flight of imagination, and she began picturing what she might do for the science fair.

   How might a flight of imagination be like the flight of a bird?

   > If our thoughts take off in a flight of imagination they move freely and easily from one idea to another. A flight of imagination may at times be like the flight of a hunting hawk. At one level our mind is relaxed and rides out currents of ideas wherever they may take us—as the hawk rides the currents of air. Our mind is alert, ready to pluck and hold on to a really good idea if it arises—as a hawk is ready to dive and pluck its prey from the ground.

4. *The fledgling sparrows fluttered and flapped as they made their first awkward flight from the barn rafters to the floor.*
   The newspaper sent the fledgling reporter out on her first assignment, to cover the flood in a nearby town.

   What is a fledgling reporter? Does she have lots of experience? A fledgling bird flaps and flutters as it learns to fly. What things might be involved in "learning to fly" for a reporter? How might a fledgling reporter "flap and flutter" while learning the trade?

   > In "learning to fly" a reporter must learn how to get interviews with the right people, learn what is involved in digging out all the facts of a situation, learn how to put all the information together quickly and well in order to meet the deadline for the paper going to the press. Fledgling reporters need lots of practice before all these things come easily.

I, Icarus

There was a time when I could fly. I swear it.
Perhaps, if I think hard for a moment, I can even tell you the year.
My room was on the ground floor at the rear of the house.
My bed faced a window.
Night after night I lay on my bed and willed myself to fly.
It was hard work, I can tell you.
Sometimes I lay perfectly still for an hour before I felt my body
    rising from the bed.
I rose slowly, slowly, until I floated three or four feet above the
    floor.
Then, with a kind of swimming motion, I propelled myself toward
    the window.

Outside, I rose higher and higher, above the pasture fence,
    above the clothesline, above the dark, haunted trees
    beyond the pasture.
And, all the time, I heard the music of the flutes.
It seemed the wind made the music.
And sometimes there were voices singing.
All of this was a long time ago and I cannot remember the words
    the voices sang,
But I know I flew when I heard them.

—*Alden Nowlan*

Daedalus and Icarus

Long, long ago the island of Crete was ruled by the powerful King Minos. Minos, who wished to live in the most splendid palace the world had ever known, hired a brilliant architect and inventor named Daedalus to build it for him. The palace at Knossos rose up story upon story, over a forest of columns. Winding stairs and intricate passageways connected the many halls and courtyards. Fountains splashed in the gardens and the bathrooms even had running water. Murals decorated the walls and ornaments of the purest gold crowned the roofs. Daedalus gained fame and honor for his great accomplishment.

Daedalus was content with his life. His wife, Naucrate, bore him a son, Icarus, who grew up to be a spirited, boldly adventurous young man. Icarus loved to join in the dangerous bull dances, to go hunting, and to climb the high hills of Crete, where he was as sure-footed as a mountain goat.

But one day Daedalus found himself dishonored and imprisoned with Icarus in the very palace he had built. He was treated harshly, for he had helped a young hero named Theseus escape from King Minos, along with Minos' daughter, Ariadne. Daedalus could not bear to be locked up, unable to use his talents. Secretly he made two sets of wings, one pair for himself and one pair for Icarus. They were cleverly fashioned of feathers in beeswax. He showed Icarus how to use the wings but added a warning:

> Fly not too low, my son, lest you fall into the cold depths of the sea.
> Fly not too high, my son, lest you perish in the burning rays of the sun.
> Fly not too fast, my son, lest your fragile wings fail you.

Daedalus and Icarus climbed to the highest tower, and, flapping their wings, they flew off like two birds. Icarus, exulting in his powers, rose on soaring wings. He could not resist the temptation to rise ever higher into the sky; the whole world shimmered below him. He flew too close to the sun and the wax began to melt. The feathers came lose, the wings fell apart, and Icarus plunged into the sea and drowned. Daedalus, powerless to help his son, sadly flew on alone to safety on the island of Sicily.

—Adapted from *D'Aulaire's Book of Greek Myths*; Gerald McDermott's *Sun Flight*; and Ian Seraillier's *A Fall From the Sky: The Story of Daedalus*

Wings

Lorenzo
Wrote a poem
About a Hitchhawk
How that bird could fly
Fly high and mean and strong
Fly like smoke
Like a terrible kite
Fly out and into light
Out doors and windows long green corridors
Basement lavatory principal's office
Nurse's room Out the center
Of the desk The bird could wing it
Teacher say This the first thing
Lorenzo here has done all year
Most likely be the last
Lorenzo smile
A high dark smile
He knew the bird could fly
He knew how wicked well
He knew how shining
Lovely was the
Flight

—Elizabeth McKim

The Negro Speaks of Rivers

To W.E.B. Dubois

I've known rivers:
I've known rivers ancient as the world and older than
      the flow of human blood in human veins.

My soul has grown deep like the rivers.

I bathed in the Euphrates when dawns were young.
I built my hut near the Congo and it lulled me to sleep.
I looked upon the Nile and raised the pyramids above it.
I heard the singing of the Mississippi when Abe Lincoln
      went down to New Orleans, and I've seen its
      muddy bosom turn all golden in the sunset.
I've known rivers:
Ancient, dusky rivers.

My soul has grown deep like the rivers.

                —*Langston Hughes*

Runagate Runagate (excerpt)

Runs falls rises stumbles on from darkness into darkness
and the darkness thicketed with shapes of terror
and the hunters pursuing and the hounds pursuing
and the night cold and the night long and the river
to cross and the jack-up-lanterns beckoning beckoning
and blackness ahead and when shall I reach that
      somewhere
morning and keep on going and never turn back and
      keep on going.

    Runagate

        Runagate

           Runagate

Many thousands rise and go
many thousands crossing over

              O mythic North

                —*Robert Hayden*

Upon Julia's Clothes

Whenas in silks my Julia goes,
Then, then, methinks, how sweetly flows
The liquefaction of her clothes!

Next, when I cast mine eyes and see
That brave vibration each way free,
—O how that glittering taketh me!

—*Robert Herrick*

Floating

                                          I'm floating
                                               on
                                          my back
                                                 on
                                          the waves

up I
  go
down I
  go

                                                                              I hear
                                                                               the
                                                                               smaller
                                                                                  kids
                                                                              shouting and

playing
  but
I'm not

                                                                              I'm floating
                                                                                on the
                                                                                        waves

WHEE
   I SHOUT
up I go
   down
I go

                                                                              I kick
                                                                                   my legs
                                                                              up and

down a
bigger
wave

                                                                              "Help!"   I
                                                                              shout
                                                                                       I go
                                                                              flying through
                                                                                        the
                                                              air

I'm in the
    air
and I look
   up
and see a
cloud
which
                                                 smiles at
                                                         me
                                                I hear the
                                                   ocean
                                               singing
                                               to the air like
                                               it's
                                               serenading
                                               her

Shhhh
goes the ocean
the air answers
    back
"WOOO"

                                               I land from
                                                     my flight
and I land
   with a
     big
splash
                                               I see a
                                                 dolphin
A cloud becomes   it jumps
   dark
then they all
   do
it starts raining
  "Qilasweli!" screams
     my father
I leave
   the ocean
no one is on
      it   the ocean goes
              Shoo
                 Shoo
                    Shoo
                       Shoo
                         Shoo
                           Shoo
                             Shoo

—*Shafali Jeste, grade 3*

The Idea

The idea fled from the flood of
logic that disproved it,
flying from the sleet
that burned,
from the grim silence
such as the heel of a shoe,
fleeing onto the rings of Saturn,
disoriented.
The insinuating snake
burying itself in fruit
was the logic.

In the guise of a dream the idea
came. In all the quickness
of something that you almost had.
Like the sand that a child
tries to catch
but can never quite.
The snowflake that you take in
to show your sister, it was almost
gone.
But not forever.

—Veronica Schanoes, grade 6

Discussion and Writing Ideas

- **I, Icarus**
- **Daedalus and Icarus**
- **Wings**

The FLEU family is delicious. It feels good on the tongue. Close your eyes and repeat the word "flutter" (softly to yourself) at least twenty times. Do you begin to see the rhythmic beating of wings in your mind's eye? Try repeating "flutter" louder with other people. How does your mind's picture change? Switch to *fly*. How does the movement in your mind change? Mine becomes freer, more graceful, easier, surer, as I glide through air on the *y*. Try repeating *fly* while someone else repeats *flutter*. Listen for the difference. What things might be best described using the word *fly*? What things *flutter*? Do some things both flutter and fly?

Fly and *flight* are powerful words in the human imagination. From the earliest times people have wanted to learn how to fly like birds. The ancient story of "Daedalus and Icarus" is a fine example. Now swoop to the here-and-now with "I, Icarus." What elements are the same?

Flying is not only *physical*. We also speak of flight as a spiritual and mental moving beyond limitations. The vision then becomes one of "wider vistas," the opening up of our personal "horizons." We can dream of what we want to be when we move beyond our daily earthbound selves. In the flight of the mind, we can feel freedom and power. In "Wings" by Elizabeth McKim, what does Lorenzo *know* that his teacher never suspects? Why do you think he chose to write about a Hitchhawk? Why does he smile a "high dark smile"?

Some people have dreams in which they fly. Do you? Can you describe them?

If you could fly, would you slip out your bedroom window at night, or would you astonish your friends with a graceful take-off during recess? What would flying feel like? Where would you go? What would you look for? What secret life would you live? Would you ever return?

What about flying mentally? When do you choose to fly mentally? Why? What is happening around you? Is your mind taking wing to escape or to celebrate something? Write about what flying is like for you (physically, mentally, or both). Choose any form you like. Be clear and specific.

- **The Negro Speaks of Rivers**

Langston Hughes compares the black soul to the history evoked by the Euphrates, the Nile, and the Mississippi. We all have currents of heritage that can waken special feelings in us—memories, events, and places that rouse in us a sense of being part of a larger flow of time and people. That sense might be wakened by watching a dragon wind down the street in a Chinese New Year's parade, by the beat of salsa, by the taste of fry bread, tahini, or lox, by the sound of the blues, a polka, or Mozart. It might be wakened by the smell of the sea, of freshly turned earth, of paint in an artist's studio. What things remind you that you are part of larger communities and histories—part of a larger flow than the isolated moment? Take a few minutes to list things that speak to you of your special heritage, as a member of a cultural group, as a musician or artist, as a player of sports, as part of a tradition of sailing, farming, mining, ranching. Then exchange lists with classmates, and add any new ideas you get from reading them.

If you like, use your list as a starting point for your own poem. As you write, help us see how you feel part of the heritage you describe, as Langston Hughes does in his poem. Have your people been farmers for many generations and do you feel especially at home on a farm, even though your family now lives in a city? If so, perhaps you have "known" the sounds of cows waiting to be milked. Perhaps you can say, "I have plowed the fields, I have pulled the beans from the vines, I have piled the hay in the barn," because somewhere in your bones you feel connected to these things even though you haven't actually done them. Are you a musician? Perhaps you have felt a kinship with African drummers. Perhaps you can say, "I have been Louis Armstrong playing his horn, I have blown Irish melodies on the flute and fiddled for Appalachian cloggers," because you feel part of the flow of such musical heritage. Choose your heritage and let us see how you feel part of its flow.

• Runagate Runagate

Flight from oppression arouses deep emotion in anyone who has known or imagined oppression. "Runagate Runagate" by Robert Hayden, describes the flight of black men and women through the Underground Railway with Harriet Tubman. The terror of fleeing and the determination to keep going are expressed in every line. Read "Runagate Runagate" as a choral piece. Practice until your reading sounds unified and strong. Afterwards, write or draw for ten minutes on your own.

You might want to write a poem that has lots of *and*'s in it, like Robert Hayden's. As a group, discuss your responses.

• Upon Julia's Clothes

Have you ever seen things that both flow and glitter? A river sparkling in the sun? A sequined gown? Fireworks arcing through the night? The double dance of light and movement can enchant us, as Julia's gorgeous silky clothes enchant Robert Herrick. Typical of the clothes worn by wealthy women in the 1600s, Julia's long silky dress flows and vibrates around her as she walks, reflecting light from its glossy surface and dazzling the poet. He is "taken" by the sight.

Can you think of things that flow or glitter that "take" and dazzle you because they are so attractive? Describe one in a poem so that we feel as drawn to it as you are.

• Floating

Listen to Shefali Jeste's poem. Can you close your eyes and imagine yourself floating with her? Now think up your own floating adventure. Imagine yourself drifting on a lake or river or ocean. (Lying on your back on the floor can help put you in the right frame of mind for this exercise.) What do you see above you? Is anything moving? How is it moving? Are you perfectly motionless, or are you moving your arms and legs? Now close your eyes and notice your skin. How cold is the water? Is it completely calm or can you feel currents rippling around you? What creatures do you imagine moving around you in the water? What sounds can you hear coming from shore? If your ears are underwater, can you hear your own breathing? What smells come your way as you drift along the bank? Does the water taste salty, muddy, fresh? How does the side of your body above the surface feel different from the side submerged? When you've soaked up a lot of impressions, open your eyes and write down all the details you can remember. If you've never learned to float, you're in luck! Your imagination can make a perfect buoy of your bones. Keep a copy of your poem close to you until you've memorized it. The next time you try floating again, repeat it to yourself.

- **The Idea**

This mysterious poem has a series of images and ideas that we can't quite catch in their flight. The odd thing is that, of all these things we can't quite grasp, we do "get" something.

Stretch the Meaning

1. The hawk flew across the fields looking for mice.
   The batter flew into a rage when he was called out on strikes.

2. A flood of water gushed from the hydrant.
   The newspaper ad brought a flood of mail.

3. When hawks hunt for food they soar in flight, catching a current of air and riding it in search for prey on the ground below.
   As Kim waited for the bus, her thoughts took off in a flight of imagination, and she began picturing what she might do for the science fair.

4. The fledgling sparrows fluttered and flapped as they made their first awkward flight from the barn rafters to the floor.
   The newspaper sent the fledgling reporter out on her first assignment—covering the flood in a near-by town.

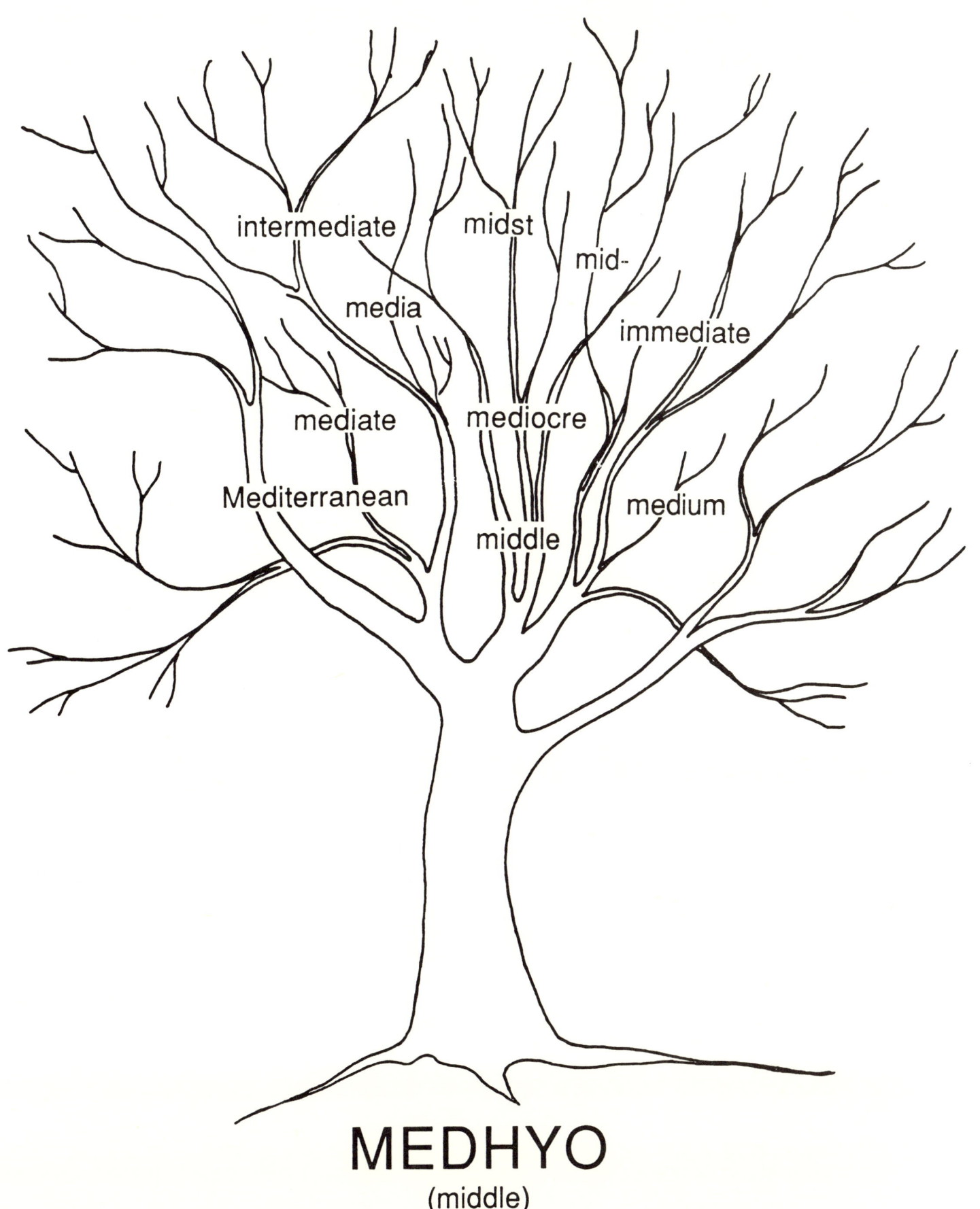

The MEDHYO family introduces a new element: a word family that includes both Germanic and Latinate vocabulary. The MEDHYO family has no Extended Meaning section as such because the meaning of Latinate words usually is extended or abstract to begin with. Before the Norman Conquest and the Renaissance, most of the "idea" words of the language were built on familiar, everyday words. Thus, a mediator might have been called a "middle-goer." After the Conquest and the Renaissance, however, many of the idea words were imported from French and Latin. As a result, it takes extra digging to find the everyday images that underlie these words. In the MEDHYO family the Germanic cousin *middle* reveals the image that underlies its Latin relatives.

You may want to refresh your understanding of how vocabulary from two different language groups might be found in one family by consulting the "Brief History of the English Language" chapter in Volume 1. The amount of historical background that you give your students is up to you. We usually introduce the family without labeling the words as Germanic or Latinate. If you want to use labels, it should be done informally and not overemphasized.

Introduction to the MEDHYO Word Family

> MEDHYO—*middle*
>
> *from Germanic*   *from Latin and French*
>
> **middle**   **mediator, mediate, mediation**
> **midst**   **medium**
> **mid-**   **intermediate**
>   **Mediterranean**
>   **immediate**
>   **mediocre**
>   **media**

MIDDLE, MEDIATOR, MEDIATE, MEDIATION

A skit of a mediation can provide a lively introduction to the MEDHYO word family. Have two volunteers dramatize a disagreement over a current issue in the school or community. A third volunteer then steps into the middle of the argument—between the two opponents—and says, "I think I can help you settle this disagreement." The dramatization ends with the mediator helping the two sides reach a solution.

> What were the opponents arguing about?
> Were they able to solve the problem themselves?
> Where did the third actor stand after stepping into the scene?

> In the *middle*—between the opponents.

> *Middle* is the root meaning of today's word family and also one of the words of the family.

If you have Spanish-speaking students, you will want to introduce the Spanish *medio* ("middle, medium") and *medianoche* ("midnight").

> What did the outsider do after stepping into the middle of the situation?

> Helped the two sides stop arguing and come to an agreement.

> Does anybody know the name we use to describe a person who steps into the middle of a situation to help two sides settle a disagreement?

> A *mediator*.

There are other forms of the word *mediator*: *mediate* and *mediation*. *Mediation* does not have to involve physically stepping into the middle of a situation; it is simply the *idea* of stepping into the middle of a disagreement to help settle it.

Are there any mediation efforts to settle strikes currently in the news? Use any examples that might be familiar to students to help reinforce the meaning.

MIDST (IN THE MIDST OF)

Because *midst* is seldom used by itself, give students the whole phrase.

If recess ends and you are *in the midst of* a game, has the game ended?
If you are *in the midst of* an argument, has anything been settled?
If you lose your way *in the midst of* a crowd, where are you?

MEDIUM

Dogs come in all sizes. Some are large, some are small. Those in the middle might be called middle-sized or...

medium-sized.

You might have students brainstorm for other examples of the use of *medium* to identify something as being in the middle between two extremes. Possible examples: *medium* height, *medium* build, *medium* temperature, *medium* as a label for clothing sizes, a *medium* rare hamburger.

Using *medium* as a label to describe things as being in the middle between two extremes is the most common use of the word. The scientific use of the word is slightly different. Here are some examples:

Water is the *medium* in which fish live.
Air is the *medium* for human life.
Soil is a *medium* for plant life.

How is *this* use of *medium* connected to the idea of middle?

Fish must live in the middle of water, humans must live in the middle of—surrounded by—air, most plants must begin life in the middle of soil.

MEDITERRANEAN

Use a globe or a map that includes the Mediterranean Sea.

South of Europe and north of Africa is a sea that is mostly surrounded by land. Its name gives a clue to its location. Who knows the name?

The *Mediterranean* Sea.

Terra is an old word meaning "land or earth." So Mediterranean means "in the middle of the land."

INTERMEDIATE

Children who are just leaning to swim may be in a beginners' swimming class, others who have learned to swim very well may be in an advanced class. What's the name of the class between beginners and advanced?

The *intermediate* class.

We often use *intermediate* to describe a middle stage of ongoing development. A person who starts off as a beginner may expect to move forward to an intermediate level and later an advanced level.

Have your students come up with other examples of *intermediate* (intermediate school, etc.).

IMMEDIATE

Choose two volunteers to dramatize *immediate* and coach them on lines such as the following:

Sam: Lucia, come quick! I can't hold the dog any longer! He jumped the fence and I can't get him back inside.
Lucia: I'll be there in a minute. Let me put my shoes on.
Sam: No! Don't wait for anything! Come right away!

When did Sam want Lucia to come?

Right away, *immediately*.

Immediate comes from the prefix *im-* ("not") and the root *mediatus* ("in the middle"). Record these elements on the board and discuss how they were combined to create the idea of "nothing in the middle."

What did Lucia want to do "in the middle" between Sam's call and going to help? In an emergency there is no time for something "in the middle"—a response must be *immediate*.

MID-

In some communities the *mid*day meal is the largest meal of the day. When would a midday meal be served?

In the middle of the day, around noon.

Mid- is used as a prefix for some words in place of writing *middle*—*mid*east for Middle East, for example. What term do we use to describe the part of the country where Iowa, Illinois and Kansas are located?

The *Mid*west.

Ask students to brainstorm some other examples of *mid-* words. Here are some examples you might elicit: *mid*week, *mid*night, *mid*-twenties, *mid*field, *mid*-air.

MEDIOCRE

Ask for two volunteers to act out this brief scene. They are shopping for a birthday gift for a younger sister or brother and are examining a shelf of display toys—various trucks, cars, trains, buggies, or the like.

> "These look like great toys for a four-year-old."
>
> "I really like this red car. It looks well-made, sturdy, as if a kid could play hard with it and it wouldn't break."
>
> "Look at this big green car. When I first saw it, I thought it looked great, but if you look closely you see it's only mediocre."
>
> "You're right. The red car was made by someone who knows how to make something that will survive a lot of handling. It's high quality. Let's buy it."

In the conversation, did you hear an *m*-vowel-*d* word that means not very good—not entirely bad, but not very high quality either?

> *Mediocre.*

What else might be described as only mediocre—not totally bad, but not high quality?

> The food at a not-so-terrific restaurant.
> A book or story that doesn't hold your attention.
> A research paper that didn't get revised or edited.

Mediocre comes from an old word which meant "halfway up the mountain." Today our meaning emphasizes the idea of getting only half way to a goal but failing to reach it. We always use the word in a negative way.

MEDIA

Three or four actors can clarify the connection of *media* to *middle*. An important athletic event (or a speech, press conference, election, concert) is taking place and it is being covered on TV. (Additional volunteers could play the roles of newspaper reporter taking notes, radio announcer describing the action.) One actor represents the camera crew, one the on-screen reporter, one or two are the athletes pantomiming their sport. The reporter stands between the camera crew and the event itself, holding a microphone and speaking to the camera. For example:

> It's the last inning of the game, folks, and the score is now tied, 5-5, with two men on base. Will the home team be able to pull it off? For those of you at home today, stay tuned to WMED to see the exciting conclusion of this championship game.

Does anyone know an *m*-vowel-*d* word which refers to newspapers, television, radio and other means of mass communication?

> *Media.*

Where did the reporter stand when speaking to the television audience?

> Between the event and the camera, or audience. In the middle.

The root meaning of *media* reminds us that newspapers, television, radio, etc. stand in the middle—between us and the events they report. The media give a wider view of events than any one person could gain, but the view comes through a middleman. The picture we get is not the event itself, but somebody else's view of it.

Note: In Latin, *media* is the plural form of the word *medium*. The Latin plural was adopted into the English language and is usually used with a plural form of a verb. Example: *The media are giving the event extensive coverage.* However, because many people are not aware that *media* is in fact plural, the word is often used in its collective sense and treated as a singular. Example: *The media has developed a lot of new technology in recent years.*

The Root: Meaning and Spelling

Review the root meaning and the words of the family.

> What is the spelling pattern for today's family?
>
> > *m*-vowel-*d*
>
> The root for today's family is MEDHYO, which, as we've discovered, means *middle*.

Sound Cousins

Moderate is often proposed as a member of the MEDHYO family. It happens to come from the root MED, which means "to take appropriate measures," but since *moderating* a meeting often involves being "in the middle" in some way, and a *moderate* quantity is a middle point between too little and too much, the word can be considered a sound cousin. It shares both imagery and a spelling pattern with the MEDHYO words.

Wrap-up

Have students record the root, its meaning and the words of the family on the class word tree and on their individual word trees. Brainstorm ideas for a "picture that tells a story" to launch students on their illustrations for the family.

Definitions to Record

mediator: a person who comes in to help settle a dispute or disagreement
intermediate: in the middle, between. Used especially to describe something that comes between a beginning and an advanced level.
mediocre: of medium quality
media: newspapers, magazines, radio, television and other means of mass communication

Story Puzzle

When introducing the story puzzle, "The Pinball Mediation," remind students that in some cases they may need to add endings (such as *-ly*) to make words from the MEDHYO family fit the blanks.

Note on the *Im-* of *Immediate*

The *im-* of *immediate* is a variant of the prefix *in-*, "not." The prefix traces back to the Indo-European root NE, "not." NE is the ultimate source of the Germanic words *no, not, nothing, none, never,* and *neither*. In a vowel-consonant reversal, it gave rise to the prefix *un-* as well. (See the "Linguistic Background" chapter in Volume 1 for discussion of vowel-consonant reversals.) NE is also the source of the Latin-based *nil, null*ify, *neg*ate, de*ny,* and the prefix *in-*.

The other *in-* prefix often found at the beginning of Latinate words means "in" and comes from a different Indo-European root: EN, "in." You have to look at the context or the specific derivation in the dictionary to tell the two prefixes apart.

Although the two *in-* prefixes have two separate meanings, they both behave in the same manner when they attach themselves to words. The *-n* of the prefix often changes to become the same as the first letter of the word. Before the letter *p*, the *n* usually becomes an *m*. Thus, *immobilize, impatient, impossible, illegible, illiterate, irresponsible,* and *irregular* are all based on the "not" version of *in-*, as are the more obvious *inactive, indecisive, incredible, inflexible, insensitive,* etc. *Immigrate, immerse, important, impress, illuminate,* and *illustrate* are based on the "in" version of *in-*, as are the more obvious *include, increase, indent, inhabit, inquire,* and *inscribe*.

Additional Related Words and Phrases

MEDIAN: the middle number of a series

MEDIEVAL

Medieval comes from the Latin *medium* (middle) and *aevum* (age). *Primeval*, which shares the same ending, refers to the "first ages."

MIDDLEMAN

MIDRIFF

MEDIUM OF EXCHANGE

A medium of exchange, such as money, stands in the middle between us and what we wish to have. Instead of trading a sack of grain for a length of cloth, we let money stand for a value, and we then exchange it for something we want.

Story Puzzle for Students

Read the entire story to yourself before filling in the blanks from the MEDHYO word tree. The challenge is to see if you can use all the words of the family.

The Pinball Mediation

Cherisse and Ray and some of their sixth-grade friends were hanging out at Cherisse's dad's store, playing pinball and video games. In the _____ of an exciting game, an older boy named Duke stopped Ray and demanded to use the game. Duke was only of _____ build, but he looked tough.

"Listen," snarled Duke, "I'm the best player around. If you don't let me play right now, I'll toss you all the way to the _____ Sea!" Ray was mad. He'd taken karate and was already in the _____ class, but he didn't want to fight over a game.

Cherisse took one look at them and stepped into the _____ of the situation. "There's no need for you to fight. I know how to settle this," she said like a real _____. "You two would argue until midnight over who's the best pinball player. Pretty soon the police would arrive and the _____ would be here to report on the disturbance. Now here's what you do. Each of you will play three games and the player with the highest score will be the winner."

Duke was strutting like a peacock, sure he would win. Ray was nervous. But halfway through the playoff, it was clear that, for all his talk, Duke was only a _____ player. Ray won easily and was called, forever after, the Pinball King.

114

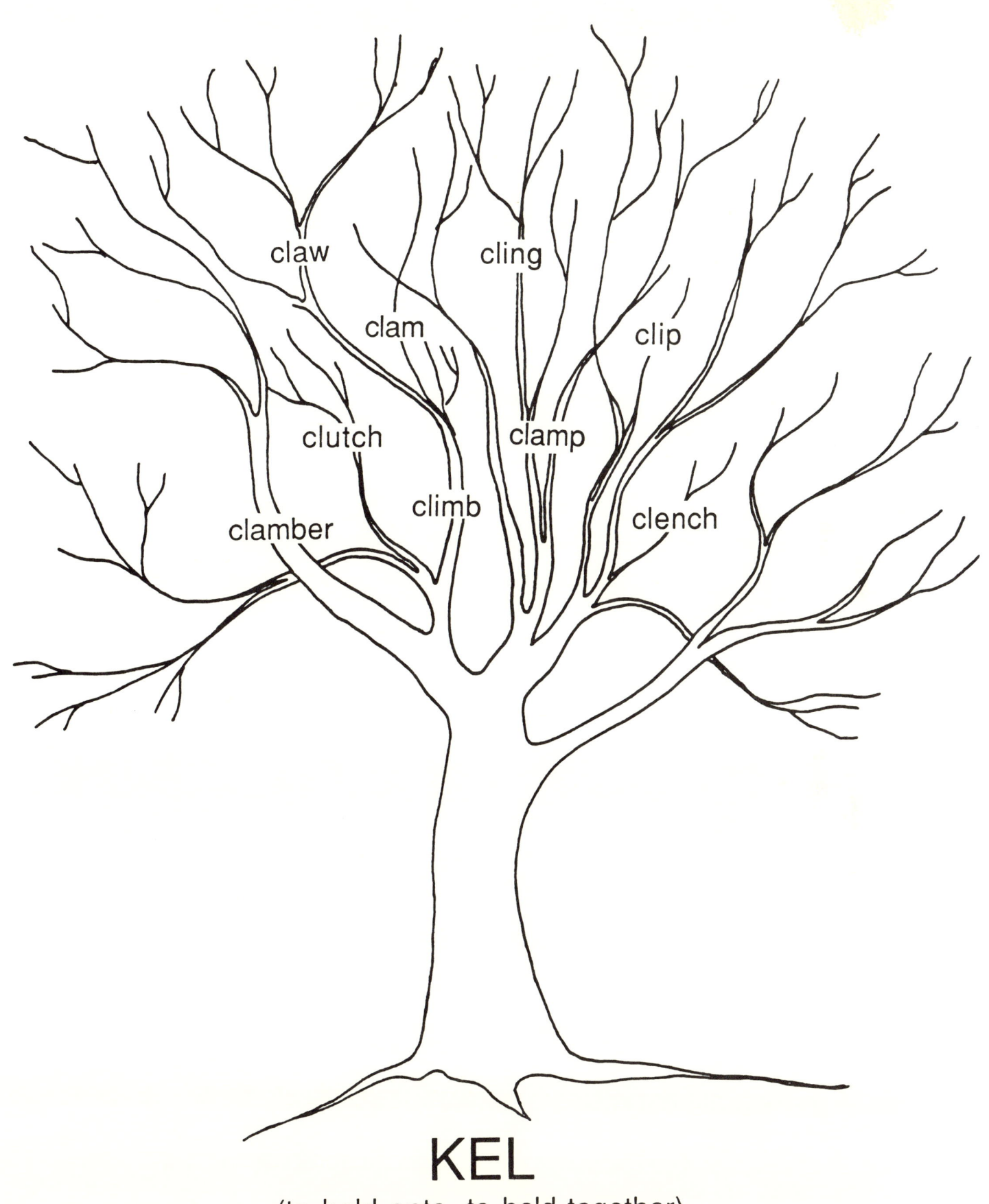

In this chapter the focus is on how the homely, down-to-earth reality of the KEL words becomes a vehicle for expressing ideas—as seen in the "Exploring Extended Meanings" and "Regional Sayings" sections. You can move through the introduction at a quick pace, then look at figurative uses of the words. Then comes the playful part—inventing your own metaphors and sayings, which in turn can be used as an inspiration for writing.

Materials useful for introducing the family are paper clips, a clamp, a clamshell. A clamshell makes vivid the implied comparison to the mouth in the regional sayings based on *clam*.

Introduction to the KEL Word Family

> **KEL**—*to hold onto; to hold together*
>
> | clip | climb | clench |
> | clamp | clamber | clutch |
> | clam | claw | cling |

CLIP, CLAMP

Gathering loose papers to be held by a paper *clip*, and using a C-*clamp* for holding pieces of wood together, or clamping a piece of wood to the table provides a quick introduction to the root image that underlies the family (*to hold onto, to hold together*) and to a pair of words that will establish the "look" of the family: *clip* and *clamp*.

CLAM

What is a sea creature that can *clamp* itself shut, *holding* its shell shut tightly for protection?

A *clam*.

CLIMB, CLAMBER, CLAW

How do you get up a ladder? You have to do more than step with your feet, you have to...

climb.

Originally *climb* referred to getting to the top of things by holding on with your hands as well as feet. Today we often use the word more generally: if we climb a hill, we may just hike up. We can use a closely related word—*clamber*—to emphasize the kind of scrambling up that requires hands *and* feet. What are some examples of clambering?

Hikers clambering up a cliff.
Window washers clambering down scaffolding.

How does an animal *climbing* or *clambering* up a tree *hold on*?

With *claws*.

What else do animals hold onto with their claws?

Cats, lions, and tigers use claws to capture and hold onto prey, as do lobsters, crabs, and crayfish.

CLENCH, CLUTCH, CLING

Get everybody on their feet for some quick pantomimes.

> You're coming out of your corner in the ring, ready to meet your opponent. How are you holding your fists?

> *They're clenched.*

> Now you've got a football and you're running for the goal line (in place!). Hold that ball tight! Don't drop it! A word that can describe how you're holding onto that ball is...

> *clutching.*

> O.K., now you've been climbing a rock cliff, inching up slowly, searching for handholds and footholds. You're holding onto a ledge with your hands when suddenly the piece of rock you've been standing on peels off and you're left hanging by your hands. Hold on tight! A friend is running for help. Don't let go! This kind of holding tight can be described by the *cl-* word...

> *cling, clinging.*

> What are some other examples of clinging?

>> Plastic wrap clinging to a surface.
>> Clothes coming out of the dryer that cling to each other because of static electricity.
>> Sweaty, wet clothes that cling to your body.
>> Small children who cling to their parents because of shyness or fear.
>> Vines clinging to trees, fences, etc. as they climb.

The Root: Meaning and Spelling

> The words of the family all begin with *c-l-*vowel. What's another way to spell that beginning sound?

> *k-l-*vowel

> The root for today's family is KEL. Just as in the GHEL family, the *l* and the vowel switched places over time.

Additional Related Words

CLASP: 1. a thing to fasten two parts or pieces together, such as a buckle or hook
2. to hold closely with the arms; a hug or embrace

The metal clasp on my rain slicker is stuck.
I clasped the puppy and ran home.

CLAY: The stiff, sticky kind of earth that tends to "hold together" rather than crumbling

CLINCH: 1. to hold one another tightly in a boxing or wrestling match
2. to settle definitely or fix firmly

Clinch and *clench* both refer to securing or holding on to something. Usually *clench* is used to describe holding onto an object, holding your hand tightly to make a fist or closing the teeth together tightly. *Clinch*, by contrast, refers to a whole-body hold—one that results in the other person not being able to move. In popular speech, *clinch* may be used to mean a romantic embrace.

Only *clinch* is used when talking about settling an argument or finalizing an agreement. In an argument, the *clincher* is the deciding factor, the fact or remark that settles the issue, and brings any further verbal moves to a halt.

CLUMP

CLOT

CLUTTER: to litter or pile things in a confused way

Clutter evolved from *clot* and originally referred to things grouped or gathered together in little heaps.

Exploring Extended Meanings

The following sentences provide a resource for helping students discover how word meanings are extended. (See the "Exploring Extended Meanings" section in the "Using *Origins*" chapter for further background.)

The discussion sentences are reproduced for students on a separate page in the "Stretch the Meaning" section at the end of this chapter.

1. *Damali climbed the hill in back of her house.*
   The singer's latest hit is climbing the record charts.

   How is climbing the charts similar to climbing a hill?

   The record is headed for the top—of the popularity charts.

   What are other examples of things that climb the way a record climbs?

   Prices climb; temperatures climb.

2. *The clamp held the corners of the frame together until the glue dried.*
   The police said they were going to clamp down on speeders.

   Are the police talking about using C-clamps to catch speeders? How is what the police do similar to what a clamp does?

   The police are planning to hold something—traffic speed—firmly where they want it, which is similar to the way a clamp holds pieces of wood where you want them. A clamp uses physical pressure to keep things in place. The police create pressure by giving speeding tickets.

3. *Juan clutched the ball and ran for the goal.*
   On the night of the first performance, Felix clutched and forgot all his lines.

   Is clutching a ball a tight, tense movement or a loose, relaxed movement? Was Bobby tense or relaxed?

   When you clutch, you "tighten up" inside.

Ask students to describe or pantomime situations in which they have "clutched."

4. *The fish wriggled out of the clutches of the raccoon and swam away.*
   "Aha, now I've got you," chortled the witch as she grabbed Hansel and held him in her clutches.
   The country fell into the clutches of an evil tyrant.

   Did the evil tyrant actually hold the country in his hands the way a raccoon might hold a fish in the clutches of its paws or the witch might hold Hansel in the clutches of her hands? How is the tyrant's having the country in his clutches like the other examples? Do people in his country feel free to move about as they like and say what they think?

5. *The baby clings to his mother whenever they go to new and unfamiliar places.*
   My grandfather clings to memories of his youth and tells us wonderful stories about his boyhood days on the farm.

   > Can you hold onto a memory with your hands? When someone clings to his memories, how is that similar to a child clinging to his mother?

   >> Neither wants to let go of what is important to him. They hold on to what they treasure—with hands, in one case, with the mind in the other.

6. *After the kids teased her, Emily clammed up.*

   > Was Emily talkative or silent?

   Ask students to demonstrate clamming up.

   > How is this kind of clamming up similar to what a clam does to defend himself?

   >> You close your mouth tightly. A clam closes its shell up tightly so that it can protect itself.

Wrap-Up

Have students record the words of the family, the root, and its meaning on their word trees. Brainstorm ideas for a "picture that tells a story."

Definitions to Record

clench:	to close or press tightly together
clutch:	to grasp or hold on tightly or firmly
clutches:	1. grasping hands, paws, claws, etc.
	2. control or power
cling:	to hold fast or stick closely
clamp down:	to become more strict

Regional Sayings

CLAM

tighter'n a clam

> In Maine "tighter'n a clam" can mean two things:
> closed-mouthed
> locked up tight.

clam mouth

> A New England term for close-mouthed

clam it

> A phrase heard in North Carolina—an abrupt way of telling somebody to be quiet

How did these phrases grow out of familiarity with the ways of a clam? Why did these phrases spring to life in New England and North Carolina, rather than in Minnesota and Illinois, for example?

You won't hear him blabbin' about it; he's tighter'n a clam.
We got them things done up tighter'n a clam.
That one's a real clam mouth, she is.
O.K., clam it. I've heard enough.

CLAW

claw out, claw off

> These two phrases heard in New England, North Carolina, and Tennessee mean to get out of an embarrassing or threatening situation. A claw-off can be an excuse.

> What sights or experiences might have inspired these sayings? Seeing a cat or squirrel scramble up a tree? Or a raccoon, a bear, a possum? Do you want to get out of an embarrassing situation quickly or slowly? How do claws relate to a quick exit?

Soon as he heard the law was on its way, he clawed out of there.
When his old girlfriend came back to town, he clawed off and we ain't seen him since.
Aw, that's just a claw-off. You coulda done it if you'd a tried.

CLUTCH

In certain areas of Pennsylvania, if a child says, "Give me a clutch," he or she may mean, "Give me a piggyback ride."

In certain areas of southern Maryland, you might hear someone describe a clump of trees as a "clutch" of trees.

Give me a clutch, Mom, I can't walk any farther.
You go for a couple of miles, pass the gas station on your left, then, just past a clutch of woods on your right you'll see the old farm.

Inventions

Now it's time to coin some expressions of your own. They needn't have anything to do with the KEL family. Just look for words that will inspire you. Here are a few examples to give you a sense of the possibilities:

I'm feeling a bit *chairish* today.

> If I say I'm feeling *chairish*, do you think I'm feeling like running and jumping and dancing? Am I likely to move around a lot?

Real *shouty* weather we've got today, isn't it?

> What's happening outside? What's the wind likely to be doing?

They *clapped* out of here and I haven't seen them since.

> Did they move slowly? Drag their feet as they left? How did they move?

We just *rugged* around all day.

> What picture comes to mind? What kind of things might you do if you rugged around all day?

Work on your own or in small groups. First, brainstorm a list of words you can use as resources. Looking around the room or looking out the window can provide you with a starting point, as can imagining a favorite place. Then invent new uses and meanings for your words. Be playful. Your meanings can be silly or serious, whichever you like. When you're finished, read your inventions to the class. Can anyone figure out what they mean? Are they a hit? Will you be hearing them around school for weeks to come? Perhaps you should get together with friends to make your own dictionary. Alternatively, the inventions can be inspiration for a group poem or story or for individual poems and stories.

Stretch the Meaning

1. Damali climbed the hill in back of her house.
   The singer's latest hit is climbing the record charts.

2. The clamp held the corners of the frame together until the glue dried.
   The police said they were going to clamp down on speeders.

3. Juan clutched the ball and ran for the goal.
   On the night of the first performance, Felix clutched and forgot all his lines.

4. The fish wriggled out of the clutches of the raccoon and swam away.
   "Aha, now I've got you," chortled the witch as she grabbed Hansel and held him in her clutches.
   The country fell into the clutches of an evil tyrant.

5. The baby clings to his mother whenever they go to new and unfamiliar places.
   My grandfather clings to memories of his youth and tells us wonderful stories about his boyhood days on the farm.

6. After the kids teased her, Emily clammed up.

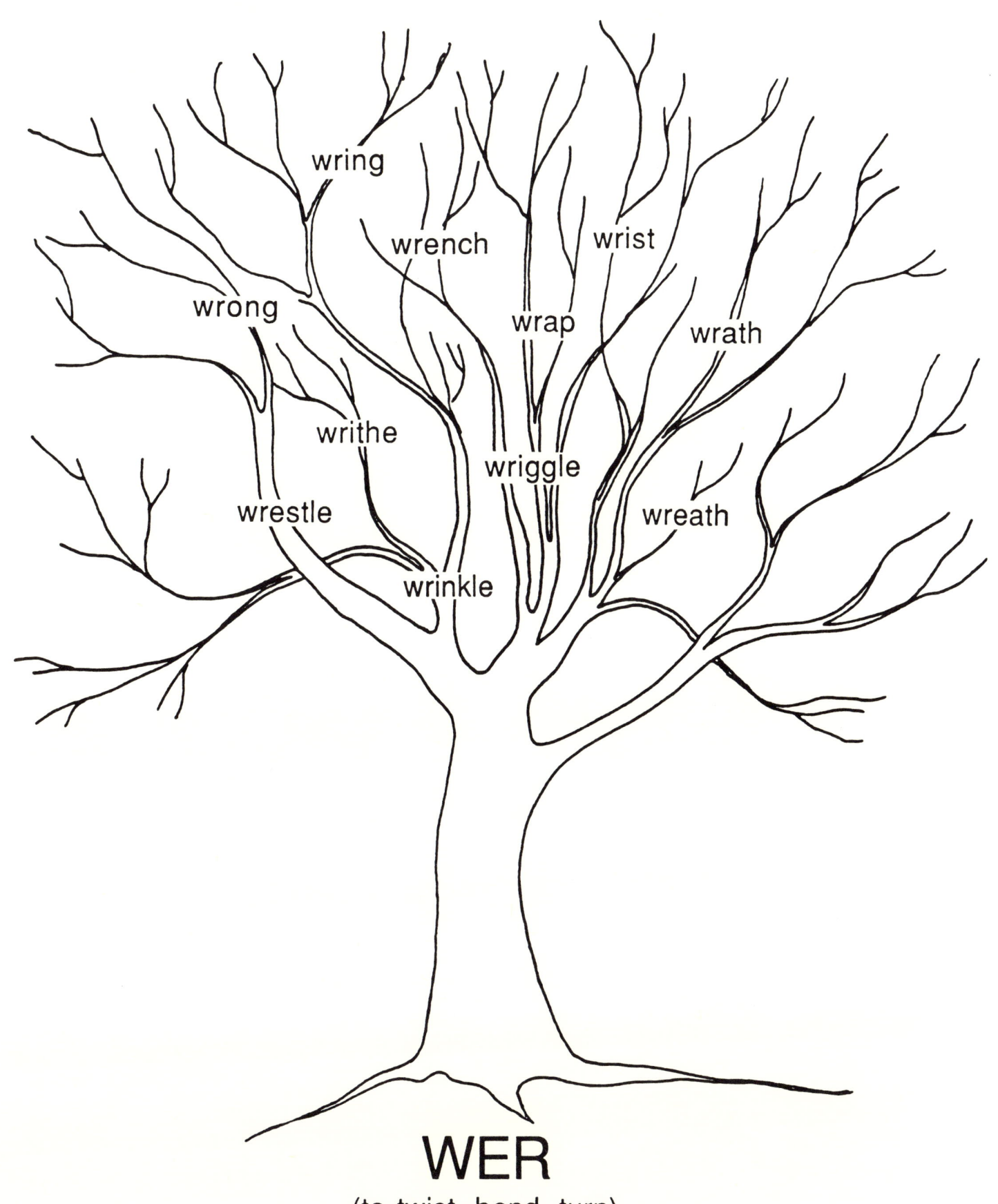

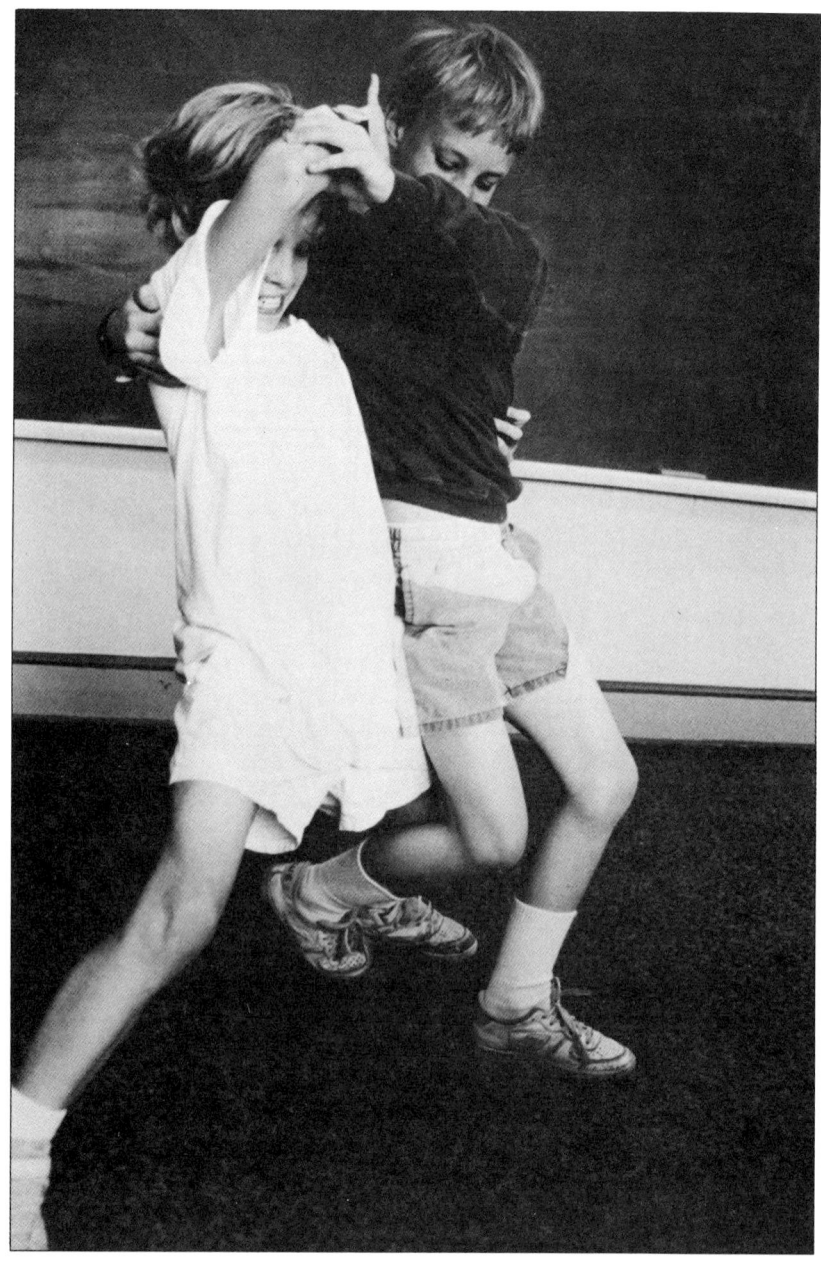

The vocabulary of the WER family invites pantomime and remains especially vivid in students' memories as a resource for their own writing. The poetry in this chapter and the "Exploring Extended Meanings" section both show how the imagery of the words has been used to express figurative meanings.

Examining the spelling pattern of the family can lead to an understanding of silent letters and an understanding of why beginning spellers often invert vowels and *r*'s.

Materials useful in exploring this family are: a wrench, a rag, and a basin of water, wrapping material, and a wreath.

Introduction to the WER Word Family

> **WER**—*to twist, bend, turn*
>
> | | | |
> |---|---|---|
> | wrestle | wreath | wrong |
> | wring | wrap | writhe |
> | wrench | wriggle | wrath |
> | wrist | wrinkle | |

WRESTLE

Begin with a pantomime of an amateur wrestling match. (Emphasize that this is a good-humored demonstration, not a fight.)

What are the actors doing?

Wrestling.

How can we describe their movements? Are their bodies straight? Do they move in a straight line?

No, they twist, bend, turn.

WRING, WRENCH

Have one volunteer pantomime wringing a wet cloth into a basin (or use the real thing). Ask another actor to pretend to loosen a bolt with a wrench. Or ask all the students to take part in both pantomimes.

What kind of movement do both of our pantomimes have in common?

Twisting, turning.

What do you think the root meaning of today's word family might be?

To twist, bend, turn.

What word describes the twisting movement being used to squeeze water from a cloth?

Wring.

Our second actor is a plumber. What tool is he using?

A wrench.

We talk not only about using a wrench to loosen a bolt or pipe fitting. We can also talk about wrenching, or twisting, a knee or shoulder.

The halfback wrenched his knee when he spun into a quick turn to avoid being tackled.

What do you think the spelling pattern for today's word family is going to be?

w-r-vowel

WRIST

What part of the body twists and turns and shares the *w-r*-vowel spelling pattern with the words on our list?

The *wrist*.

WREATH

During the winter holidays, people often twist branches of evergreen into a circle to form a...

wreath.

Are there some other occasions when people make wreaths?

WRAP

Have volunteers wrap an object with paper, a doll with a blanket, themselves with a shawl.

How is *wrap* connected with our root idea *to turn, bend, twist* ?

You bend the covering around the object.

We wrap things to cover or protect them; often the word carries a feeling of coziness and warmth in such cases.

The mother wrapped her baby in a warm blanket.
When he got out of the swimming pool shivering with cold, Mario's dad wrapped him in a big soft towel.

WRIGGLE

How does a worm move across a sidewalk after a rain?

It moves by twisting and turning; it *wriggles*.

Here are possible pantomimes:

You are bored and restless and start wriggling in your seat.
You wriggle your toes in the sand.

You try to wriggle into a pair of pants that have grown too tight.

The twisting and turning movement involved in wriggling makes it a good method of escape from a tight situation.

The child wriggled out of her mother's arms and ran back for one last turn on the swings.
The thief wriggled through a hole in the fence and escaped down the alley.

WRINKLE

If your clothes have been lying in a twisted heap in the corner, what word might describe them?

Wrinkled.

Where else might we find wrinkles?

WRONG

When a person who has been in trouble decides to start following the law and doing the right thing, we sometimes say that he or she is "going straight." What is a *w-r*-vowel word we might use to describe the opposite of "going straight"?

When people get in trouble they take the *wrong* path; they "turn away" from doing what they should.

WRITHE

Picture a football player getting hurt, falling to the ground, and twisting back and forth in pain. Can anybody think of a *w-r*-vowel word that describes this twisting back and forth in pain?

Writhing.

Can you think of other examples when a person or animal might writhe in pain? *Writhe* can also describe twisting or squirming with embarrassment.

To make the meaning of *writhe* memorable, use pantomime. Students might like to experiment with the contrast between the relatively gentle movement of *wriggling* and the more violent, out-of-control movement of *writhing*.

ᛞ

If your class happens to be familiar with Greek myths, you might remind them of Medusa, who had writhing snakes in place of hair on her head and turned men to stone with her horrible looks.

WRATH

> The last word we are going to add to the family describes a feeling. The word describes very strong anger—anger that twists and turns inside you until it explodes with rage or fury. Does anybody know a *w-r*-vowel word that describes this kind of anger?
>
> *Wrath.*
>
> Wrath is reflected in a person's face. An angry person's face is sometimes described as being "twisted with rage."

To make *wrath* vivid do contrasting pantomimes of a peaceful face and a face twisted with rage:

> Close your eyes and remember a completely happy, peaceful time or place. Let your face show the contented feelings of that memory.
>
> Now, think of something that makes you very angry. Remember the time when you were the angriest you have ever been—and let your face show your feelings. If you are making an angry, twisted face, we could describe you as looking *wrathful*.

Ruth Whitman's poem "Listening to grownups quarreling" and two student poems, "Parents Fighting" and "Fights," can be used to introduce *wrath*.

The Root: Meaning and Spelling

> All the words in today's family grew from the root WER. What is the meaning of the root?
>
> To twist, bend or turn.
>
> And what is the spelling pattern for the words of the family?
>
> *w-r*-vowel

Silent Letters: Their History Is a Spelling Clue

> In the *w-r*-vowel spelling pattern, which letter is silent? Today we no longer pronounce the *w*, but hundreds of years ago, people pronounced both the *w* and the *r* in the words of the family.

Have students experiment with pronouncing the words as they were originally pronounced, sounding both the *w* and the *r*. (E.g. pronounce *wrap* more or less as *wuhrap*.) Such playfulness can help students remember the silent *w* in their spelling.

For further discussion of silent letters, see the "Different Spelling Patterns of Several Languages Thrown Together" section of the "Brief History of the English Language" chapter. Discussion of the silent *w*'s of the WER family can be a touchstone for discussing silent letters wherever students may encounter them. Understanding that a now-silent letter represents a clue to how a word was pronounced hundreds of years ago makes its spelling more interesting and more memorable.

Inverting Vowels and R's: Common in the History of Our Language and in the Work of Beginning Spellers

Do any of you remember spelling *first f-r-i-s-t* or *birthday b-r-i-t-h-d-a-y* when you were first learning to spell? Switching *r*'s and vowels around is a common mistake for beginning spellers—and the same kind of switch or inversion sometimes takes place in the historic development of words. Where do we see this inversion in the WER family? How is the spelling pattern of the root different from the spelling pattern of the words of the family?

※

For a more complete description of why *r*-vowel and vowel-*r* inversions tend to take place, see the "Linguistic Background" chapter. Understanding this inversion can be useful to students who have trouble with it in their own spelling. They are often reassured to find that their "mistakes" have been a common occurrence for centuries. The knowledge does not provide a magic cure, but it can help make the problem interesting.

Note on Connections between Images of "Twisting" and the Idea of *Wrong* and between Images of "Straightness" and the Idea of *Right*

It is interesting to note that images of *twisted, bent,* or *crooked* have often been used to express the idea of something being wrong. In legal language, a *tort* is a wrongful act and *tort* is based on the Latin *tortum,* "twisted." *Distort* comes from the same root. If someone *distorts* the facts of a situation, we get an account of it that is wrong. If we describe someone as having a *warped* or *twisted* mind, we think of their perspective on things as wrong. Someone who is depraved (from the Latin *pravus,* "crooked") has likewise veered onto the wrong path, as has someone whose values are *perverted* (from the Latin *vert,* "to turn").

By contrast, the word *right* comes ultimately from the Indo-European REG, "to move in a straight line"—as do *correct, rectitude, regular,* and *regulation.* Staying on the right path has sometimes been described as staying on the "straight and narrow."

Note on "Sound Cousins"

Write and *wreck* are often proposed as members of the WER family. Although they happen to come from different roots, they can certainly be considered "sound cousins" because they share both a spelling pattern and the imagery of twisting and bending—things that are *wrecked* are often twisted and bent out of shape and *writing* often involves twisting and bending movement. *Write* comes from a root that means "to scratch," which reminds us of its origins in carving, and *wreck* comes from a root that means "to push or shove." Since the *w* of *write* and *wreck* is no longer pronounced, it might be more accurate to call them "spelling cousins," but it won't hurt to stick with "sound cousins," since the visual pattern does, at some level, evoke a sense of the sound they once shared.

Wrap-Up

Hand out the word trees and ask students to fill in the root and the words of the family on the class word tree and on their individual word trees. Brainstorm for ideas for WER family "pictures that tell a story."

Definitions to Record

wrath: very great anger; rage
wreath: a circle of flowers, leaves or branches twisted together
wrench: 1. to twist sharply and suddenly
        2. a sharp, sudden twisting
        3. a tool for turning nuts, bolts, etc.
wriggle: to move by twisting and turning
writhe: to squirm in pain or embarrassment; to twist and turn with strong or violent movement

Additional Related Words

WARP: 1. to turn, bend or twist out of shape
       2. to turn away from a natural or healthy course; to distort true meaning or understanding

The door has warped and we can't close it.
The players were so angry at the umpire, it warped their good judgment. They lost their concentration and lost the game.

How is having your judgment warped like having a warped door that won't close?

Notice that *warp* follows the *w*-vowel-*r* spelling pattern of the root WER.

WORM

What creature wriggles through the earth or across the sidewalk, or twists and turns at the end of a fishhook? It too follows the *w*-vowel-*r* pattern of WER.

WORRY

Another word that follows the *w*-vowel-*r* pattern describes a feeling of concern that might cause you to frown—or wrinkle your brow. What is a *w*-vowel-*r* word that you would use to describe how you would feel if you were nervous about taking a hard test?

WRY

Some smiles are ear-to-ear; others are smaller smiles that twist one corner of the mouth. Do you know a word to describe this crooked, slightly twisted smile?

James made a wry smile when he heard the pun.

Scientists studying the nature of smiles have discovered that spontaneous smiles tend to be symmetrical, using both sides of the mouth and face equally. Conscious, deliberate smiles, on the other hand, tend to use only one side of the mouth and face—and thus look wry.

AWRY

A closely related word (built on the word *wry*) describes things that have gotten turned or twisted to one side, as your clothes might be after an energetic game.

Juan's clothes were all awry after wrestling with a friend.

An extended meaning of *awry* refers to situations getting out of order.

Our plans went awry and we never made it to the baseball game.

WRANGLE: 1. to argue in a noisy way
               2. a noisy quarrel
               3. to herd or tend horses on the range

The experience that underlies the idea of *wrangling* is similar to the experience that underlies the idea of *wrath*. Angry feelings twist and turn inside—and in this case they burst forth in noisy quarreling.

Do you think controlling horses—some of them wild—was a quiet business for the cowboys?

Exploring Extended Meanings

As usual, the discussion sentences are reproduced for students at the end of this chapter.

1. *Ravi won the wrestling match.*
   Later, he wrestled with a math problem as he did his homework.

   > Did Ravi use his arms and legs as he wrestled with the math problem? Did he roll around on the floor with it as he would with a wrestling opponent? How is wrestling with a problem in your head similar to an actual wrestling match?
   >
   >> It is difficult—as a wrestling match is difficult.
   >> You struggle. Just as a wrestler moves back and forth trying to get a hold on his opponent, you move back and forth in your mind, trying one thing and then another as you struggle to "get hold of" a solution.

   By accident, Mr. Pennywhistle rode his bicycle through the glass door and shattered it. He felt guilty about smashing the door and wrestled with his conscience about what to tell Mrs. Pennywhistle. Should he tell her the truth or should he blame the accident on George, their St. Bernard?

   > How did Mr. Pennywhistle's wrestling with his conscience involve moving back and forth in his mind?
   >
   >> One minute he might say to himself, "I must tell the truth; it's not fair to blame poor old George." The next minute he might say to himself, "I can't tell the truth. Mrs. Pennywhistle will be furious! Let George take the blame." He twists back and forth from one thought to another as he struggles to make his decision.

2. *Emilio wrapped up a birthday present for his sister.*
   Detective Brenda Chang wrapped up her case.

   > What happened to the detective's case?
   >
   >> She solved it.
   >
   > How is wrapping up a case similar to wrapping up a present?
   >
   >> When you wrap up a case, you cover all the questions that need to be covered, tie all the pieces of evidence together, and present it to the judge.
   >
   > Can you think of other things you might wrap up the way you wrap up a case?
   >
   >> You might wrap up: the evening news
   >>   a meeting
   >>   a discussion
   >>   a story you are writing

Just before she wrapped up the case, Brenda Chang warned her partner to keep the information under wraps.

> If somebody asks you to keep something under wraps, do they want you to talk about it or keep it a secret? Is a wrapped present supposed to be a secret or are you supposed to know what is in it?

3. *Dicey's sneakers made no noise on the roadway. No cars overtook her. There was no sound at all, except the occasional distant barking of a dog or lowing of a cow. The silence wrapped around her like a quilt....*
   (from Homecoming by Cynthia Voight)

> *Wrap* can describe a practical process such as tying up the loose ends of a meeting to bring it to a close or it can suggest the mystery of keeping something under cover. It can also suggest feelings. What kind of feeling is suggested by "the silence wrapped around her like a quilt"?

4. *Angela tripped while playing soccer and wrenched her knee.*
   Andre found it wrenching to say goodbye to his best friend, who was moving away.

> How is the feeling Andre had about his friend's leaving similar to the feeling Angela had when she wrenched her knee?
>
>> Saying good-bye pulled at Andre's feelings in a painful way and his friend's absence left him with an ache that took a while to heal.

5. *The ball rolled into the alley, and Claudia wriggled between the garbage cans to get it.*
   For the last two days Mrs. Morton has tried to wriggle out of her promise to take her children out for ice cream one afternoon.

> Was Mrs. Morton actually twisting and turning as she tried to get out of doing what she had promised?
>
>> No. Instead, she moved back and forth in her mind, looking for ways to avoid carrying through on her promise.
>
> If a person is described as trying to wriggle out of keeping a promise or doing a job, do you think he or she is more likely to say straight out, "I won't do it," or to try to get out of keeping the promise or doing the job by giving lots of excuses?
>
>> The phrase *wriggle out of it* usually suggests ways of getting out of something that are not straight and to the point. You don't say "no" straight out. You give excuses.

The Dream Keeper

Bring me all of your dreams,
You dreamers,
Bring me all of your
Heart melodies
That I may wrap them
In a blue cloud-cloth
Away from the too rough fingers
Of the world.

—Langston Hughes

Listening to grownups quarreling

standing in the hall against the
wall with my little brother, blown
like leaves against the wall by their
voices, my head like a pingpong ball
between the paddles of their anger
I knew what it meant
to tremble like a leaf.

Cold in their wrath, I heard
the claws of the rain
pounce. Floods
poured through the city,
skies clapped over me,
and I was shaken, shaken
like a mouse
between their jaws.

—Ruth Whitman

Parents Fighting

watching T.V.
not really watching,
I'm listening to my parents
    fight! fight! fight! fight!
    I don't want to,
but I can't help it,
    I feel like a
    yo-yo going up
and down up and
    down.
        I'm really not
    sure whose
        side I'm on,
nobody's really,
    I just pretend
I don't notice
    but I do
        notice
    and I do care,
I feel like I've
    been struck by
lightning
        and it's
    stuck inside
    me and
can't get out—
parents fighting—
    It keeps punching my
        insides
        like a
        raging bull.

—V.W. Fowlkes, grade 4

Fights

when my
    parents fight
it feels like
    an earthquake
with nowhere to
    go except
run through my
    house and
        destroy everything
    I feel
      like
    an ant
      with
          two
      giants
        stomping
    and yelling
I can't see
    anything
but I
    can hear
    it like
      an ant
    would
it's like
    the world
    is about
      to blow
    up and
      my parents
are trying
    to say
      as many
things as
    they can
before they die.
Both of
    them stop
fighting   it
      feels
queer or almost lonely
    the house is
      filled
        with
      silence
at last
    I hear a
    few
soft words. I
then sit back in relief.

                —*Anonymous, grade 4*

Discussion and Writing Ideas

- **The Dream Keeper**

Wrap can be a practical, business-like word, describing what you do to your peanut butter and jelly sandwich. It can also be a personal, private word suggesting worlds of comfort and protection when you need them most. Read "The Dream Keeper" for an example of this use of the word. Hughes is collecting dreams and "heart melodies," wrapping them in pieces of sky, and protecting them from all possible harm.

All of us would like magical protection at times, a soft, encircling something to defend us from harm. What might you wrap around yourself to give you this guarantee of well-being and invincibility? Would you fashion your cloak from pleasant materials: bee pollen, butterfly wings, clear running streams, your mother's long hair? Or would you seize and sew a more dangerous element into your design: thunderbolts, jaguars' growls, broken glass? Think of possible magical materials to wrap yourself in. Begin your writing by telling us what you're wrapped in. How does it protect you? Where can you now go and what can you now do? What special powers do you now possess? How will you use them?

- **Listening to grownups quarreling**
- **Parents Fighting**
- **Fights**

Wrath is like a thunderclap. In its strongest uses, it may remind us of the awesome anger of Zeus on Mt. Olympus or the power of Jehovah in the Old Testament. In milder form, it has its place in mortal lives as well. Have you ever been very angry with a friend? A brother? A sister? Your mother or your father? Has anyone ever expressed anger toward you? Where were you at the time and what was happening? What did it feel like inside? Were you arguing, shouting, or using silence as a weapon?

When we argue with someone, we know we will probably have some say in what will happen next and what the final outcome of the argument will be. We have at least some control over the situation. It can feel quite different when you overhear a quarrel between two people you love. You feel helpless, especially when you're a child. Read "Listening to grownups quarreling" by Ruth Whitman. Why does she feel "blown like leaves against the wall by their voices"? How is their anger like paddles in a pingpong match? When you feel frightened and helpless, everything around you can feel ominous and threatening. How does she express this in the second half of her poem?

Read "Parents Fighting" and "Fights." How do the authors feel about hearing their parents fight? They compare their feelings to many things—being a yo-yo, being struck by lightning, being an ant next to two giants stomping, and yelling. Which comparison is strongest?

How do *you* feel when grownups you care deeply about are quarreling? Try to get the feelings you remember down on paper. It's not necessary to tell what the quarrel was about. What comparisons can help you to express the impact of the quarrel as you felt it at the time? If you can't remember ever being affected by a quarrel between grownups, try to remember a quarrel between friends or other family members, or even an argument in which you were involved. The feelings will probably be similar. When you are finished, you may want to read your work with classmates. Are your feelings yours alone or are they shared by others?

Stretch the Meaning

1. Ravi won the wrestling match.
   Later, he wrestled with a math problem as he did his homework.

   By accident, Mr. Pennywhistle rode his bicycle through the glass door and shattered it. He felt guilty about smashing the door and wrestled with his conscience about what to tell Mrs. Pennywhistle. Should he tell her the truth or should he blame the accident on George, their St. Bernard?

2. Emilio wrapped up a birthday present for his sister.
   Detective Brenda Chang wrapped up her case.

   Just before she wrapped up the case, Brenda Chang warned her partner to keep the information under wraps.

3. Dicey's sneakers made no noise on the roadway. No cars overtook her. There was no sound at all, except the occasional distant barking of a dog or lowing of a cow. The silence wrapped around her like a quilt, a silence made up of trees growing and corn ripening, of the bright sky glowing and the distant water following its tides. This was not an empty silence.

4. Angela tripped while playing soccer and wrenched her knee.
   Andre found it wrenching to say good-bye to his best friend, who was moving away.

5. The ball rolled into the alley, and Claudia wriggled between the garbage cans to get it.
   For the last two days Mrs. Morton has tried to wriggle out of her promise to take her children out for ice cream one afternoon.

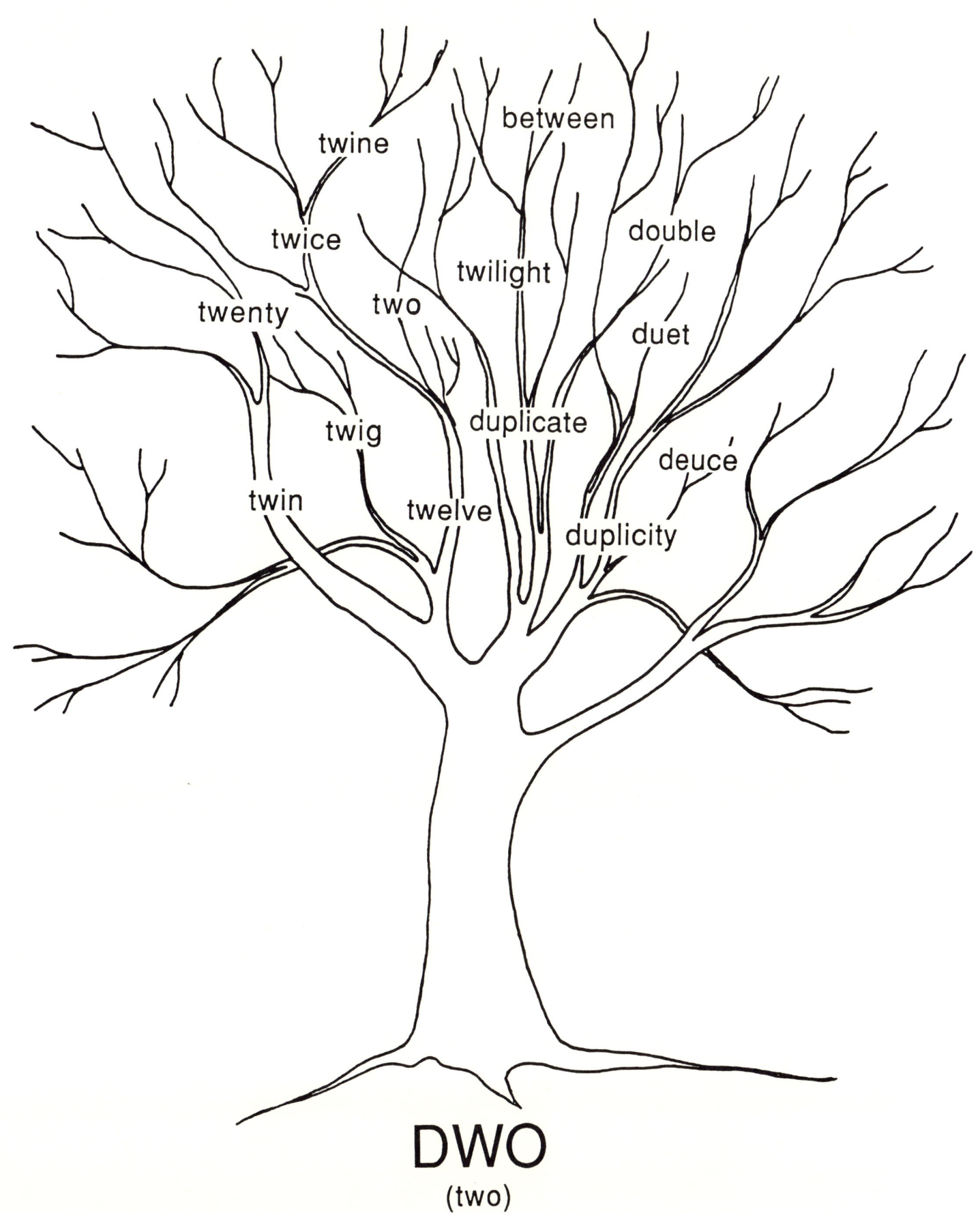

Like the MEDHYO family, the DWO family includes both Germanic and Latinate vocabulary. In addition, it introduces a consonant shift that takes place as you move from the Germanic to the Latinate words. Students enjoy the introductory exercise that invites them to play with sounds and discover the "logic" that underlies the *d/t* shift.

The liveliness of the DWO lesson comes partly from the ease and fun of generating such a large family. The "twoness" that is so obvious in the number words of the family illuminates the more complex vocabulary. The poetry selections explore *duplicity* and *twilight*. "Double Dutch Song," a jump-rope chant, allows the DWO family to infiltrate recess.

Materials useful for introducing the family are: twine, a twig, a deck of cards, and dice.

Introduction to the DWO Word Family

DWO—*two*		
two	twine	double
twelve	twig	deuce
twenty	between	duplicate
twice	twilight	duplicity
twin	duet	

Preparation

Before introducing the family, have students experiment with making *d* sounds and *t* sounds to discover how closely related they are. Have students follow your lead, making each sound in unison. Switch back and forth from one sound to the other as often as necessary as you ask the following questions.

> First, let's notice what is the same in the way we make these two sounds. When you make a *d* sound, what does your tongue do?
>
> > It hits the roof of your mouth just behind your teeth.
>
> When you make a *t* sound, what does your tongue do?
>
> > The same thing—it hits the roof of your mouth just behind your teeth.
>
> As we make *d* sounds and *t* sounds, then, the "mouth action" is exactly the same for both sounds. Now let's look at what's different about how we form the two sounds.

Have students place their fingers on their throat (and press down slightly on the vocal chords) to feel what happens as they switch back and forth between making a *d* sound to a *t* sound and back again. Be sure they make only the consonant sound of the *t* without adding any subsequent vowel sound.

> Which is louder—the *d* sound or the *t* sound? When do you feel your vocal chords vibrating? When you make the *d* sound or the *t* sound?
>
> Because we vibrate our vocal chords when we make the sound of *d*, we call *d* a "voiced consonant." The only way *d* and *t* are different is the *d* is voiced and *t* is unvoiced. In speech we often switch back and forth from one sound to the other without realizing it.

At times, for instance, we pronounce -*ed* with a *t* sound, sometimes with a *d* sound. Which sound do you give to -*ed* in the following words?

walked	discovered
jumped	passed
landed	traveled
cried	copied

How many of you pronounce the *t*'s in the following words as though they were *d*'s? Say the words as you ordinarily do. Listen to yourself. Listen to each other. Do you hear *t*'s being pronounced as though they were *d*'s? They often are in these words.

little	later
metal	battle
butter	decorated

In today's word family we have an example of shifting between *d* sounds and *t* sounds. Some of the words begin with *t*, some with *d*.

The root of today's family is DWO. Keeping in mind our discussion of *d*'s and *t*'s, who can guess what the meaning of our root is going to be?

Two.

If any of your students speak Polish, you might want to introduce the Polish word for two, *dwa,* which closely resembles the Indo-European root.

The Word Family: First Session

Students often come up with the words of the DWO family without much prompting. Use the following ideas to elicit words and to discuss the connection between individual words and the root meaning.

TWO, TWELVE, TWENTY, TWICE

Two is both the meaning of DWO and one of the words in today's family. Can you think of any other number words that begin with *t-w*-vowel?

Twelve, twenty, twice.

How is the idea of two involved in the number twenty?

Two times ten.

Why two times ten? Why is our number system based on ten? How many fingers do we have? Our number system is based on a "handy" system of counting—our ten fingers.

How is the idea of two involved in the number twelve?

Ten plus two.

The word twelve comes from roots that mean "two more than ten."

TWIN

If two children are born to the same mother on the same day, what are they called?

Twins.

TWINE

Unravel a length of twine for students:

There is a kind of string that is especially strong because it has two or more strands twisted together. That kind of string is called...

twine.

When things twist around each other the way strands twist around each other in a piece of twine, they can be described as *twining* around each other....

A vine twines around a tree, a branch, a porch railing.
Red and white stripes twine around a candy cane.
A boa constrictor twines around its prey.

...or as being *entwined* with one another...

The vines were so entwined with the branches of the tree that it took us hours to pull them off.

TWIG

As trees grow, new branches grow from the old. The name for the young branch reminds us that there are now two branches where there was one. The new little branch is called...

a *twig.*

BETWEEN

Choose something that is between two students and, to elicit the word, ask where it is.

What clue in the spelling of *between* tells us that we use the word when talking about being in the middle of two things or people?

*t-w-*vowel

When we talk about being in the midst of several things or people, we use *among*:

Examples: Kwame sat *between* his mother and father during the show.
After the show, he sat *among* his friends, talking and eating ice cream.

Can you think of other examples for *between*?

During an eclipse, the moon moves between the sun and earth, blocking the light from the sun.
The Potomac River runs between Maryland and Virginia.
An argument came between the two friends and made them lose interest in each other for a while.

❧

Some students might have heard the old expression *betwixt and between*, which suggests being in the middle without being clearly one thing or another.

TWILIGHT

A *tw-* word describing the fading light that comes between sunset and darkness is...

twilight.

Twilight is related to the idea of two through the idea of between— between the light of day and the darkness of night.

❧

If students in your class watch "The Twilight Zone," you might explain the connection between the idea of twilight and its use in the show. The TV show is science fiction that takes place between one world and another, between one time zone and another.

Shifting to the *D*-Vowel Pattern

The spelling pattern changes for the next group of words. These words keep the *d* of the root DWO, as do the words for two in Spanish, French, Italian, and Portuguese. Who knows the word for "two" in these languages?

Spanish: dos
French: deux
Italian: due
Polish: dwa
Portuguese: dois

Like the words for "two" in these languages, the other members of today's family have a *d*-vowel spelling pattern.

DUET

To elicit the word, ask two volunteers to dramatize a duet.

> Duet also describes a piece of music written for two singers or players. What word describes music written for three players? Can you see evidence for how the words *three* and *trio* might be related?

DOUBLE

> If a batter gets a hit and makes it safely to second base, he or she has a...

> *double.*

DEUCE

From a deck of playing cards, pull out a two and ask for its name. Ask students to compare the spelling of *deuce* with the spelling of the words for *two* in French, Spanish, Italian, Polish, and Portuguese. Which of them does it most closely resemble? *Deuce* entered American English from the French-speaking Louisiana Territory. Gamblers on the Mississippi river boats popularized the word.

> Deuce also describes...

> The two spots on the sides of dice (sometimes called "snake eyes").
> A tie score of 40-all in tennis.
> A sports car with two doors—a *deuce coupe.*

DUPLICATE

> If you lose the key to your house or your car, you need a second key which is an exact copy of the first. Can you think of a *d*-vowel word we might use to describe the second key?

> A *duplicate.*

You might have visited a hardware store and seen someone operating a machine for *duplicating* keys. Who can describe how it works?

২৯

Notice the shift in pronunciation that occurs between the verb and noun forms of the word. This shift is typical of words of Latin and Greek origin. By contrast, in words of Germanic origin the accent remains on the root element of the word and pronunciation of the root element remains the same, as in *like, unlikely, likelihood, likeable, likeness.*

Ending the First Session

We suggest dividing the introduction of this family into two sessions. We have found this a convenient place to make the division, but the division can be made in any way that best suits your situation.

A Note on Spelling

You might keep your eye out for spelling mistakes that involve substituting a *d* for a *t* or a *t* for a *d*. Often such mistakes are "logical" in that they accord with the way a student pronounces a word. Students sometimes find it helpful to understand the logic of their mistakes.

The DWO Word Family: Second Session

At first this section focuses on words and phrases that suggest the idea of being deceptively two-sided. The "Optional Independent Activity" section looks at phrases built on *two* and *double* that simply mean "twice as much."

DUPLICITY
TWO-FACED, TWO-TIMING
DOUBLE-DEALING, DOUBLE-CROSSING, DOUBLE AGENT

Read the dialogue "The Double-Dealer" near the end of this chapter. This brief tale of double-crossing works best as a radio play, with the audience hearing the voices coming from behind a screen or divider of some sort. The radio play approach works best because there is little visual interest in the scene, but if no screen is handy, have the listeners close their eyes. Alternatively, you can use the poem "The Flattered Flying Fish" to introduce the concept of duplicity.

> Old Tom and Maria discovered that their partner Casey had been two-faced. They use phrases built on *two* and *double* to describe Casey and his behavior. Listen for those phrases as the actors read the end of their scene again. They are...
>
> *double-crossed* and *two-faced*.
>
> There are other phrases built on *two* and *double* that you might use to describe someone who is acting two-faced—acting one way to your face and another way behind your back. You might say they were...
>
> *two-timing* or *double-dealing*.
>
> Another word, similar in appearance to the word *duplicate*, that can be used to describe the kind of deceptive two-faced behavior that Casey used to trick his partners is...
>
> *duplicity*.

In spy stories someone who engages in duplicity by pretending to work for one country while really working against it and for another country is called a...

double agent.

A good way to discuss the concepts of *duplicity, double-crossing,* etc. further is to ask students for examples of such behavior from stories and television shows.

Students enjoy stringing the words and phrases of this section together to make a magnificent insult. Let a few students roll these off their tongues for their classmates.

Wrap-up of the Second Session

Have students select their favorite words from the DWO family and brainstorm for ideas for illustrations or use the suggestion for illustrating twilight (below).

Definitions to Record

twine: 1. strong string made by twisting two or more strands together
2. to twist together or wind around
twilight: the time of day just after the sun sets and before it rises, when there is a faint light in the sky
duet: 1. two singers or players performing together
2. music written for two singers or players
duplicate: 1. an exact copy
2. to make an exact copy
duplicity: acting one way openly and another way secretly in order to deceive

Illustrating *Twilight*

Have you ever scanned your yard expectantly waiting for the first fireflies to appear? Do you like looking at trees or hills at the hour they turn bluish? Have you ever noticed the hour at which the birds in your yard suddenly go silent?

Twilight has sometimes been described as "the gap between two worlds." The phrase allows twilight a period of time in which to be itself. The light has changed, yet night has not closed in. Everything seems to stand out with great clarity, neither flattened by the sun nor swallowed by the darkness. Colors darken and soften, yet edges and outlines grow bold.

Try this experiment. Divide a sheet of paper in three parts. Let one end represent day, the other night. Give twilight the space in between. Draw or paint your idea of the different times of the day. You can be literal if you like, or you can simply use colors, tones, shapes.

Story Puzzle

Students may enjoy doing the story puzzle in a straightforward way or playing with mixing the words around. For example, could *twins* be *deuces, doubles, duplicates, twigs*?

Optional Independent Activity

Some students enjoy thinking up a list of expressions built on *two* and *double*. Most of the expressions will suggest the idea of "twice as much." A group could do this independently, then check their list against the dictionary. Alternatively, groups could compete to see which group could generate the longest list. Consulting an unabridged dictionary adds to the fun of the activity by providing a wonderfully long list of expressions.

Additional Related Words

TWAIN

Who is the author of *Huckleberry Finn* and *Tom Sawyer* ?

Mark Twain

Samuel Clemens' pen name, Mark Twain, came from his days as a Mississippi River pilot. The call "mark twain," which meant "by the mark two fathoms," assured a river pilot that the water beneath his boat was comfortably deep. (*Fathom*, which came to be standardized as a six-foot unit of measure, derives from a root that means "the length of two arms stretched out.")

TWIST

Twist, which is related to *twine*, originally referred to the entwining of two or more threads to produce a single strand, such as rope. Strong silk thread is still known as "twist." You might mention the dance of the same name.

DUO

What phrase describes the partnership of that famous pair, Batman and Robin?

The Dynamic *Duo*.

DUPLEX

What's a duplex? It can be one apartment with *two* floors or one house divided into *two* separate homes.

DUAL

Dual means twofold or having two elements. What are *dual* controls? Where might you find them? If a teacher said, "I have a *dual* purpose in giving you this assignment," what would he or she mean?

Note: *Duel* is often proposed as a member of the family as well. It happens to come from a different root—the Latin *duellum,* which means "war"—but since it sounds like *dual* and in fact always takes place between two people, including the word as a "sound cousin" is legitimate.

DOUBT
DUBIOUS

Doubt and its close relative *dubious* come from a word that meant "hesitating between two alternatives." If you are in doubt, have you made up your mind about what you're going to do?

If you have students pantomime "hesitating between two alternatives" or "not being sure of which path to take," they will see how the general idea of being unsure or uncertain emerged as a common meaning of the word *doubt*.

Twilight

Dove-colored shadows merge,
Color has faded, sound fallen asleep—
Life and motion have settled
Into an undulant dusk, a distant rumbling...
The invisible flight of the moth
Is heard in the night air...
Hour of inexpressible melancholy!
All is within me, and I am in everything!

Silent twilight, sleepy twilight,
Pour yourself into the depths of my soul,
Gentle, languid, sweetly fragrant,
Rise in flood and then become still.
By darkness senses are selfless
Spill over the cup's lip!
Let us taste annihilation
And merge with the slumbering world!

—*Fyodor Tiutchev*
Translated by Christopher Edgar

The Flattered Flying Fish

Said the Shark to the Flying Fish over the phone:
"Will you join me tonight? I am dining alone.
Let me order a nice little dinner for two!
And come as you are in your shimmering blue!"

Said the Flying Fish: "Fancy remembering me,
And the dress that I wore at the Porpoises' tea!"
"How could I forget?" said the Shark in his guile:
"I expect you at eight!" and rang off with a smile.

She has powdered her nose; she has put on her things;
She is off with one flap of her luminous wings.
O little one, lovely, light-hearted and vain,
The Moon will not shine on your beauty again!

—*E.V. Rieu*

The Giraffe

The 2 *f*'s
in giraffe
are like
2 giraffes
running through
the word giraffe

The 2 *f*'s
run through giraffe
like 2 giraffes

—*Ron Padgett*

Double Dutch Song

One	Twelve
We've just begun	A green elf
Two	Duet
Tie my shoe	Don't forget
Three	Twice
Duplicity	Mighty nice
Four	Double
Shut the door	Trouble
Five	Deuce
Bee in a hive	What's the use
Six	Twig
In a fix	Eat a fig
Seven	Between
Saw some twins	Pork and beans
Eight	Twilight
Duplicate	Almost night
Nine	Twenty
Ball of twine	Up a tree
Ten	So long
Try again	End of our song.
Eleven	
Monkey's grin	

—*Kate Rushin*

Discussion and Writing Ideas

- **Twilight**

What mood does Tyutchev set to show what twilight means to him? Is this how you feel at twilight? What are your favorite lines?

What are your memories of twilight? How are the memories of summer different from those of winter? Have you ever played after-supper softball (or basketball or stickball) in the summer? As the light begins to fade, distances become indistinct; the ball becomes harder and harder to see. You swing and miss. Perhaps the game dissolves into tag or hide and seek in the shadows. How is winter twilight different? Do you retreat into the house more eagerly when cold deepens with the shadows? Or do you like the stillness of a winter twilight? Collect twilight images with your class. What is your family doing? What are you hearing, seeing, smelling, waiting for? Talk about which images are the most powerful for you, which word choices the most effective. You may want to expand one of your favorites into a poem or story. Make it suit your own feelings and experiences. Your twilight is your private gap between worlds.

- **The Flattered Flying Fish**

In "The Flattered Flying Fish," notice how the genteelness of the conversation is reinforced by the order and niceness of the rhyme and meter, which highlights the Shark's duplicity even more.

- **Giraffe**

How does our sense of something change when it is set beside its twin? *Giraffe* plays with how the double letters of the word inspire the poet to see them as creatures. Did you know that all letters originally were pictures? (Who says spelling is boring?) Do double letters inspire pictures in your mind? What about the two *s*'s of *expressway*? The two *t*'s of *attention*? The two *m*'s of *summer*? Choose any word with double letters, and try using it to inspire your own poem.

- **Double Dutch Song**

"Double Dutch Song" really does work as a jump-rope song. Try it.

The Double Dealer

Narrator: During California gold rush days, back in the 1840s and 50s, men and women had a lot of high adventure as they scrambled to stake their claims and get rich quick. As people raced to claim gold for themselves before others could find it, trickery and deception were common strategies for trying to lead competitors astray. Many stories like the following took place.

Maria: Well, Tom, I think we made a good find today. That stream back up in the hills is mighty hard to get to and those gold nuggets were small, but there sure were a lot of them.

Old Tom: Yes, we've been moving from one place to another for too long. I think we should settle down and stake our claim by that stream and see what it brings us.

Maria: Should we share the claim with Casey? What should we tell him when he gets back to camp tonight?

Old Tom: Well, Casey's an old friend, Maria. He has stuck with us during all these long days of searching. It was only because he was off getting us food and supplies that he wasn't with us today when we stumbled on that stream. We've shared the hard times, we should share the good.

Maria: Look, here he comes. Let's tell him our news.

Narrator: Maria and Tom tell Casey all about their find, and the next morning they show him the trail to the stream and the gold nuggets. When they finally reach the edge of the stream, though, Casey says he's not very impressed.

Casey: Well, I'll tell you, this don't impress me too much. Sounded good when you told me about it back at the camp, but these nuggets look awful puny to me now that I see them.... I guess this is the time to tell you about what I found down the track a ways. I wanted to see what you'd found here before figuring where we should settle in, but now I've seen this spot, I have to tell you I've found a better one. It's about two days journey south of here. Stopped for the night, I did, and I was pushing my way a good distance off the main track so as nobody could lift the supplies while I was sleeping. Came to the edge of a stream and found nuggets there three, four times as big as these. I say we head south to stake our claim there.

Narrator: Old Tom, Maria, and Casey pack up, travel south for a day, then camp for the night. When Old Tom and Maria wake up the next morning, they're in for a rude surprise.

Maria: Where's Casey?

Old Tom: He's gone! Clean gone! And he's made off with all the horses and supplies as well. We're stranded!

Maria: We've been double-crossed! He never did find any gold! Casey made up that story to lure us away from our gold...and now he's hightailing it back there to grab all the gold he can before we can catch up with him.

Old Tom: And with no horses and no food, it's going to be a good long while before we can catch him.

Maria: And we thought he was our friend!

Old Tom: I guess it turns out he was a two-faced guy. All we saw was his friendly face, and we really got took.

Story Puzzle for Students

Read the story to yourself before filling in the blanks with words from your DWO word tree. See how many different DWO words you can use.

A Case of Duplicity

Once there were _____ in the sixth grade named Richard and Lee-Ann. They were _____ years old. Their _____ favorite things were solving crimes and playing cards. Lee-Ann also really liked to sing. Her best friend, Ruby, tried to get her to join her singing group. But Lee-Ann said, "No, I just like to sing _____ with Tiffany."

"Du-et," said Richard, laughing at Lee-Ann.

"Well, I wouldn't talk if I was skinny as a _____ the way you are."

"I'd rather be a twig than a tree trunk," said Richard. (You can tell they also like to tease.)

One evening just after _____, Richard and Lee-Ann were in the street. Lee-Ann was jumping up a storm playing _____ dutch, and Richard was playing a game of cards. Richard had just picked up a wild _____ card when Fredo ran up and yelled, "My bike just got stolen!"

"How did it happen, Fredo?" Lee-Ann asked.

"I tied it up for just a few minutes outside of the Seven-11."

"Tied it up? With what?" asked Richard.

"_____."

"Twine? Why didn't you use your lock?"

"I lost my key."

162

"Don't you have a _____?"

"No, and besides, my cousin Tony said he would watch it."

"If I told you once, I told you _____ times, always put a heavy-duty chain around your bike," Richard said.

Just then _____ two parked cars they saw a flash of red. "What was that?" Richard asked.

"That's my bike!"

"If that's your bike, who was riding it?"

"Tony!" Fredo said and took off.

"That's a case of _____ if I ever saw one," said Lee-Ann.

"Ah, Lee-Ann, will you quit using those big words," Richard said.

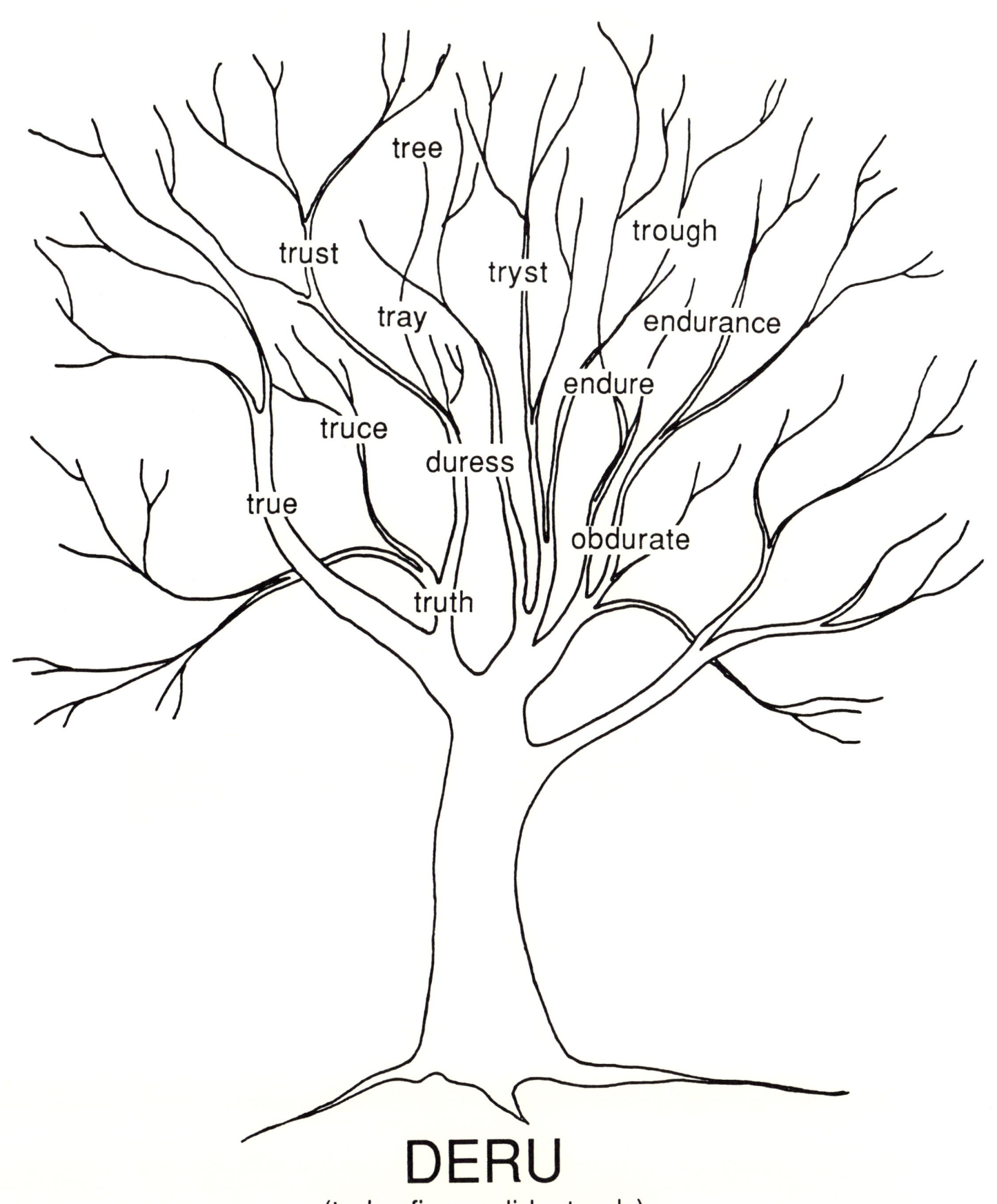

Most words of the DERU family are "idea" words. The pantomimes suggested in the introduction and the poetry that accompanies the family connect the words to experiences of being "firm, solid, steady"—the root meaning of the family.

Like the MEDHYO, OINO, and DWO families, the DERU family includes two distinct sets of vocabulary: one Germanic (the *t-r*-vowel words) and the other Latinate (the *d*-vowel-*r* words). Use the introduction to the DWO family to review the *d/t* shift.

An object useful for introducing the family is something to serve as the "prized object" in the pantomimes for *obdurate* and *duress*.

Introduction to the DERU Word Family

> **DERU**—*to be firm, solid, steady*
>
> | | |
> |---|---|
> | true | endure |
> | trust | endurance |
> | truth | obdurate |
> | truce | duress |
> | tryst | |
> | tree | |
> | tray | |
> | trough | |

TRUST, TRUE, TRUTH

A pantomime of two people helping each other climb to a high ledge can dramatize the root meaning that lies at the heart of the DERU family. One climber interlaces the fingers of both hands to provide a foothold for the first climber; the other then extends a hand to pull his/her partner up. You can simply have students visualize such scenes from books and movies, experiences on the playground, etc., but it's preferable to get a physical sense of the experience by acting it out.

> If you're going to find a partner to help you climb, who are you going to look for? Someone who is unsteady or likely to collapse?

For fun and contrast you might have volunteers dramatize an experience with a partner who collapses or shakes and almost collapses every time a climber places a foot in his or her hold. Contrast is helpful in clarifying an image or idea.

> What kind of a partner would you want if you were climbing? Someone you can count on; someone who can maintain a *steady* hold, a *firm* grip; someone you can *trust*; someone who gives you *solid* support.

> Two variations on the word *trust* describe being able to count on somebody's word. If we know we can count on a person's word, we know what they say is...

> *true,* the *truth.*

What is the spelling pattern of the family?

> *t-r*-vowel

TRUCE

If two enemies are going to stop fighting, they have to count on each other's word. A word related to *true, truth,* and *trust* can describe such an agreement—

truce.

TRYST

Tryst is an old word found mostly in "days of yore" stories, but one that we've found to be a favorite with students. It describes a time and place for meeting someone, often in secret, often a lover. *Tryst* comes from an even older word that means "a place where one waits trustingly." Introduce this archaic and seemingly irrelevant word and you may be surprised at how often you hear it bouncing around the classroom. It's good to encourage delight in language, unrestricted by utility. If your students enjoy *tryst,* discuss *troth* and *trow* in "Additional Related Words," as well.

TREE, TRAY, TROUGH

Why do you think *tree* might have come from a root that means firm, solid, steady? Think back to the primeval forests when trees grew undisturbed for hundreds of years—no bulldozers, housing developments, shopping malls then. Do you have any 'primeval' trees in your area? Any wonderfully sturdy and solid trees, ideal for climbing? How does it feel to sit in the branches of such a tree?

Two *tr-* words come from *tree* and describe objects originally made from the wood of a tree—one originally a flat piece of wood used for carrying things, the other originally a hollowed-out log used to hold water for animals to drink.

Tray and *trough.*

A Shift in Spelling Pattern

The next words of the family are Latin-based and have a *d*-vowel-*r* pattern. (See the DWO family for a review of how vowels and *r*'s often shift places over time.) All of the words may involve stretching students' vocabulary. If you think it best, mention the words first, then discuss their connection to the root meaning of the family.

ENDURE, ENDURANCE

Ask students to imagine ancient trees, mountains, rock formations, and planets, solid things in our universe that have endured for hundreds or thousands or millions of years. These things have a solid strength that allows them to last through the ages—others a more fluid strength. What of oceans, whales, cockroaches, stars?

What qualities do we need to endure hard times, athletic competitions, a difficult challenge? Steadiness of purpose? A firm resolve to make it through? A solid sense of our own abilities?

OBDURATE

Have volunteers stage a skit in which two or three try to persuade another to lend something valuable, such as a tape player or radio, a baseball glove, or a bicycle. The owner of the prized object is battered by a series of pleas and arguments designed to persuade him or her to give it up. The owner firmly resists every plea and argument. Remind the "owner" to be steady as a rock—unwavering. This kind of stubborn, unyielding behavior can be described as...

>*obdurate.*

DURESS

Now change the outcome. A group of volunteers applies steady, unrelenting pressure to the owner of the prized object. One after the other they insist on borrowing the object, and perhaps even become a bit threatening. Finally, overwhelmed, the owner gives up and lends the object.

> Did the owner give up the radio (or whatever) willingly and freely? What kind of pressure was brought to bear? We can use the word *duress* to describe this kind of firm, steady, unyielding pressure.

> We usually use the word *duress* in the phrase "under duress." For example: The prisoner signed the confession *under duress.*

Wrap-up

Provide the root, DERU, and be sure the root meaning and words of the family are all recorded clearly so that students can record them on their own word trees. Brainstorm ideas for illustrations of some of the words.

Note on the "Sound Cousin" *Durable*

Durable usually comes up as students explore the DERU family—and it seems as though it ought to be part of the family. In fact it comes from a different root that means "long"—as in "something that lasts a long time." Obviously the qualities needed in order to last a long time overlap with the qualities needed to *endure*. Because of the shared sound patterns and overlap in meaning, the two words can be considered "sound cousins."

Definitions to Record

truce: a stop in fighting, a temporary peace
endure: 1. to continue to exist; to last
2. to put up with; to bear
endurance: power to last and withstand hard wear, hardship, or pain without giving out
obdurate: stubborn or unyielding
duress: the use of force or threats to get something
tryst: appointment to meet at a certain time and place, especially one made by lovers

Additional Related Words

DRYAD: a tree nymph

DRUID: a member of an order of priests in ancient Gaul and Britain. From "one whose knowledge is firm."

TROTH: good faith, fidelity. As in "thereto I plight thee my troth" from the marriage ceremony in the *Book of Common Prayer*.

BETROTHED: promised in marriage. From "being in relation to truth."

TROW: to think, suppose

Learn to Be a Rock

Learn to be a rock
To sit in the dirt for days
Without moving a muscle

To stare up at the towering trees
To look like a small mountain
To be shelter for the little bugs
    that hide under you

You could be as rough as sandpaper,
As smooth as silk,
As sharp as a knife,
And as blunt as a pencil.

—Matthew Barzun, grade 5

sugarfields

treetalk and windsong are
the language of my mother
her music does not leave me

let me taste again the cane
the syrup of the earth
sugarfields were once my home.

i would lie down in the fields
and never get up again
(treetalk and windsong
are the language of my mother
sugarfields are my home)

the leaves go on whispering secrets
as the wind blows a tune in the grass
my mother's music is in the fields
this music cannot leave me.

—Barbara Mahone

Overheard on a Saltmarsh

Nymph, nymph, what are your beads?

Green glass, goblin. Why do you stare at them?

Give them me.

        No.

Give them me. Give them me.

        No.

Then I will howl all night in the reeds,
Lie in the mud and howl for them.

Goblin, why do you love them so?

They are better than stars or water,
Better than voices of winds that sing,
Better than any man's fair daughter,
Your green glass beads on a silver ring.

Hush, I stole them out of the moon.

Give me your beads, I want them.

        No.

I will howl in a deep lagoon
For your green glass beads, I love them so.
Give them me. Give them.

        No.

—Harold Monro

Discussion and Writing Ideas

- **Learn to be a Rock**
- **sugarfields**

Endure can suggest many kinds of staying power. We can use it to describe things both large and small, real and ideal. In "Learn to be a Rock," Matthew Barzun describes something both small and steady. How does Barzun convey the patience of a rock? The fixedness of its experience? Is it necessary to be hard to endure? Read "sugarfields" by Barbara Mahone. How is the idea of *enduring* expressed in this poem? How is memory a connecting thread through time? If Mahone's sugarfields disappeared years ago, can they be said to still be enduring in her mind? Why or why not? Can you think of things that will endure because you carry them in your own mind?

Close your eyes for a minute and think about the word *enduring*. What kinds of pictures flash through your mind? Try not to censor them in any way. If you have trouble picturing anything, think small and specific. How does an apple seed endure? A diamond buried underground? A weed? How does a drop of rain endure past its moment of falling? Now think big. How does a mountain endure? A river? The North Star? Make a list of all the different things you thought. Choose one and let it be the start of a poem or story. If you get stuck, close your eyes and try to *become* the thing you have chosen. Ask yourself, "What do I see? What is happening to me? What am I enduring? How do I feel?"

- **Overhead on a Saltmarsh**

Obdurate is a wonderful word for arguments. If you feel obdurate right down to your bones, you can resist all pleas and threats. How does the nymph resist the begging of the goblin in Harold Munro's "Overhead on a Salt Marsh"? (You'll need to read the poem once all the way through to separate out the parts.) Who uses the louder voice? The greatest number of words? Who has the final word? Find a partner for a dramatic reading of the poem. Practice your lines, finding the voice and stance that best suits your character.

When have you been obdurate in real life? What pleas and threats were used against you to get you to change your mind? Can you imagine any fantasy arguments similar to Harold Monro's? What might a dragon demand of a drawbridge? The moon from a mountain? A snake from a snail? How might one threaten the other to get what it wants? Try writing an obdurate poem or conversation yourself. Take a clear, firm stance and refuse to budge. After you've read yours with classmates, choose the most obdurate ones to act out. Experiment with voices and stances. (You might find the loudest voice is not necessarily the most effective.) When everyone has had a chance, take an imaginary eraser and wipe this assignment out of your mind. Be *reasonable* for the rest of the day.

Story Puzzle for Students

Read the entire story before filling in the blanks with words from your DERU word tree. Three of the words from the family are *not* included. Which words?

Overland Trail Diary

The year was 1852. I was but a young woman of sixteen and traveling with my family in a covered wagon across the Overland Trail, on the way to California. Here is part of my diary, in which I wrote near every day, so that I might give a _____ account of the adventures and hardships which befell us.

April 23, 1852

Our wagons have been following the Platte River in Nebraska Territory for nigh on three weeks now, heading west toward the mountains. If _____ be known, I'm sorely tired of trudging these muddy miles in the drenching rain. My mother took ill and she and the babies are riding under the canvas but my brothers and I are walking. Our poor, tired ox teams won't be able to _____ the whole long journey if they have to pull any extra weight. This morning at dawn, Father went to spy out the land to see if we might make the river crossing by noon. The river crossings test our courage and _____. Some people say that if the snakebites, the cholera or the coyotes don't get us, the rivers will. In the spring, the rivers are icy cold, overflowing their banks, ripping up the few, scrawny prairie _____ by their roots and sending them downstream amidst whirlpools and rapid currents.

Father returned with the news that two wagon trains were ahead of us and were getting ready to ford the muddy river. Some of the men agreed to meet us at the riverbank to help us cross. You would think that traveling next to a river would provide plenty of drinking water, but not the Platte. It's a river of moving sand, too dirty to bathe in and too thick to drink. Back home, the cattle could drink fresh, clean, well water from wooden _____ in the barnyard, but on the trail we collect whatever water we can in pots and buckets to give to the animals and to use for cooking. I never thought I'd actually look forward to taking a bath.

We arrived at the crossing point and saw dozens of cattle swimming the swift current, with men on horseback trying to guide them with shouts and waving hats. Mother, Father, and I began taking apart our wagon so the men could float it across the river. Mother and the younger children will stay inside. We _____ that our sturdy prairie schooner will get them safely across. Father, the boys, and I must swim across on the backs of mules which have been lent us. I am very frightened, for we have heard that three people drowned here last week. But under such _____, somehow we find the strength to keep moving on toward our goal.

It is nightfall now and we're all thankful that the day is done and we're safely on the far side of the river. My little mule was strong but stubborn. When Father tried to lead him into the river, with me clutching his neck, he became _____ and refused to budge. Finally he began swimming, and although I was terrified as the cold, gray waters closed around us, my mule was an expert swimmer and we scrambled up the opposite bank to welcoming arms. Mother and I made camp and cooked dinner and tucked in the young ones. Tomorrow we move on.

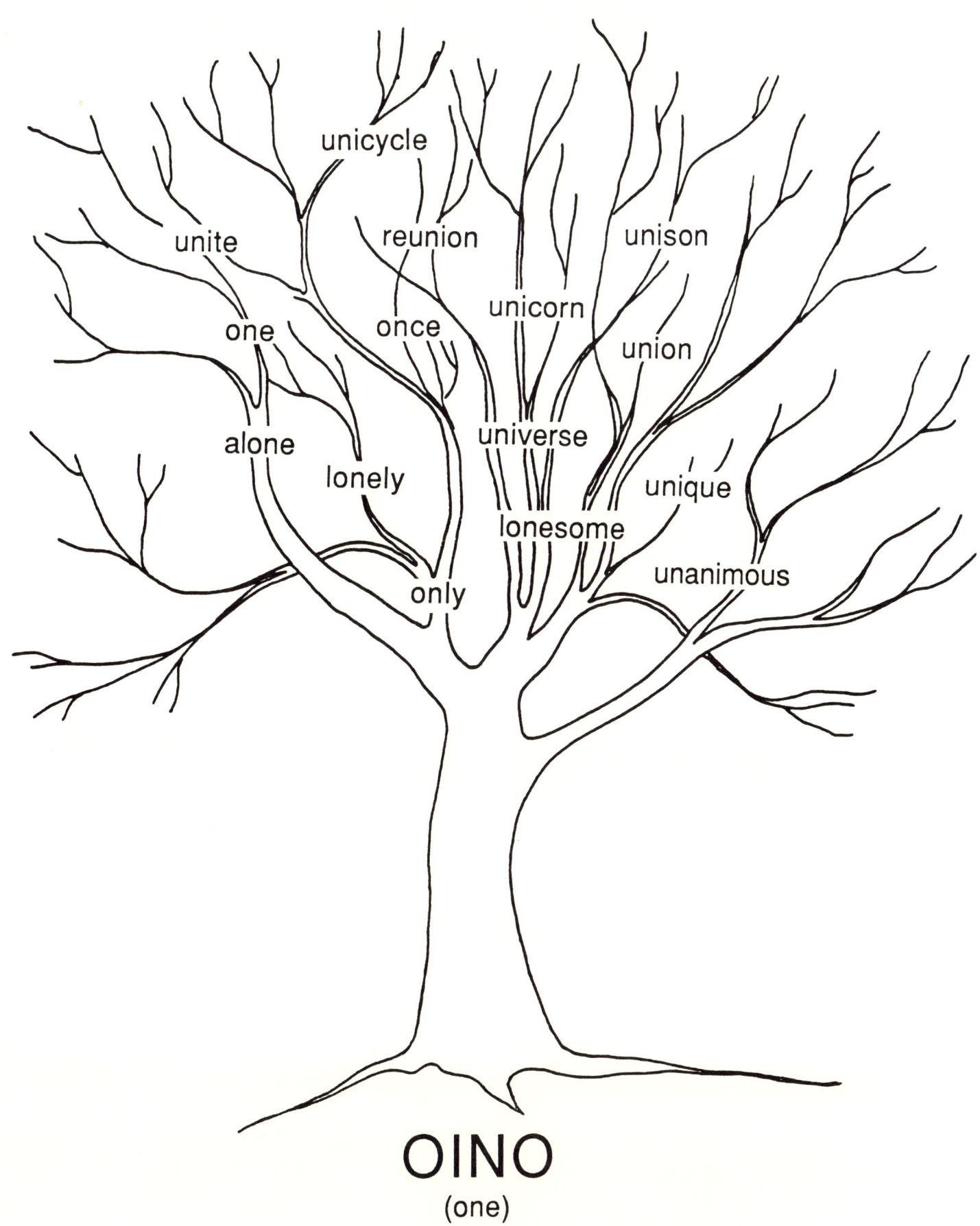

One can evoke the peace of solitude, the desolation of loneliness, the wonder of being unique, the joy of a reunion, the power of unity. The words of the OINO family and the poetry found toward the end of the chapter offer opportunities to explore oneness in many modes. The *solus* family, presented briefly towards the end of the "Introduction," can extend discussion to another vocabulary of aloneness.

Like the DWO family, the OINO family is large and includes both Germanic and Latinate vocabulary. The chapter does not include a separate section on extended meanings because the primary meanings of most words in the family are themselves "extended" or metaphoric. The pantomimes suggested in the lesson can revive a sense of the down-to-earth experience that underlies meanings that have moved away from their roots.

This chapter includes poetry related to the word family.

Introduction to the OINO Word Family

OINO—*one*		
one	unique	unite, united
once	unicycle	union
only	unicorn	universe
alone	reunion	unanimous
lonely	unison	uni-
lonesome		

Words for *one* that also come from OINO:

Spanish:	uno
Italian:	uno
French:	un
Greek:	ena
German:	ein
Yiddish:	aince

ONE, ALONE, LONELY, LONESOME

A good way to introduce the OINO word family is to put on a skit that dramatizes the image of one in contrast to that of many. Have five or six volunteers stage the following scene. A group gathers and starts talking and laughing fairly noisily. One actor, whom we'll call Sam, breaks away from the group, saying, "I'm tired of all this noise and all these people. I want to be by myself." Sam crosses to the other side of the room and, with a sigh of relief, settles into being alone.

> Sam left the group and went away to be by himself. Another way to say you want to be by yourself is to say, "I want to be...

> *alone.*

> If you are all alone in the room, how many people are in the room?

> *One.*

> *One* is the root of today's family as well as one of the words of the family. Can you find the word *one* in *alone*?

> *Alone* comes from "all one," which got combined and shortened into *alone*. When the words were combined, the pronunciation changed, so it is easier to see the *one* in *alone* than it is to hear it.

At times you may be happy to get away from crowds and be alone, but at other times being alone may make you sad. That sadness can be described by another *one* word...

lonely, lonesome.

ONCE, ONLY, ONE, AND ONLY

Can you think of other words and phrases built on *one* ?

How does the spelling of *one* change in *once* and *only* ?

The phrase *one and only* suggests a person who stands out from the crowd and has a talent that nobody else can match. Can you think of somebody who is so special and talented that you would describe him or her as the *one and only*? Or as *my one and only*?

Shifting to the u-n Spelling Pattern

In the next group of words the spelling pattern changes from *o-n* to *u-n*. The *u-n* words share a spelling pattern with the words for one in Spanish, Italian, and French. Who knows these words?

Spanish: *uno*
Italian: *uno*
French: *un*

Latin, the language from which these languages developed, also spells the word for one with *u-n*.

UNIQUE

If you describe someone as the *one and only,* you are saying that he or she is a special, one-of-a-kind person. Does anybody know a word that begins with *u-n* and describes a special, one-of-a-kind thing?

Unique.

One and only is often a boastful phrase. The word *unique* says the same thing, but in a quieter way.

You might read the poem "Fable" and use it as a starting point for making a list of the unique talents of various creatures.

UNICYCLE, UNICORN

Have you ever seen a clown in the circus riding a one-wheeled cycle? What is it called?

You might point out the relationship of a *uni*cycle to a *bi*cycle and a *tri*cycle.

Long ago there were tales told about an animal that was supposed to be magical because it had just one horn, instead of the two that animals with horns usually have. What was this magical creature called?

REUNION

Have seven or eight volunteers dramatize a family reunion. Assign bits of dialogue, such as the following, to bring the scene to life as the family gathers:

"My, how you've grown."

"Kofi, I want you to meet your Aunt Doris."

"Well, at last I get to meet my new nephew."

"What an adorable baby!"

"Charlene, I want you to sit down with your grandmother and listen to her story about your cousin Bill."

"I can't believe it's been five years since we saw you. You don't look a day older."

"I can't believe how big this family is getting to be."

The scene ends after a photographer calls everybody together for a picture:

"Okay, let's get everybody together in one place here for a photograph. We're going to want a record of having this family all together."

What's happening in the scene? When a family travels from different cities and towns to gather together in one group, we often call the gathering a ...

family *reunion.*

Who can underline the spelling pattern that tells us that *reunion* is connected to the idea of "one"?

The *re-* of reunion means "again." People who hold reunions have been together once before and now are meeting again. What are some other kinds of reunions besides family reunions?

> High school reunions
> College reunions

UNISON, UNITE, UNITED

Have your students imagine they are sailors on a large, eighteenth century sailing ship. Explain that sailors used to chant or sing songs (sea chanteys or shanteys) to establish a rhythm for hauling the heavy canvas sails up the masts. The physics of hauling the sails was such that much greater force was applied if everyone pulled on the rope at the same time. The whole crew would chant or sing to establish a beat for hauling the sails.

Ask several students to volunteer for a pantomime of hauling the sails and ask everybody to establish a beat with either of the following chants:

1. Heave her up and away she goes   2. Heave ho
   Haul away, haul away   Away she goes

The beat is on the accented words. Have the "sailors" listen to each other and practice the chant until they are all speaking together and in rhythm and the sailors who are raising the sail are hauling the rope on the beat.

> Terrific! You achieved the power of a chant—which is to sound like one very powerful voice. When many voices speak as if in one voice, we say that people are speaking in...
>
> *unison.*
>
> And your chant helped the others to join together to exert as much power as possible. People often join together because they can achieve more power working together as a group than they can working as separate individuals. One of the words from our family that describes this kind of joining together is...
>
> *unite.*
>
> In the early days of our country the American colonies wanted to join together to defeat their British rulers and win independence. They chose a name for themselves that emphasized their vision of separate states combining as one nation...
>
> The *United* States of America.
>
> Can you think of other nations or organizations that use the word *united* to emphasize that they have come together into one group?
>
> United Nations.
> United Arab Republic.
> United Auto Workers.

The motto, *E Pluribus Unum,* which appears on the Great Seal of the United States, is Latin for "Out of many, one."

UNION

> When workers join together to increase their power to negotiate better working conditions, the organization they form is called a...
>
> *union.*

UNIVERSE

> What word describes the sun, the planets, the stars, the galaxies, and everything in space? The word emphasizes thinking about everything in space as all part of one system.

> *Universe.*

UNANIMOUS

Offer a set of choices likely to elicit a unanimous vote on one side or the other, such as: Who would like to go out for recess? Who would like to stay after school and do extra work?

(If for any reason the vote is not unanimous, persuade the dissenters to join the group for the sake of the demonstration.)

> What happened?

>> Everybody voted to go out.

> Yes, you were all "of one mind." Does anyone know a *un-* word that means everyone is "of one mind"—that everybody agrees on the same thing?

>> *Unanimous.*

> The *-animous* in *unanimous* means "mind" or "spirit."

The Root: Meaning and Spelling

> The spelling pattern in today's words is a little bit tricky. Who can figure out how to describe it?

>> vowel-*n*

> The root from which all the words of today's family grew is OINO. And OINO means...

>> *one.*

A reminder about the "logic" underlying vowel shifts: ask if any students have toddler brothers or sisters at home who are just learning to speak, and if so, ask them to listen to those early toddler words. Does the toddler's version of a word have the same vowels as the version used by the older members of the family? There is often a difference. Vowel shifts are part of our personal history, as well as part of the history of the language.

Note

Many words of the OINO family begin with the prefix *uni*. You might want to suggest that students keep an eye out for this prefix in other words, as well.

Wrap-up

Ask students to fill in the root and words of the family on the class word tree and on their individual word trees. Brainstorm for inspiring ideas for illustrations of the family.

Definitions to Record

unite:	to bring together into one; join together
union:	a group united for a special purpose
unique:	one-of-a-kind; remarkable
universe:	the whole of all existing things, including the earth, planets, stars, and galaxies; all existing space and matter
unanimous:	in complete agreement; of one mind
unison:	speaking or singing together as if in one voice

A "Companion" Family for OINO

Latin: **Solus** ("by oneself")

> **solo**   **desolate**
> **solitary**   **soliloquy**
> **solitude**

The words of the *solus* family focus on the idea of self apart from others. The words are in fact related to the Germanic word *self* through the common ancestry of the Indo-European root SEU, which refers to the idea of *self* and reflexive pronouns generally, as in the French "Il se lave" (literally "He washes himself").

Solitude and *solitary* are words we often use in describing the kind of serenity in being alone that one feels in the Chinese poems "In the Mountains on a Summer Day" and "Riding at Daybreak." *Desolate* evokes the unhappiness, the loneliness of being alone. The *de* prefix, which means "down" or "away from," suggests, in a loose fashion, feeling "down" and feeling "away from" others in a negative sense. *Desolate* often carries with it a sense of being abandoned. What's the difference between a *soliloquy* and a *monologue*? Could you be accompanied by a friend on a *solo* flight or in a *solo* performance?

Isolated happens to come from another root, the Italian *isolato,* which means "converted into an island." Our sense of the word is nevertheless influenced by its strong resemblance to the *solus* vocabulary, and it can certainly be considered a "sound cousin."

Story Puzzle

Students may want to do the puzzle in a straightforward fashion or play with how putting some of the OINO words in the "wrong" spaces gives them another slant.

Additional Related Words

UNIVERSAL: shared by all or everyone

Food and water are universal needs.

UNIVERSITY: an institution of learning that includes both graduate and undergraduate schools

The connection with the root meaning comes through the idea of many schools being united as one institution.

Howard University includes an undergraduate school and schools of law, medicine, dentistry, engineering and education.

UNIFORM: 1. all the same, not varying
2. clothes—all of the same kind—worn by members of a group when they are on duty

The foreman asked the head carpenter to make sure all the door frames were of a uniform height.

The marching band held bake sales and car washes all year to raise money for new uniforms.

UNIT: 1. a single part of something larger
2. a group of things or people treated as one

A foot is a unit of measure.

Three National Guard units were called up to help with disaster relief after the flood.

ONION: a vegetable in which many layers are wrapped into one bulb

ATONE: to make up for doing something wrong

Atone comes from blending the words "at one." When you have injured a person in some way, you are no longer "at one" with him or her—the hurt or injury divides you. When you do something to atone for the hurt or injury, you try to end that division and regain the state of being "at one" with the person.

Eric tried to atone for hurting his brother's feelings by offering to take him fishing.

In the Mountains on a Summer Day

Gently I stir a white feather fan,
With open shirt sitting in a green wood.
I take off my cap and hang it on a jutting stone;
A wind from the pine-trees trickles on my bare head.

—Li Po
Chinese, 8th century
Translated by Arthur Waley

Riding at Daybreak

Not a man is stirring
In the early light,
As my horse trots
Through the rustling yellow leaves.

The pale waning moon
Fades slowly in the dawn,
And a temple bell calls
Through the frosty air.

Far off,
Where forest trees loom through the mist,
A mountain torrent
Rushes down its stony bed.

—Sun Yun Feng
Chinese, Ch'ing Dynasty
Translated by Henry H. Hart

Number 5—December

Nobody knows me
when I go round late at night
scratching on windows
& whispering in hallways
looking for someone
who loves me in the daytime
to take me in
at night

—David Henderson

Those Winter Sundays

Sundays too my father got up early
and put his clothes on in the blueblack cold,
then with cracked hands that ached
from labor in the weekday weather made
banked fires blaze. No one ever thanked him.

I'd wake and hear the cold splintering, breaking.
When the rooms were warm, he'd call,
and slowly I would rise and dress,
fearing the chronic angers of that house,

Speaking indifferently to him,
who had driven out the cold
and polished my good shoes as well.
What did I know, what did I know
of love's austere and lonely offices?

—Robert Hayden

l(a

le
af
fa

ll

s)
one
l

iness

—e.e. cummings

Fable

The mountain and the squirrel
Had a quarrel,
And the former called the latter "Little Prig";
Bun replied,
"You are doubtless very big;
But all sorts of things and weather
Must be taken in together,
To make up a year
And a sphere.
And I think it no disgrace
To occupy my place.
If I'm not so large as you,
You are not so small as I,
And not half so spry.
I'll not deny you make
A very pretty squirrel track;
Talents differ; all is well and wisely put;
If I cannot carry forests on my back,
Neither can you crack a nut."

—*Ralph Waldo Emerson*

Autobiographia Literaria

When I was a child
I played by myself in a
corner of the schoolyard
all alone.

I hated dolls and I
hated games, animals were
not friendly and birds
flew away.

If anyone was looking
for me I hid behind a
tree and cried out "I am
an orphan."

And here I am, the
center of all beauty!
writing these poems!
Imagine!

—*Frank O'Hara*

Discussion and Writing Ideas

Oneness can range from the pleasure of solitude to the pang of loneliness to the glory of uniqueness. The poems above reflect these varied ways of experiencing *one*, and the ideas below invite students to write about their own oneness. The irony in Frank O'Hara's poem might make it more challenging to teach than most of the other poems in *Origins*.

- **In the Mountains on a Summer Day**
- **Riding at Daybreak**
- **Number 5—December**
- **Those Winter Sundays**
- **l(a**

Picture the words *alone* and *lonely*. What images appear for each? Do they overlap in places? Have you ever felt glad to be alone? Alone and lonely? Lonely even though you were with other people? Have you sympathized with the loneliness of others and wondered how to help?

"Riding at Daybreak" and "In the Mountains on a Summer Day" are both expressions of contentment in being alone. Where would you go to find these feelings? Imagine yourself there and notice what's around you. What are you seeing and thinking? Do your thoughts open into wider worlds when you step away from the routine of daily life? Do you have moments of feeling "at one" with the universe around you?

"Number 5—December" by David Henderson hits a different note: "I am alone *and* I am lonely." Added to loneliness is the misery of searching for a place to sleep on a cold night. Try to picture a time when you were alone and lonely. Where were you? Was it night? (It doesn't have to be.) What could you hear around you? What other feelings go with loneliness?

Read "Those Winter Sundays." What are "love's austere and lonely offices" as described by the poet? (*Austere* means "severely simple" and *offices* is used here to mean "tasks.") How do the father's lonely tasks show his love? Why can't the son respond? Can you think of times when you could not respond to what someone did for you—could not even say "thank you?" Do you think your lack of response made the other person feel lonely? Did *you* feel lonely because you weren't able to say thanks?

E.E. Cummings plays with the idea of loneliness by inserting a falling leaf into the word *loneliness*, playing up the resemblance between the *l* of loneliness and the number *1*, letting pieces of words fall in (lonely?) isolation on the page. Does this visual word play make you *feel* loneliness—or does it leave you cold?

Now try this free-association exercise. Give yourself one minute—no more—to write down anything that comes to your mind when you think of *alone* and *lonely*. Don't censor any thought, no matter how farfetched or off the subject it may seem. Then choose those thoughts from your list that seem closest to your own experience and write about them in any form you'd like. (Sometimes simply rearranging and adding words to your list will give you a poem in itself.) Anytime you're alone with nothing to do, or feeling lonely, try writing about it. You might find that writing about it changes the way you feel.

• **Fable**

Imagine a world in which everyone did, thought, and felt the same things. How would we each know who we are? What if I dreamed your dreams? You tasted my food? I had your toothache? In fact, we know who we are, in part, because we're all different. Each cucumber, mountain goat, and human being is unique.

In Emerson's "Fable," what advantages does the squirrel have? The mountain? They have chosen to argue about their talents. What other nonhuman elements in nature might enjoy such an argument? How might a stone and a stream quarrel about their unique abilities? An elephant and a mosquito? A cabbage and a centipede? List as many interesting non-human "partners in argument" as you can with classmates. With a friend, choose one of these combinations you would most like to argue. Decide which you will be, and allow yourselves five minutes to think about the advantages of being exactly what you are. (You may want to jot down a few notes to help you remember your good points.) Now, with a group of classmates as your audience, allow yourself one minute to argue your case aloud with your partner.

• **Autobiographia Literaria**

The title of Frank O'Hara's poem means "the story of the writer's life." His poem is about being lonely, unpopular, and withdrawn as a child, but it ends on a funny note. It's rare when poems about painful feelings turn out to be funny, but then, this is a rare and tricky poem.

It's tricky because at first it's hard to tell if the "I" in the poem is the author or if it's a character the author invented. If the "I" in the poem is the author, he must be kind of nutty to think he's "the center of all beauty," unless he's just making fun of himself. The other possibility is that Frank O'Hara imagined a character who is speaking in this poem, a character who was extremely shy as a child and extremely weird as an adult. All of these possibilities make this poem tricky and interesting, like an optical illusion.

Think about a time when you felt shy or out of place, isolated from the people around you; or, if you want, just make up such a time. Feel free to exaggerate, the way Frank O'Hara probably did (it's unlikely that he really hid behind a tree and yelled out that he was an orphan). Write a poem in short lines, describing what happened, and end it with something very happy about the way you are now. It's good to exaggerate the happy part, too.

Story Puzzle for Students

Read the story before filling in the blanks with words from your OINO word tree. The challenge is to see if you can find a way to use all the words of the OINO family.

Topper Barnes, the Unique Unicyclist with a Touch of Magic

_____ there was a guy named Topper Barnes. He got his name because, as he put it, he was the "top of the line." Topper was so cool he wore a black satin jacket with his favorite weird animal, a _____ painted on the back. There were little gold letters on his collar that said, "The _____ and only Topper Barnes."

I said, "Topper, why do you have that animal on your back?"

"It's magic," he said, "just a touch of magic."

Now you may think old Topper was conceited with his name and fancy threads. But I'll tell you the truth, that guy was _____. You could tell he was lonesome just the way he walked (when he thought no one saw him); hands in his pockets, head down, feet dragging. And even though he had a lot of brothers and sisters, most of the time Topper didn't hang with anyone. He was just _____.

I'll tell you a couple of _____ things about our man Topper. In our neighborhood, if you are cool, you have wheels; and if you don't have a car you at least have yourself a ten-speed. Now, Topper, what did he have? He had a _____. I'm telling you, he could ride that thing like he was king of the _____. Up there, high, cycling smooth as you please, he could even carry groceries for his mama without falling off.

The other thing about him was the way he could play basketball. Why, he even got a scholarship to go to the university on account of his moves. (He's smart, too; I don't want you to think he can only handle a basketball.) I remember the time there were tryouts for the _____ States Olympics basketball team. Did you hear me? I said U.S. of A. tryouts. I'm telling you, no one from this neighborhood was even trying out for that stuff.

The day came. Topper arrived outside the stadium and what do you think he saw? He saw a picket line walking back and forth in front of a store across the street. Well, Topper always supports any _____ on strike, but he needed to hurry to get into that stadium for the tryouts. It was his big chance. It was his _____ chance.

So what do you think he did? He ran across the street to the picket line and began to chant:

> Give us a brand new day;
> We want higher pay.

Before you knew it, this line of folks, who had been silent as a mouse, began to chant, first one voice, then all of them in _____. I tell you, it was powerful!

Topper wanted to stay with the strikers, but even more, he longed to try out for the U.S. Olympic basketball team. So he dashed off into the stadium. When he got inside, that boy played the best he ever had. They say he was faster than Magic Johnson, smoother than Michael Jordan. That day he was the _____ choice of the judges, the only player they all agreed on. And that's just got to be as tough as riding a unicycle, if you ask me.

(Sound cousins)

194

PE 1576 .R6 1989 v.2

DATE DUE

PE 1576 .R6 1989 v.2

ORIGINS

Volume 1
Bringing Words to Life

À droit

ORIGINS
Volume 1
Bringing Words to Life

by
Sandra R. Robinson

Teachers & Writers Collaborative
New York

Origins: Volume 1

Copyright © 1989 by Sandra R. Robinson. All rights reserved. Printed in the United States of America. No part of this publication may be reproduced, stored in a retrieval system, or transmitted, in any form or by any means, electronic, mechanical, photocopying, recording, or otherwise, without prior permission of the publisher.

"American Gothic (To Satch)" by Paul Vesey is reprinted here by permission of Samuel Allen.

Teachers & Writers is grateful to the following foundations and corporations for their support of our program: American Stock Exchange, Mr. Bingham's Trust for Charity, Columbia Committee for Community Service, Consolidated Edison, Aaron Diamond Foundation, Manufacturers Hanover Trust Company, Mobil Foundation, Morgan Stanley Foundation, New York Telephone, New York Times Company Foundation, Henry Nias Foundation, Helena Rubinstein Foundation, the Scherman Foundation, and the Steele-Reese Foundation. T&W also receives funds from the New York State Council on the Arts, the National Endowment for the Arts, and the New York Foundation for the Arts Artists-in-Residence Program, administered by the Foundation on behalf of the New York State Council on the Arts and in cooperation with the New York State Education Department with funds provided by the National Endowment for the Arts and the Council.

Teachers & Writers Collaborative
5 Union Square West
New York, N.Y. 10003

Library of Congress Cataloging-in-Publication Data

Robinson, Sandra R. (Sandra Rockwell), 1944-
    Origins: bringing words to life / by Sandra R. Robinson
  with Lindsay McAuliffe
      p.   c.m.
      Bibliography: p.
      ISBN 0-915924-90-0 (set) — ISBN 0-915924-91-9 (v. 1). —0-915924-92-7 (v. 2).
    1. English language—Etymology—Studying and teaching. 2.
English language—Studying and teaching. 3. Vocabulary—
Studying and teaching.
I. McAuliffe, Lindsay. II. Title.
PE 1576.R6 1989
422 .071´073—dc20   89-31355
                                                  CIP

Photographs: Sally Halvorson
Illustrations: Mary Azarian
Maps and word trees: Trevor Winkfield

Printed by Philmark Lithographics, New York, N.Y.

Table of Contents

Acknowledgments	ix
Preface	xiii
Introduction	1
Bringing Words to Life by Understanding How They Grow	5
Using *Origins*: The Teaching Materials in Volume 2	16
Overview	16
Introducing *Origins*	17
Exploring Extended Meanings	27
Reading Poetry	28
Writing and Ideas for Other Activities	29
Developing Your Own Word Families	34
How Meanings Change over Time	36
Exploring Popular Speech and Cross-Cultural Metaphors	38
Sound and Meaning	41
Sound and Spelling	43
A Brief History of the English Language	44
The Anglo-Saxon Invasions	45
Old Norse	48
The Norman Conquest	50
The Conquest Reshapes the Language	54
The Renaissance	57
English after the Renaissance	60
The Mixed Heritage of English	61
Indo-European Origins	69
American English: The Story Continues	71
Linguistic Background	76
Additional Word Families Based on Indo-European Roots	82
Body Metaphors in English	92
Exploring Popular Speech	94
Sound Families	97
An Annotated Bibliographical Note	99
Appendix: The Words Project	103
Using *Origins* as a Base for a Literacy Program	103
Inventing Stone Age Languages	105
Using *Origins* in French Class	105
Exploring Cross-Cultural Metaphors	106
A Final Word	106
Student Word Tree	108

Acknowledgments

Origins reflects the contributions of many individuals and organizations. I want to express particular thanks to those who played major roles in moving *Origins* from its tentative beginnings through to an active life in diverse classrooms and on to publication. The path was a long and winding one, and it seems remarkable, in retrospect, how the right people appeared at the right moment, by turns, to nurture, inspire, prod, push, and support the project.

When the first glimmers of *Origins* began to inspire my thinking, Bea Lindsten, head of the Potomac Middle School where I was teaching, offered generous encouragement. When I proposed teaching a new course based more on enthusiasm and ideas still bubbling to the surface than on any detailed curriculum, she responded with a sense of adventure. Her trust sustained my confidence and her office was a haven where I could share doubts, triumphs, and a love of language and history. Her whole-hearted support of my teaching experiments made the beginnings of *Origins* possible.

At the next stage of the project, David Hackett, then director of the Robert Kennedy Memorial, challenged me with a fellowship and a broader vision of the potential of *Origins* than I had initially conceived. From the moment I began talking with Dave about the material, he seized on its wide-ranging possibilities and pushed me to run with them. His support, through three years of fellowships from the Memorial and through major help with other fundraising, launched us (I was soon joined by my colleague, Lindsay McAuliffe) into piloting *Origins* in numerous classrooms in Washington, D.C., both in the inner city and in independent schools. His assistant, John Cheshire, instigated the Job Corps pilot, which further expanded our understanding of the possibilities of the material. Dave Hackett's challenge and support were catalysts that evoked many possibilities for *Origins* that would otherwise have lain dormant.

As I began to feel the need to write up new insights and ideas generated by four years of piloting a field edition of *Origins*, Jill Wilkinson appeared on the scene and offered support from the Stillwater Foundation. I am deeply grateful for Jill's patience, enthusiasm, and belief in *Origins*. She offered support for the final stage of writing this book at a time when we had no publisher in sight. I have greatly valued her personal support, as well as the financial support from Stillwater.

As I worked to prepare *Origins* for publication, Ron Padgett, my editor at Teachers & Writers Collaborative, and Christopher Edgar, editorial associate, made vital contributions to improving the clarity and organization of the text. I appreciate their help in pointing me toward revisions that were very much needed.

Calvert Watkins, editor of *The Dictionary of Indo-European Roots* (which is the source of the word families of Volume 2), provided an invaluable scholarly review of *Origins*, as well as its preface. He took time from a crowded schedule to go over two successive versions of the text and to help me clear up various points of confusion. I have appreciated both his help and the kind spirit in which he has offered it. Walt Wolfram, co-director of the Research Division of the Center of Applied Linguistics and professor at the University of the District of Columbia, also provided valuable advice and encouragement.

I would like to thank, as well, Sally Smith, head of the Washington Lab School, who had a major influence on my understanding of how children learn. Like my colleague and fellow author, Lindsay McAuliffe, I spent a year as an apprentice at the Lab School, where Sally trained us in using the arts and all the senses for learning. The Lab School overflowed with sculptors, dancers, musicians, and actors, and all of the artists and their arts were integrated into the teaching of spelling, math, reading, writing, and history. At the Lab School *kinesthetic* did not refer to the experience of moving a pencil across a page (touted by many workbooks as the "kinesthetic" element of an exercise); it meant that you got to your feet and *moved*. Being immersed in the Lab School for a year was formative. Many activities suggested in the word family chapters of *Origins* have their roots in that experience.

My collaboration with Lindsay McAuliffe had its beginnings in the Lab School connection. We shared a commitment to the kind of innovative teaching that had influenced both of us at the Lab School, and, when looking for a partner to help pursue the development of *Origins*, I turned to her. Her participation in *Origins*, from its early stages through toward its final form, has been invaluable. She took half-time leave from her teaching at the Sidwell Friends School and gave up summers to help write word family chapters, develop adaptations of the material required by the District of Columbia Public Schools, gather feedback from teachers who were piloting *Origins*, and prepare workshops for teachers. I could not have shepherded *Origins* through its many incarnations without her help. The opportunity to spend uninterrupted summer days bouncing ideas back and forth between the two of us was particularly valuable to me, as was her expertise in running workshops for teachers.

As a result of Lindsay's work, other teachers at Sidwell Friends became actively involved in the development of *Origins*. Susanne Saunders broadened the scope of *Origins* and greatly enriched it by collecting poetry and developing writing ideas to accompany word families. Priscilla Alfandre generated great excitement among her students by having them speculate on the origins of words through inventing Stone Age languages. I would like to add a special thank you to Lisa Hirsh, friend and teacher extraordinaire, who spent a summer helping write materials for the word family chapters, and to Celia Alvaraz, my partner in the Job Corps project, who taught me a great deal about *Origins* as a resource for minority students through her own inimitable combination of generosity and unvarnished truth-telling. Her encouragement has meant a great deal to me. Eva Dömötör, partner in years of conversations that helped develop my teaching ideas, offered valuable insights. I would also like to thank Carol Kranowitz, Judith Steinberg, Bruce Boling, and Adrienne Carlee who provided important help and support along the way.

All the teachers who participated in piloting *Origins* played vital roles in its development as they plunged into using the material with their own students, posed questions and offered their own ideas. Working with the teachers who took part in the project was stimulating and a real privilege. Grateful thanks go to all of them: Vergaline Campbell, Doris Giles, McCoy Humes, Carol Robinson, and Yvonne Robinson in the District of Columbia Public Schools; Priscilla Alfandre, Michelle Jeffrey, Robert Peterson, Susanne Saunders, and Jennifer Swanson Voorhees at the Sidwell Friends School; Ann Craig, David Pines, and Ena-Mai Kvell at the Capitol Hill Day School; and Margaret Valiante at the Parkmont School. Carol Robinson provided invaluable help in adapting materials to the requirements of the D.C. schools. Cheri Bridgeforth, a doctoral student in linguistics, helped with interviewing teachers and gathering their ideas.

Lindsay McAuliffe and I are grateful to administrators at all of these schools for welcoming us. Particular thanks go to the District of Columbia Public Schools and the Sidwell Friends School for extensive help and in-kind contributions. We would especially like to thank Floretta McKenzie, Dr. William

Brown, Dr. Sheila Handy, Anabelle Strayhorn, and Leila Head of the D.C. schools, and Earl Harrison, Helen Colson, and Dr. Richard Lodish of Sidwell Friends for important administrative support for our work.

Gratitude is also due to writers and artists associated with Teachers & Writers Collaborative: Larry Fagin, Herbert Kohl, Bernadette Mayer, Jessica Sager, Daniel Sklar, and Felice Stadler.

Three artists have enhanced *Origins* by their contributions. Kate Rushin wrote the poems "Blues Song," "The Rapper as Light," and "Double Dutch Song" especially for *Origins*, contributions that have been favorites among students. Sally Halvorson made students' responses to *Origins* vivid through her photographs. Mary Azarian has captured a sense of the history that underlies English in her illustrations for the "Brief History of the English Language" chapter. We are honored to have these contributions.

The work that resulted in *Origins* would not have been possible without generous financial support from a variety of funders. In addition to major support from the Robert Kennedy Memorial and the Stillwater Foundation, the WORDS Project—the entity organized to receive funds and pursue the development of *Origins*—received major support from the Lyndhurst Foundation, the Cafritz Foundation, the Strong Foundation, and the Dreyfus Foundation. Additional support came from the April Trust, the Lucas Foundation, the Miller and Chevalier Charitable Foundation, the Riggs Bank, the Fairfax Hotel, PEPCO, the Chesapeake and Potomac Telephone Company, IBM, Hechinger's, Oliver T. Carr, and four individuals.

My own work in completing *Origins* would not have been possible without the patient and expert work of Judy Miller, who helped type the manuscript; the wonderfully reliable help of the young women who lived with us and helped care for my daughter—Rose Bailey, Fabienne Van der Keer, and Marty Cooper—and the support of my family. I would like to say a special thank you to Marty Cooper, who, with great patience and geniality, helped keep our household on an even keel during the pressured last months of completing the manuscript. The patience, good humor, and generous spirit of my husband David has undergirded my work on *Origins* at every step. I am deeply grateful for his belief in my work, which has never faltered over many years and many ups and downs, and for all his day-to-day help in freeing me to complete it. Finally, I would like to thank my daughter, Kate. The joy she brings to my life is an important source of energy in my work.

Preface

By Calvert Watkins
Department of Linguistics, Harvard University

Sandra Robinson begins *Origins* by emphasizing the role of verbal play in language: the creating of new combinations of words and forms and the stretching of expressions to apply to new situations. Likewise, initial language learning, which begins in the crib, is a very playful process. Children play-talk when by themselves, and they are well aware of this learning process. Many years ago my just-turned-four-year-old daughter and a friend of the same age were talking about—and illustrating—how they used to say words when they were "babies." The friend picked up her glass of milk and said, "I used to call it *mook*." Knowing her current pronunciation, I asked, "What do you call it now?" "Mook." "What's the difference?" With an air of complete self-possession, she replied, "Now I say it louder." If teachers can preserve, enhance, and foster that initial magical fascination with language, they will have accomplished their most enduring single task as educators.

Being creative with language is fun. What were the feelings of the first person to say *input-output*? Probably something akin to those of a precocious pre-school poet I knew, who on learning that a playmate's name was Ferdie, said, with a wicked gleam in his eye, "Ferdie-Berdie."

The particular creativity of American English shines forth in the words and phrases surveyed in the "Brief History of the English Language" chapter of *Origins*. A comparable list, equally poetic, picturesque, and exotic, could be drawn up for Australian English, as anyone who has tried to explain the lyrics to "Waltzing Matilda" will know. The same applies to all of the many other varieties of English, whether in Britain, Canada, Central America, Southern Africa, or the Indian subcontinent.

Being creative with language is not the only thing that is fun. Figuring things out is also fun. And knowing *why* can be very satisfying indeed.

There are a number of approaches to knowing *why* in human language. Some have to do with the psychological make-up of all human beings and seem to be characteristic features of most or all human languages: these are termed "language universals." In respect to such features, all languages are in some sense the same the world over. All languages have things like nouns and things like verbs. All languages have sentences, and these sentences have things like subjects and things like predicates. Most languages have in their lexicons forms like *boo-boo, cuckoo,* and *yum yum,* or expressive patterns like *wishy-washy* or *shilly-shally.* Studying and understanding such features (and others more complex) tells us something about the organization of the human mind.

But of course all languages are different, too, and the variety of languages is above all a product of language change. English is fortunate in having a fairly long period of documentation, and the history of the language, based on its written records, has been thoroughly studied and very well described. But historical linguistics—the scientific study of language change—is not limited to the study of written records. We know that English is not an isolate, but is closely related to other languages that make up the Germanic group, and this group in turn is one of the ten or so branches of the Indo-European family of languages. All these are descendants of a single prehistoric proto-language spoken perhaps some six or seven thousand years ago, termed Indo-European or Proto-Indo-European. The principal features of this language, its grammar and vocabulary, have been reconstructed by the techniques of historical linguistics.

The great originality of *Origins* lies in its utilization of both the documented history of English and of its reconstructed Indo-European prehistory as a touchstone to the teaching of language skills, particularly in elementary school. The method can work precisely because it evokes the spirit of verbal play, the magical pleasure in manipulating language. May *Origins* win new friends for the endlessly fascinating study of language, our language, and its roots.

Introduction

Beginnings and Development

Origins had its beginnings when a turn of fate led me to design a course on the history of the English language for a class of sixth graders. As I worked to gather materials that would inspire this energetic band of thirteen boys, I stumbled across the resource that gave rise to *Origins*—the "Indo-European Root Appendix" of the *American Heritage Dictionary*. The appendix revealed word families that appeal to students at an elementary level, families that reflected the poetry and playfulness of the language in particularly vivid ways. After a year of experimenting with ways of using the material and finding it did indeed seize the attention of the restless characters in my class, I knew I wanted to find ways of developing it for other teachers as well. When a request for support to run a summer workshop caused a year-long fellowship to fall into my lap, I was launched precipitously into trying an early version of *Origins* in two Washington, D.C., classrooms—one at the Brent School, a public school, and one at the Sidwell Friends School, a private school. Seeing students in these two very different settings respond with the same enthusiasm and lively participation to *Origins* classes presented by their own teachers confirmed my belief in the material. Students who felt hesitant in the world of books and writing felt at home with the get-on-your-feet, get-the-images-in-your-bones activities that introduced the word families; students adept at reading and writing responded creatively to the imagery and verbal playfulness reflected in the historical growth of the words. All were intrigued by seeing how the latest street language and popular speech spring from the images of our experience in the same way that words developed centuries ago.

Over the next several years, the project grew to include three third- and fourth-grade classrooms at the Sidwell Friends School; four upper-elementary classrooms in the District of Columbia Public Schools; three upper-elementary classrooms at Capitol Hill Day School, a Washington private school; a junior high class at the Parkmont School, an alternative school in D.C.; and a pilot literacy program for a class of Job Corps students, ages 19-21, who were reading at second- and third-grade levels. When Job Corps students took a lively interest in exploring items of their own speech and then, in spite of initial aggressive indifference, started competing to be first on their feet to embody the images of a word family, I was once again convinced of the power of the material.

In all settings I—and Lindsay McAuliffe, who joined me in writing up materials—worked in partnership with teachers who were piloting *Origins*. We met to toss around ideas for presenting particular word families and then, after a class, to chat about what worked and what fell flat. The materials in Volume 2 of *Origins* reflect the play of ideas set loose as we worked together—both in pairs and in larger gatherings of all teachers who were working with the project. One of the many ideas that sprang from these gatherings—and was given shape by Susanne Saunders—was the formal inclusion of the poetry and of writing ideas that Lindsay and other teachers were already beginning to use as a natural outgrowth of exploring the word families. Later contributions to the poetry and writing ideas were made by writers-in-the-schools associated with Teachers & Writers Collaborative as they used *Origins* in New York City public schools.

Purpose

The purpose of *Origins* is to get students excited about language by tracing the histories of particular word families in ways that illuminate all vocabulary as well as important elements of reading and writing. The origin of a word has much in common with the origin of a poem or story. All have their beginnings in the stuff of our experience and take place through playful leaps of imagination. This broad understanding of word meaning animates all the word family chapters, as exploring the imagery of words flows into reading poetry and writing poems and stories. *Origins*, then, is a "vocabulary" book only in the broadest sense. We have found that its greatest value lies in fostering a delight in words. That delight has a solid foundation because, as students trace the development of word families, they acquire insights that help them understand all vocabulary in a more powerful way, habits of analysis important in reading, and resources for creating vivid language in their own writing.

Sources and Materials

The word families in Volume 2 of *Origins* came from Germanic and Indo-European roots. Drawn from *The American Heritage Dictionary of Indo-*

European Roots, the families have not previously been presented as teaching materials for students at elementary and junior high levels. We chose these families for many reasons: the vocabulary of the families is lively and down-to-earth and has great appeal for younger students; the vividness of the words makes them an inspiration and resource for writing; the abundance of words that have both a down-to-earth primary meaning and a secondary abstract meaning provides an excellent opportunity for exploring how abstract meanings develop. In addition, some of the families reveal ties of kinship between words of Germanic origin and words of Latin origin in ways that provide students with additional resources for detecting the many networks of relationship that permeate English vocabulary.

The scholarship that revealed the family ties in the word families we have chosen to explore was first made readily available to the general public in the "Indo-European Root Appendix" edited by Calvert Watkins and published in the 1969 edition of *The American Heritage Dictionary* (Boston: American Heritage Publishing Company and Houghton Mifflin). The Appendix was revised and updated by Watkins and published in 1985 as an individual volume, *The American Heritage Dictionary of Indo-European Roots* (Boston: Houghton Mifflin). If you check the Indo-European roots presented in *Origins* against this source, you will find a few minor changes were made. These were made in consultation with Calvert Watkins and are described in the "Linguistic Background" chapter. Examples of regional speech referred to in *Origins* are drawn from the following sources: *The Dictionary of American Regional English, Volume 1*, edited by Frederic G. Cassidy (Cambridge: Harvard University Press, 1985), *Maine Lingo* by John Gould (Camden, Maine: Down East Magazine, 1975) and *Down in the Holler: A Gallery of Ozark Folk Speech* by Vance Randolph and George P. Wilson (Norman: University of Oklahoma Press, 1953).

Structure

Volume 1 of *Origins* presents background material for the teacher. The materials include a general analysis of how meaning develops in words ("Bringing Words to Life by Understanding How They Grow") and a brief survey of the history that has shaped English vocabulary ("A Brief History of the English Language"). Although written for teachers, these materials can also be read by older students. The "Using *Origins*" chapter discusses ways of using *Origins* in the classroom and the "Linguistic Background" chapter presents a general discussion of the linguistic information found in the teaching materials.

Volume 2 presents teaching materials in chapters that explore individual word families. Ideas for exploring the families are presented in considerable detail in the beginning chapters in order to provide a full and lively sense of the possibilities that have emerged as students and teachers in many settings have used the material. Once students and teachers have explored a number of families, they begin to shape the material to their own needs and style, and therefore teaching ideas are presented in a more abbreviated form as the chapters progress. Most chapters include poetry and writing ideas, as well as ideas for exploring the word family.

How to Use This Book

For teachers who would like to get started using *Origins* without having to read the entire book, we suggest the following plan.

• In Volume 1: Read the "Bringing Words to Life" chapter. Then read pp. 16-28 and 38-40 of the "Using *Origins*" chapter.

• In Volume 2: Present the material in the BHEL, KER, GHEL, and WER families, and add the FLEU or DWO family, whichever is appropriate for your students. This plan works well as an introduction to the material. Later you can delve into other parts of the book and branch out to other word families.

Bringing Words to Life by Understanding How They Grow

Who made up the words we use? How does language grow? How did the words *glint, glad,* and *glass* grow from the root GHEL ("to shine")? How did *rip off* and *spaced out* grow from the words *rip* and *space*? Language has always grown through the inventiveness of those who use it. Word families that developed hundreds of years ago and phrases of popular speech coined yesterday and today are the legacy of people who have been playful with root meanings, extending them to make new connections. The new connections—the new meanings—often reflect the experience of a particular time and culture. What is a "free-lance" artist? Standing in the historical shadows behind the free-lance artist or writer is the medieval knight who, rather than being attached to one particular lord, hired himself and his lance out to many different lords.

The teaching materials of *Origins* are designed to recapture a sense of the playful inventiveness that fuels the growth of language and a sense of how meaning is rooted in experience. Inventiveness is the lifeblood of all the ways we express ourselves in language—new words and phrases, poems, stories, plays. In *Origins*, exploring word histories spills over into reading poetry, writing poems and short plays, inventing new words—participating in the drama as well as reenacting it.

At the heart of *Origins* are the word families, which we explore with lots of up-on-your-feet, get-into-the-act, get-the-imagery-in-your-bones activities. We emphasize word families of Germanic origin because their words are often both colorful and down-to-earth. For example, from a root that means "to swell" we get the words *ball, balloon, belly, bulky, bulge, boulder, bold,* and *billow*. We also include families that, by going back to Indo-European roots, reveal relationships between familiar Germanic words and more abstract Latinate vocabulary. From the Indo-European root MEDHYO, for example, come the Germanic *middle, midst,* and *mid-* and the Latinate *medium, mediate, intermediate, Mediterranean, immediate, mediocre,* and *media*.

As we suggest ways to explore word families, our focus is on the images

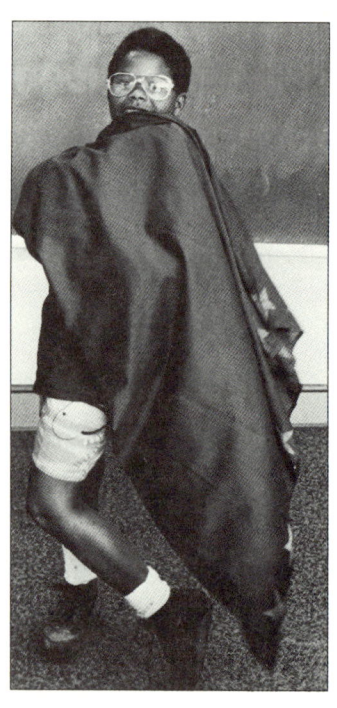

and experience that underlie a word's "definition." In a typical lesson we might begin with a pantomime—of a wrestling match, for example. How do the wrestlers move? They twist or bend. *Wrestle* comes from the root WER, which means "to twist or bend." That image of twisting and bending was a resource for coining many other words, as well—*wrap, wreath, wriggle, wrinkle, wrist, writhe, wrong,* and *wrath.* Students examine the twisted strands of a wreath, wriggle into an imaginary pair of almost-outgrown pants, imagine the coziness of being wrapped in a blanket, writhe with pain after an imagined soccer injury, wrinkle their foreheads in surprise or in a frown. The root image springs to life in many forms, illuminating the words of the entire family.

Why search out the images that underlie *wrestle* or *wrap* or *wriggle*? Aren't the meanings of these everyday words easy enough to grasp without digging into their roots? The meanings of such words are indeed accessible. Many of these words, however, also leave their down-to-earth beginnings and journey forth to suggest abstract ideas. What do we mean when we say "Tony wrestled with the math problem" or "Demali wrestled with her conscience"? We wrap a child in a blanket, but we also wrap up a report and keep a secret under wraps—and become so wrapped up in the book we are reading that we forget to notice the time. We may watch a worm wriggle across a sidewalk, but we may also watch a politician wriggle out of campaign promises. The images we have explored as we first encountered the WER family become a resource for understanding these "extended" or abstract meanings. When Tony "wrestled with the math problem," did he get down on the floor and use his arms and legs to grapple with the problem? How is the *idea* of wrestling with a math problem related to the twisting, bending, and sweat of a physical wrestling match? Both involve struggle, both are difficult. When you wrestle with a problem in your head, you move back and forth in your mind, trying one thing and then another as you struggle to "get hold of" a solution—just as a wrestler moves one way, then another, trying to get hold of his opponent.

Tracing the evolution of the WER family words from their earliest roots to their latest abstractions dramatizes how we use our down-to-earth experience to express our flights of thought and imagination. Abstraction—literally "drawing away"—is one term that describes such evolution. Metaphor—literally "to carry beyond"—is another. Abstraction highlights the movement from experience to idea. Metaphor highlights the inventiveness that springs from our urge to coin new words and create new meanings. We tend to think of metaphor as an item of high culture. In truth, metaphor lives as vital a life on the streets and in the back hills, on farms and in computer rooms as it does in Shakespeare. It is a vehicle by which language—and indeed our very thinking—develops. *Chill out, bedcord strong,* and *he doesn't have both drives on line* are all as genuinely metaphorical as Shakespeare's "Sleep...balm of hurt minds." From the intuitive perception that our body temperature is lowered when we relax (*chill out*) to the experience of finding strong rope to hold the mattress of a homemade bed (*bedcord strong*); from frustration with the limits of a computer that lacks a second drive (*he doesn't have both drives on line*) to the experience of feeling balm heal a wound, the varieties of human experience are the clay we reach for to shape new meanings—or express old meanings in a fresh way. To express intangible feelings and ideas, we draw on what we know through the senses. Scenes from baseball and boxing become a resource for describing thoughts about somebody's conduct: *he's way off base*; *that's a low blow*. The unexpected twists of improvisation that occur as a jazz musician departs from the melody line to play "changes" become a resource for describing difficult times that put you through ups and downs: "Problems with her job have really been *putting her through changes*." An image of winds blowing "toward the harbor" is at the root of the word *opportunity*. The sensation of light and warmth suggested by the root idea "to shine" is at the base of a word that describes happiness: *glad*.

Exploring the word families of *Origins* provides a background for detecting the human experience and inventiveness that underlie the formal definitions of all words, whether they be words in the dictionary, the latest popular speech, or simply an unusual turn of phrase. Students studying the settling of the American West, for example, encountered the puzzling phrase "proving up on the homestead." What experiences on a homestead might lie behind the idea of "proving up"? The students had been immersed in *Origins* for several months, and the strategy of posing such a question was a familiar one. They were quick to come up with a list: clearing the land, building a house and barn, digging a well, planting crops. By the time they finished their list, they had a good sense of what the pioneers must have meant when they used the term "proving up."

Evoking the experience suggested by a root meaning provides a fuller understanding of how meaning develops than the unadorned this-comes-from-that approach. What, for example, is the meaning of the word *construct*? The root meaning of the word is to build (*struct*) together (*con-*). Why build *together*? If we simply set *together* beside *build*, its meaning may be puzzling, but if we delve into the experience it suggests, it can point us toward a vivid understanding of the word. What comes together in construction? A pile of logs, a stack of boards, a heap of stones or bricks. Or young saplings bent into a dome and covered by branches. Window frames, doors, plaster board. Water pipes, electric wires, insulation. Or chunks of ice carved for an Eskimo home. What holds these things together? Wooden pegs, animal sinew, nails, cement. By the time we have explored the experience suggested by the *con-* of *construct* (in conjunction with our understanding of *build*), we have a full-bodied sense of the word.

The same approach—What is the experience at the root of this word?—can illuminate the multiple meanings of a word. In *The American Heritage Dictionary*, for example, more than thirty-five meanings are given for the word *draw*. Such a long list of meanings can be daunting. The list becomes manageable, however, if we see the many meanings not as separate and discrete, but as a family of related meanings that have grown from the experience of *pulling* that lies at the root of the word—an experience we can discover in its primary meaning. A chimney that *draws* well is one whose air currents *pull* smoke upward; the concept of money *drawing* interest is a metaphorical *pulling* of one thing toward another; someone who *draws* a picture *pulls* a pen or pencil across a surface; and a fiction writer who *draws* a scene in a novel does so by a metaphorical extension of an artist's drawing.

The *Origins* angle of vision on language also provides a foundation for valuing students' own speech. Whatever background and interests students may have, their conversation will include lively figures of speech that reflect the kind of inventive thinking that has fueled the growth of language throughout history. From the latest popular speech to the vocabulary of a non-standard dialect or the vocabulary of strikingly different languages such as Chinese or Arabic, there are words and expressions in a student's own language that can be illuminated by delving into the experience that underlies their meaning. Exploring such expressions often generates an enthusiasm that then carries over into exploring the word families. When students feel they are part of the story, they are more interested in studying it. The "Using *Origins*" chapter provides additional thoughts on digging into the roots of popular speech.

Even when students' home language is wholly unrelated to English, exploring metaphors based on shared experience can establish a sense of connection between the language of home and school. In all languages, vocabulary is rooted in experience, and basic to all of us, whatever language we speak, is that we experience the world through our bodies. In English, many metaphors are rooted in this experience of the body. We may aspire to be *head* of a company, our achievements may inspire us to hold our *heads* high, we may be *head*strong in pursuit of what we want, or we may take on more than we can *handle* and find ourselves in over our *heads*. A person who is deceitful may be described as two-*faced*. We may be *nosy*, we may *nose* into a parking space, or we may look down our *noses* at others. If we want to ignore something, we may turn a blind *eye* to it—or turn a deaf *ear* to it. On the other hand, we may lend an *ear*—or even be all *ears*. You can be firm and put your *foot* down—or you can throw up your *hands* and give in. You may *shoulder* a burden or get cold *feet* and avoid it. A person may be cold-*hearted* or warm-*hearted*, hard-*hearted* or soft-*hearted*—or *heartless*. We can take *heart* or lose *heart*—and we can attack a job half-*heartedly* or whole-*heartedly*. Any group that sits down to brainstorm such a list will come up with many other examples. Such examples provide a jumping off point for eliciting similar metaphors in other languages. So far, all the languages we've investigated have yielded such expressions. In Arabic, the word for the *head of a company* or *head of state* is also built on the Arabic word for *head*—and the same is true in Thai. In Hungarian, the word for disorder or anarchy is "headlessness." In Hebrew, Rosh Hashanah means "head of the year." In Tagalog, a language of the Philippines, the word for generous means, literally, "with open palm." In Temne, one of the languages of Sierra Leone, having a "good hand" means, figuratively, that everything you do turns out well. In Wolof, an African language, to have a "clean heart" is to be sincere.

Exploring students' own speech helps to awaken the sense fostered by all of the *Origins* material—that the story of how language grows belongs to us all. A group of reluctant Job Corps students became interested in spite of themselves when we started exploring word origins by examining items in their own speech. Nineteen- to twenty-one-year-olds who were reading at second- and third-grade levels, these students were hardly eager learners. By the end of a week, however, they were claiming the first word family as their own and competing to be first on their feet to dramatize a word. They developed a grudging admiration for those people of the past who, by coining the words of the BHEL family, knew how to be as slick with words as they were.

We have found that the *Origins* approach to exploring word families and students' own speech sparks a delight in words and illuminates many corners of the language arts curriculum. "That's one of our words!" echoes through classrooms where students have been tracing the life history of *Origins* vocabulary. In one inner-city class, virtually the entire group turned to their teacher, whispering and smiling with recognition as a *duet* (a member of the DWO family they were studying) was announced in assembly. Most important, the sense of family feeling developed for the particular vocabulary of *Origins* begins to spread to words in general. Where do they come from? What are their relatives? "I bet *handle* comes from *hand*, right?" "Hey, *split* is like *rip off*. When you split, you separate yourself—you get going away from where you've been." "*Nestle* must be related to *nest*! If you're going to nestle down in something, it's like getting in your nest." Everyday words take on new life. Unfamiliar words kindle new interest. Where do they come from? Do they have any word cousins? Students who have been immersed in *Origins* are eager to hear such stories—and teachers who have been using the material are alert to the pleasures of finding and telling them. When a third grader was puzzled by the meaning of the word *cardiac*, encountered in a book she was reading, her teacher not only helped her discover the root meaning of the word ("heart") but also introduced her to two other members of the family—*courage* and *accord*. How might *courage* and *cardiac* be related? "Because you have to have a big *heart* to be courageous," came the immediate reply. And *accord*? Together they explored its meaning as a "meeting of hearts." Because exploring *Origins* word families—including reasons for frequent vowel shifts within a root pattern (*car-, cour-, cor-*)—had been so much a part of the classroom experience, the discussion took only a moment. The territory was familiar. Several days later the third grader referred, with a smile, to her "heart" family.

Delight in words begins to animate students' writing, as well. The lively vocabulary of *Origins* word families shows up with growing frequency in

stories and poems. The images and words of a family can also be a formal inspiration for writing. A brainstorming meditation on *gold* (another member of the GHEL family), launched a writing session for a class of Washington, D.C., fourth graders. Here is one of their poems:

Gold

>Gold,
>>its reflection bends
>
>>the earth
>>>with awe.
>
>It tempts
>>the gangsters
>
>>and
>>>touches the
>
>>heart.
>
>It speaks coldly
>>>and
>
>>answers softly
>>while whistling
>
>>a tune of
>
>the sun's rays.
>Kissing the galaxy
>>and warming the
>
>>seas
>>>it opens
>
>>all feeling
>>and greed.
>
>It tackles the
>>mind
>
>and touches
>the bones.

>—*Amy DuRoss*

Writing has grown naturally from the experience of exploring *Origins* in the classroom. The clusters of vocabulary that share images, the alliterative play of sound found in many of the word families, the inventiveness with sound and meaning revealed by many word histories, the use of images and experience to express ideas in lively ways that catch the mind's eye—these elements fundamental to how language grows are natural resources for writing. In addition, many word family chapters in this book present specific writing ideas. These are based both on the words of the family and on the poetry included in the chapter. Writing ideas that can be used with any of the families are found in the "Writing" section of the "Using *Origins*" chapter.

Exploring the *Origins* word families can also be a resource for "getting the picture" in reading. Understanding how we seize the images and details from our experience to express ideas illuminates the meaning not only in individual words, but in poems and stories and histories as well. Students who have explored how the root image "to shine" was used to express an idea of happiness in the word *glad* have a feel for how the more extended images of Paul Vesey's poem express a feeling of celebration:

> **American Gothic**
> *to Satch*
>
> Sometimes I feel like I will *never* stop
> Just go on forever
> Til one fine mornin'
> I'm gonna reach up and grab me a handfulla stars
> Swing out my long lean leg
> And whip three hot strikes burnin' down the heavens
> And look over at God and say
> How about that!

What feelings are evoked by the scene that opens Madeleine L'Engle's *A Wrinkle in Time*?

> In her attic bedroom Margaret Murry, wrapped in an old patchwork quilt, sat at the foot of her bed and watched the trees tossing in the frenzied lashing of the wind. Behind the trees clouds scudded frantically across the sky. Every few moments the moon ripped through them, creating wraith-like shadows that raced along the ground.

In the following lines from Gwyneth Morgan's *Life in a Medieval Village*, do Robert Fitzralph and the sheriff represent only themselves, or are they presented as a way of pointing beyond themselves to general realities of the medieval world?

> As part of his duty as a tenant, John has to help mend the road that runs through the village. Like most lords, Robert Fitzralph does not take much interest in the work and thinks it a great nuisance and expense and waste of time. But since the sheriff's horse stumbled in a rut a few years back, and the sheriff hurt his arm and lost his temper, the lord feels obliged to do something about repairing the worst parts of the road each autumn. All the tenants are pressed into service to quarry and cut the stones and to fill up the holes and ruts.

"Getting the picture" as we read often requires having a sense of how meaning moves beyond specific and literal details to suggest larger ideas. This movement takes place in many various ways. Sometimes it involves formal metaphor—as it often does in poetry—but sometimes it involves a looser, less formal process of pointing beyond specifics to more general ideas—as in the story of Robert Fitzralph and the sheriff.

As students learn how meaning moves from experience to idea in individual words, they begin to extend that understanding to poetry, stories, and nonfiction.

Using *Origins*:
The Teaching Materials in Volume 2

Overview

In Volume 2 of *Origins*, each chapter presents material for introducing and exploring a word family. Most chapters also provide poetry that includes images or concepts of the word family and writing ideas based either on the poetry or on playing with words and images of the family. All chapters include material for exploring how concrete meanings are extended to express abstract and figurative ideas, and many chapters include a specific section called "Exploring Extended Meanings" that details ways of making the process clear. Before reading further, you should browse through one or two word families, since we refer to them often in the following pages.

The teaching materials presented with each word family may have a somewhat formal look, but they are meant to be used as a flexible resource and adapted to your own needs and interests. We found that the clearest way of presenting the material was one that preserved a sense of conversation—of us talking with you and of you talking with your students. The format is *not* meant to be a script. It is meant, rather, to evoke a sense of the lively exchange between students and teachers that has in fact taken place as they explored the word families together. The format allows us to use a light touch in presenting a lot of specific information: information about the history of individual words in a family; thoughts on how to clarify the connection between a word's origin and its present meaning; ideas for ways of bringing the material to life through skits and pantomime, through exploring objects, and through helping students explore and remember experiences of their own that illuminate the meaning of a word.

In Volume 2, teaching ideas are presented in considerable detail in the beginning chapters and in more abbreviated form as the later chapters progress. In the "Developing Your Own Word Families" section at the end of this chapter, we discuss how you might explore word families not included in *Origins*.

Introducing *Origins*

How do you begin using *Origins*? Do you plunge straight in to exploring one of the word families? Most teachers like to provide a brief introduction to the overall idea of word families first.

Vergaline Campbell, a teacher in the District of Columbia public schools, introduced the idea of word families by comparing them to family reunions. What similarities can be seen among relatives at a family reunion? She gave an example from her own family: the "Campbell eyes" and "Campbell mouth" that led one relative to say, "I could tell a Campbell anywhere." Then she talked about how, in tracing the lines of relationship in a family, people sometimes construct a family tree. She drew an example of a family tree on the board, and that became the point of reference for introducing the word tree and the concepts it represents:

- Just as new people are born into a family, creating new and larger families, new words grow from older "parent" words.
- Just as new members of a family resemble parents and grandparents in certain ways, members of a word family resemble the older "parent" word or root in certain ways. Members of a word family resemble each other through a shared meaning of the "parent" root and through a shared spelling pattern.
- Just as members of a human family have many individual differences as well as many shared traits, members of a word family have distinct individual definitions, as well as a shared connection to the same root meaning and spelling pattern.

Many teachers have used some version of this family reunion idea as a way of introducing *Origins*.

Others have begun by exploring items of popular speech current in students' own language. They explored items such as *rip off* and *chill out*, looking at how the idea expressed by *rip off* (stealing, or cheating someone out of something) grew from the image of separation and the suggestion of violence in the act of ripping, and how *chill out* (take it easy, relax) has its roots in the fact that substances move more slowly when chilled or cooled—hence, slowing down to relax. Teachers exploring such items of popular speech might discuss them along the following lines:

> You've just discovered a lot about the way language grows. Ever since language began, people have been making new words and expressions from old ones. They take some of the ideas from the old word and use them in new ways to create new words or phrases—the way someone created *rip off* from *rip*. Later, we're going to be looking at how many words grew in just that way.

Since popular speech changes rapidly, any examples we cite here will be quickly dated. If you want to introduce *Origins* via slang or expressions particular to a region or culture, you will need to be alert to what is current among your own students. Choose expressions whose origins are relatively obvious. (See the "Exploring Popular Speech" and "Cross-Cultural Metaphors" sections toward the end of this chapter for further discussion.) Using students' own speech to introduce *Origins* can be particularly powerful for students who have negative or ambivalent feelings about school. One teacher found that this approach was also very effective in her English as a Second Language class, because her students were delighted to learn some "American expressions."

Some teachers like to introduce *Origins* by drawing on the material presented in the "A Brief History of the English Language" chapter. Although the historical background is *not* necessary for exploring the word families, it is helpful for answering questions as they may arise. Beyond that, use the history in whatever ways may be appropriate or appealing for your own students—or skip it.

Introducing Word Families to Students

In each of the introductions to the individual word families in Volume 2, our focus is on showing how word meanings arise from the images of our experience. In presenting ideas for exploring how words developed from a particular root image or experience, we have tried to preserve the playfulness of the process. Have fun with the material. Entering into the playful spirit that underlies the birth of new words and meanings and developing a delight in language have down-to-earth results for students, not the least of which is a love of reading and writing. Keep this thought foremost in your mind as you introduce word families; it is more important than any particular idea presented

in the material. Better to skip something than to lose the spirit of adventure through worrying about every detail.

Here are principles to keep in mind as you use the material—and adapt it to your own purposes:

- Bring the imagery of the root to life at the outset by relating it to something concrete and familiar to your students.
- Keep things clear visually. As you go along, put the root and its meaning and the words of the family on the board in such a way that the relationships among them are obvious.
- Be sure students understand the connection between the root image or experience and the modern meaning of individual words in the family.
- Be sure students notice the other point of connection (a shared spelling pattern or sound pattern) that links the root and the words that have grown from it.
- Have students get word meanings "in their bones" through exploring objects, doing skits and pantomimes, and discussing examples of how the meanings are embodied in their own experience.

The particular ideas suggested for introducing the words of a family have evolved from the experience of using *Origins* in the classroom. These ideas can be used directly or as a starting point for your own ideas. We couldn't resist including more insights and information about some words than you will want to use in any one session—especially when you are just getting acquainted with the material. These "extras" can be included at a later time, if you wish. As you prepare for introducing a particular word family, you may find it helpful to develop a summary image for each of the words in the family rather than trying to remember ideas for introducing them in linear form. For example, you can summarize our suggestion for a pantomime to introduce the word *bold* by visualizing students crouching and hiding from danger and then standing, taking a deep breath, looking as fearsome as possible, and boldly advancing to meet the danger (*bold* comes from a root that means "to swell"). It takes a lot of words to *describe* the images, but the images themselves summarize many words.

Doing pantomimes, examining objects, and discussing how word meanings are embodied in students' own experiences can all be used either to introduce words or to investigate a word's meaning and connection to the root after it has been introduced. We have found that students enjoy discovering the words of a family for themselves. Once they have the root and two or three words of the family, they enjoy using the clues of shared imagery and shared spelling pattern, as well as pantomime, etc., to discover other words of the family. Any words that do share the imagery and spelling pattern but turn out not to be actual members of the family can be included as "sound cousins" (discussed below). Some teachers prefer to introduce the whole family first and use the teaching suggestions to explore connections between the root and the word family later. Whichever approach you may use, you will find that, after students have explored several word families and have a feel for the process, they will begin leaping ahead of any step-by-step introduction of words to generate many words of the family—and a number of "sound cousins" as well—in one quick burst. Let the suggestions flow and investigate connections between word and root as the next step. If suggestions become too random, ask students to describe a connection with the imagery of the root as they propose each word. You do want to keep the focus on *how* new words and meanings develop.

The word family chapters are loosely ordered in terms of the complexity of the material presented. The beginning chapters present core linguistic ideas and later chapters build on this base. Teaching ideas, on the other hand, are spelled out in greatest detail in the first few chapters, then presented in briefer form as the chapters progress. We suggest you start with one of the early chapters, then follow whatever order best suits your class.

How long should you spend exploring any given word family? Most teachers have spent at least two class sessions of approximately forty-five minutes on a given word family—usually in once-a-week sessions. The amount of time you spend will depend, of course, on the age of your students and on what materials and activities you find appropriate for your class. Teachers who have used the writing ideas presented in the word family chapters and elsewhere in this chapter have generally done so during class periods normally allotted for writing—and the time spent on writing may be in addition to two sessions for exploring the family itself. Teachers working with older students have sometimes focused primarily on writing and have spent no more than half an hour on an introductory exploration of the family.

We have found that the greatest value of the material lies in fully understanding the ideas in it, not in racing through as many word families as possible.

Therefore, whatever materials you choose to use, we urge you to keep in mind that their fundamental value lies not in providing a "vocabulary" list, but rather in awakening a feeling for words that will change how students read, write, talk, and think.

Sound Cousins

"Sound cousin" is a term we coined to describe a relationship based on sound patterns, not family descent. Many word families in *Origins* include groups of words that share the same beginning sounds. For example, most of the words of the GHEL family are alliterative: *gleam, glow, glimmer, glisten, glint, glass, glossy,* and *glad.* Because English has this large group of *gl-* words that share the imagery of shining (their root meaning), we have a tendency to associate other *gl-* words with images of light, as well—if their meanings allow such association. For instance, students frequently—and quite insistently—argue that *glory* and *glorious* should be members of the GHEL family. They point out that a glorious day is usually one full of sunshine, that those who achieve glory usually "shine" in what they do. (Unmentioned so far by students, but supporting the association, are the many links between light and glory in religious art and language.) Since *glory* and *glorious* do share with the GHEL words both a sound pattern and the imagery of shining, it is legitimate to affirm the connection that students intuitively feel as they argue for including the words in the family. We have coined the term "sound cousins" to describe the connection. Linguists use other terms (such as "sound symbolism") to describe the connection, but do recognize it as real. However, the tendency to associate the imagery of the GHEL family with other *gl-* words is just that—a tendency. *Gloomy* and *glum* both begin with *gl-* , but their ending sounds and their meanings cut the association short.

In the word family chapters in Volume 2, we include notes on sound cousins that have frequently been proposed by students. The word trees in those chapters include both space for recording the words of the family and a space at the side of the tree for sound cousins. When deciding whether words may be recognized as sound cousins, you need to consider whether they share both a sound pattern and an area of imagery or meaning.

Additional Related Words

At the beginning of each chapter, we list the words we most commonly introduce as members of a particular word family. There are often more words in the family than in that list. We omit words from the introductory list for a variety of reasons, usually because they are of less immediate interest than the core words of the group. Many words left out of the introductory list are listed at the end of each chapter under "Additional Related Words." Depending on the age and interests of your students, you may want to include some or all of the "Additional Related Words" as you explore the family.

For a definitive list of all members of a word family, check the "Indo-European Root Appendix" of the 1969 edition of *The American Heritage Dictionary of the English Language,* which may well be in your library, or the updated version of the "Appendix" published in 1985 under the title of *The American Heritage Dictionary of Indo-European Roots*, as a companion to the 1982 *Second College Edition of the American Heritage Dictionary.* If you look up word families in these sources, you will find that we have omitted certain words because of their general obscurity, a sound shift that requires a lot of arcane explanation, or an overcomplicated history of development. Because some roots have been adapted for *Origins*, you should read the "Word of Explanation" note in the "Linguistic Background" chapter before doing such research.

Wrap-up and Review

Discussed below are materials and activities you can use after you have introduced the words of a family. Teachers have often found it useful to have students assemble their own *Origins* notebooks where they keep word trees, illustrations, definitions, and story puzzles, as well as poetry and their own writing.

Word Trees

Word trees can provide a clear visual summary of the relationship between the root and the words that grew from it. Each word has a relationship to the root, but has branched off to establish its own distinct meaning. At the end of each volume of *Origins*, you will find a word tree that can be photocopied for students. The tree includes space at the bottom for recording the root and

Individual word tree (*right*)
and class word tree (*below*)

its meaning, spaces in the branches for recording words of the family, and space at the side of the tree for recording sound cousins.

Many teachers also have used a large word tree posted on a bulletin board. Students record the words on index cards and hang them on the tree. Some classrooms have made smaller poster-paper word trees for each family, gradually accumulating a "forest" of trees over the course of the year. The "forest" keeps the words of the family readily available as a resource for writing.

Illustrations

Asking students to use the words of a family by drawing a "picture that tells a story" can help integrate the words with their own experience and imagination. The teachers in our workshops who have expressed doubt about the value of the exercise, usually say, after doing the exercise, "Aha, you really *do* learn a lot...."

You might start by brainstorming ideas for illustrations with the class. The brainstorming alone can be a good exercise. In doing the illustrations, the emphasis should be on ideas, not perfect artwork. Speech "balloons" (like those in comic books and comic strips) can enlarge the possibilities for expressing ideas. You may want to give students the choice of working in small groups to do group illustrations together. You might want to join a group and get a feel for the process yourself. Students often enjoy showing their illustrations to each other.

Story Puzzles

Many word families include story puzzles that can provide another opportunity for playing with the words of the family. These can be done in groups or individually, as part of classwork or for extra credit. An alternative to doing the puzzles in a straightforward manner is to put the *wrong* words in the blanks, an experiment that can illuminate the words in surprising ways because of their shared imagery.

Definitions

We have provided our own brief definitions of words in each family. These definitions focus on meanings explored in the *Origins* materials, often highlighting connections with the root imagery of the family. Although you can have students look up their own definitions, you can save time by putting ours on the board for students to copy.

Student illustrations based on the WER and GHEIS roots.

Review Pantomimes

Most teachers spend at least two sessions on a given word family. Many have found that at the start of a second session students enjoy reintroducing and reviewing the words of a family by inventing their own pantomimes. Such pantomimes often inspire imaginative thinking about the words. Sometimes when the teacher has difficulty figuring out what word is being dramatized, the students are quick to identify it.

Exploring Extended Meanings

The "Exploring Extended Meanings" sections discuss how primary meanings, grounded in experience, are extended to express abstract and figurative ideas. We use the term *extended meaning* and, in student materials, the phrase *stretch the meaning*, to focus attention on this process instead of focusing on the labels used to identify the results of the process—metaphor, abstraction, figurative language, etc. You may use any labels familiar to your students, but keep in mind that the primary value of "Exploring Extended Meanings" lies in having students get the feel of the process by walking through it and focusing on how it happens rather than on how to label it.

Students are, of course, already familiar with how the imagery of root meanings has been extended to create new words and meanings. In families made up largely of Germanic vocabulary, most words have primary meanings that remain grounded in everyday experience. "Exploring Extended Meanings" follows the evolution of these words into the realm of ideas. In general, it is only in the Germanic vocabulary of the language that we see both concrete and abstract levels of meaning in the same word—both the down-to-earth *clamp* holding two boards together and the police *clamping down* on speeders, both the *glimmer* of a candle in a dark room and the *glimmer* of an idea in our minds. By contrast, much of our Latin-based vocabulary is already "extended" or abstract. (See the "Brief History of the English Language" chapter for further discussion.)

"Exploring Extended Meanings," then, takes a look at "home-grown" abstractions that occur in the development of words in the KER, GHEL, FLEU, KEL, and WER families. The exploration of abstraction in these families provides a model for exploring "extended meanings" wherever you may encounter them—elsewhere in *Origins* and in whatever reading your students may be doing in class.

Reading Poetry

Most of the word family chapters include poetry that uses the imagery of the family. Poetry flows naturally from the imagery and metaphor inherent in how new words and meanings take shape. The poems that accompany word families include both student poetry written in response to writing ideas that accompany a family and adult poetry. The adult poetry ranges from ancient to modern and includes traditional African and Native American poetry, African-American poetry and poetry from Japan, poetry translated from Russian and from Chinese, poetry from seventeenth-century England and from twentieth-century America. Three poems were written especially for *Origins* by Kate Rushin, a Boston poet. A few families are not accompanied by poetry because we could not find any that used the images or words of the family in ways we found inviting or compelling. You should, of course, feel free to add other poems.

As with all of *Origins*, these examples are meant to be used flexibly. You may use one or two poems with one word family and none with another; you may settle in with a feast of several poems if you find a group that is particularly irresistible. The poems can be used in many ways. They can be read aloud: by you, by individual students, or by students in choral groups. Some, such as "Legend" (in the BHEL family), can be acted out. Others, such as "The Rapper as Light" (in the GHEL family), invite memorization and chanting. Some lend themselves to illustration. The poetry can also be used to inspire students to do their own writing.

Writing and Ideas for Other Activities

We have found that the vocabulary of *Origins* begins to animate students' writing, whether or not we make formal attempts to make it do so. You may want to leave it at that. For those who would like to go beyond casual connections with writing, we present writing ideas particular to the words and poetry of specific families and other ideas that can be used generally with any family.

The writing ideas in the word family chapters create a sense of listening in on a classroom conversation, which you should adapt for your own purposes.

A good general approach to writing is that described by Flora Arnstein in her books *Poetry and the Child* (New York: Dover, 1962) and *Children Write Poetry* (New York: Dover, 1967). Her gentle approach focuses first on awakening children's understanding of the elements of poetry by inviting them to make choices. In discussing poems, she asks, "What are your favorite lines, words, sounds, pictures?" When prompted to make their own judgments, children begin to look closely and listen carefully. Arnstein also invites students to choose which poems they want to keep for their own personal anthology. Students feel empowered and independent when rejecting poems that don't move them and accepting ones that do. After exploring their favorite elements of two or three poems and choosing what they want to include in their own anthology, the students write. No particular instructions are necessary. Students simply are given free time to write their own poem or story. What Arnstein finds (as we have found in using the approach) is that students reach for what they can use in the poetry they've read and use it as best suits their needs. It may be an emotion or idea they want to explore, or words or sounds they want to play with. Alternatively, the inspiration may be subterranean and indirect—something is nudged awake by a chain of associations and comes to the surface, seeking a shape. Arnstein usually publishes the students' writing so they can read each other's work.

If you want to follow this approach with *Origins*, you will give students all or most of the poems that accompany a given family so that students can choose among them for their own anthology. In addition to having students choose their favorite poems, you may want to have them choose their favorite words of a family.

Many other writing teachers have used model poems to inspire their students to write. Among the best examples are Kenneth Koch's *Rose, Where Did You Get That Red?* (New York: Vintage, 1974) and Nina Nyhart and Kinereth Gensler's *The Poetry Connection* (New York: Teachers & Writers Collaborative, 1978).

Some teachers have used *Origins* primarily as a resource for writing. Larry Fagin, a writer-in-the-schools, has focused on the imagery of the families to generate vocabularies that serve as inspiration for students' poetry. When using the GHEL ("to shine") family, for example, he first invites students to generate and explore the words of the family and then to brainstorm other words that share in the imagery of "shining." All possibilities are welcomed: *sparkle, sun, diamond, firecracker, shimmer, bright, fire, flame, lightning, polish, ruby, torch, mica, sunset.* The next step is to brainstorm opposites—"dark" words: *shadow, cave, cloudy, dull, midnight, sad, dreary, twilight, black hole, shady, purple, fading*—whatever comes to mind. After a large vocabulary of "shining" and "dark" words has been generated on the board, Fagin reads a few poems by students who have done a similar exercise, writes a collaborative poem with the class, and then launches the students on their own poems and stories.

Here are some additional ideas and other activities proposed by writers at Teachers & Writers Collaborative.

- Have students combine words from a single family (such as *gladglass* from the GHEL family or *drizzledroopy* from DERU) and use them in their writing. Such amalgamations, especially from Germanic roots, suggest vivid images that might serve as the radiant center of new student poems.

- Have each student pick a word (*glimmer, belly, drizzle*), pantomime it, and then anthropomorphize it by giving it a name (Cherie Glimmer, Marvin Belly, Manuel Drizzle) and creating a character for it. Then perhaps have the kids write monologues, dialogues, or short plays using these characters. Such dramatic pieces are usually more sucessful if they involve a conflict.

- Choose a word and have students design a kind of "happening" for it, for example, a Glimmer Event in which all the students hold mirrors and bright flashlights in a dark room.

- Have students form living word trees, like an acrobatic or cheerleading team. One student plays the root, the others are arranged above him or her in the branches. (The best way might be to have the "branches" standing and sitting on a table and the "root" hunkered down on the floor.) Then they all simultaneously act out their words, using sound and movement.

- As a corollary to the above, have the same students create spontaneous sentences that link together, as in the example given below. This is just a variation on the old idea of spontaneous oral stories, with the added rule of using words from a single family.

    Example (using KER words):
    Student 1: "The burglar *crept* around the..."
    Student 2: "...uh, the *crooked* tree where..."
    Student 3: "...some *creepy* people were..."
    Student 4: "...*crocheting* a..."
    Student 5: "...picture of a *creek*..."
    Student 6: "...on a *cradle* pillow."

- Have students invent a word or words for experiences or feelings they've had, but for which there is no obvious, specific word. Say you are ten years old and you've wanted a particular toy for years. Now your parents have finally promised it to you for your birthday, but when that day comes, they give you something you don't even want! You feel both deflated and explosive. Invent a word that stands for that feeling. Then write an account of the incident, using the invented word or words. Of course, the event could also be a happy one—for example, a moment when someone you liked or admired suddenly and unexpectedly showed warmth toward you.

- Have students write a dialogue in an imaginary language. For instance, two young people, Arprizal and Colinet, meet at midnight in the town of Rogovekail. Both of them are very sad:

    ARPRIZAL: Soling to vog butig nott.
    COLINET: Fentig soling butig regonott.
    ARPRIZAL: Fo, fo nott moto pur copi.
    COLINET: Vog butig solig soling.
    ARPRIZAL: Vog butig nog.
    COLINET: Fentig nog soling.

They leave together, arm in arm, happier but still a little anxious.

- Have some students make a dictionary of the words in the dialogue above. Have other students translate the dialogue into English, with or without the dictionary.
- Have students invent the future form of contemporary words, and write sentences, poems, stories, etc., using these words. The notion of the possible future of words makes more sense if the students have an idea of how certain contemporary words are themselves products of verbal evolution. So, for example, if *God be with you* was gradually condensed to *goodbye*, perhaps the next step will involve even further condensation, to something like *gdbi*. If *goodnesse* became *goodness*, then perhaps it will be slimmed down to *goodnes*. If *breakfast* + *lunch* created *brunch*, will *lunch* + *dinner* create *linner*? (Probably not, because *linner* doesn't sound appealing.) And how about new words to describe new things? Will there be "feelovision"? A "telerose"? A "megadog"? Will the troublesome apostrophe (*it's* versus *its*) disappear? Creating a plausible-sounding future English involves a certain amount of thinking and analysis, not just a spewing forth of gibberish (which is fun, too).

Developing Your Own Word Families

How did we develop ideas for exploring word families in the classroom? And how can you develop similar approaches to word families not in this book? First, you need to think of the root meaning of a family not as a word or words on the page, but as an experience. What experience does the "meaning" of the root evoke? How can the meaning be embodied? Once you develop a full sense of the root experience, the ways in which words of the family embody facets of the experience begin to come to life for you. Then you can begin to think of ways to highlight those connections and dramatize how the experience takes shape in particular words. Dramatizing an individual word may be no more "dramatic" than discussing with students examples of its meaning in their own lives. What you're trying to get is that grounding in experience that yields a full-bodied sense of a word's meaning.

If you are exploring words of Germanic origin, you will often be tracing three stages of development: the root meaning; a primary, concrete meaning; and an extended, figurative meaning. The primary meaning will be the resource for seeing how the figurative meaning—or meanings—developed. If you are exploring words of Latin or Greek origin, you may find it helpful to remember that, although most of these words have an abstract meaning in English, many of them also had a concrete meaning in their native setting. Sometimes imagining what that meaning might have been conjures up a scene from the past. For example, a *report* is, literally, something "carried back." Pondering that meaning, the mind can travel back to a time before telephones or airplanes and visualize a messenger arriving on foot with a piece of news. Thinking about the imagery of something "carried back," one can also understand the connection between a rifle report and a report on the state of the economy.

Dictionaries

When preparing to explore a word family, we use dictionaries a lot. Our starting point is the "Appendix" of the 1969 *American Heritage Dictionary* or the 1985 *American Heritage Dictionary of Indo-European Roots*, cited above. We have listed additional families drawn from this resource in the "Linguistic Background" chapter. If you want to focus on developing word families of

Latin and Greek origin, two excellent pamphlets are Rudolf Schaeffer's *Latin-English Derivative Dictionary* and *The Greek-English Derivative Dictionary*, both available from the American Classical League (Miami University, Oxford, Ohio 45056). We also refer to *The Oxford English Dictionary* to check on how words of a family have developed over time. The *OED* provides dated quotations that exemplify how words were used, some dating back to the ninth century. We skim the quotations and the archaic and obsolete meanings of a word to see how its imagery has been used to express a variety of meanings. A revised, updated version of *The Oxford English Dictionary* was published in twenty volumes in 1989. We use the *Compact Edition of the Oxford English Dictionary* (New York: Oxford University Press, 1971) because of its convenience and relatively low cost. The *Compact Edition* micrographically reduces the thirteen volumes of the original dictionary (published in 1933) to two volumes that must be read with a magnifying glass (which comes with the volumes). Supplements updating the dictionary are produced in a third compact volume.

In addition to *The American Heritage Dictionary* and the *OED*, *The Random House Dictionary of the English Language* (New York: Random House, 1969 and 1987) and *The Oxford Dictionary of English Etymology* (Oxford, New York, 1966) are very useful. We also consult student dictionaries for clarity and simplicity in word definitions. The two we have used most frequently are the *Scott Foresman Intermediate Dictionary* (Glenview, Illinois: Scott, Foresman, 1988) and the *Houghton Mifflin Intermediate Dictionary* (Boston: Houghton Mifflin, 1986). Both dictionaries are good for students, as well, because they contain many word histories. All these resources are fun to share with older students—fifth and sixth graders, even fourth graders. Simply put the dictionaries out for whoever may be interested. Some students are fascinated and enjoy leafing through the pages. Pursuing words in the *OED* with a magnifying glass is a special favorite. Other students don't want to venture near such weighty tomes and shouldn't be required to. The point is to convey a sense of adventure, not pedantry.

How Meanings Change over Time

As you explore word histories, you will often find that the connections between root meanings and current meanings are illuminating and readily understandable. At times, however, the path of development may seem puzzling—or even illogical. The word *nice*, for example, once meant "ignorant, foolish" and the word *silly* once meant "happy, blessed." People sometimes cite such word histories as examples of how word meaning develops by unpredictable—and, by implication, mysterious—leaps. Although the ways in which meanings develop from a particular root or image cannot be predicted, they are almost always understandable in retrospect if you know something about the history and circumstances in which the new meaning took shape.

If you are puzzled by a particular shift of meaning, *The Oxford English Dictionary*, with its abundance of historical information, can often help. For example, the *OED* provides clues to why *nice* evolved from meaning "ignorant, foolish" in the 1200s to meaning "pleasant, agreeable" today. Citations from the 1500s and 1600s use *nice* to mean "tender, delicate." A leap of imagination allows us to see that the qualities of being ignorant and foolish might be seen in affectionate or indulgent terms when looking at a young child, for example, and therefore associated with a kindly attitude toward vulnerability. Once we feel kindly and indulgent toward vulnerable creatures, we can readily shift from focusing on their foolishness to focusing on their tenderness and delicacy. That is one shift toward a positive meaning of *nice*. For citations of *nice* from the 1600s and 1700s, the *OED* gives the meaning of "over-refined, luxurious." One can readily see an association between foolishness or ignorance and pretentious attempts at refinement and luxury (the concept of *nouveau riche* is an old one). Gradually, however, positive qualities associated with refinement and luxury predominated, and the association with foolishness and ignorance dropped away. Over the centuries, then, the word *nice* became associated with a variety of positive qualities. Its evolution from meaning "foolish and ignorant" to meaning "pleasant and agreeable" becomes understandable once you know the intermediate steps of development that took place between the eleventh and the twentieth centuries.

You can sometimes understand such shifts in meaning simply by using your imagination and understanding of human nature. When you stop to think about why *silly* might have evolved from its original meaning of "happy" or "blessed," you may be able to conjure up memories of people who have seemed foolishly and unrealistically happy or "blissed out." A term from the 1960s, "bliss ninnies," embodies precisely the combination of ecstasy and accompanying divorce from reality (and hence foolishness with regard to practical reality) that seems the likely pivot on which the meaning of silly shifted from "happy" and "blessed" to "foolish."

Vegetate is another word that has, over time, embodied seemingly contradictory realities. In the 1600s the word was used to mean "to animate or quicken," "to make strong or vigorous"—meanings derived from the lively growth of plants and vegetables. By the mid-1700s, however, a different meaning grew from a different perspective on the vegetable world. *Vegetate* came to mean "to live a merely physical life; to lead a dull, monotonous existence." It is probably more than mere coincidence that this pejorative meaning of the word developed as the Industrial Revolution was beginning. Agrarian life no longer seemed so exciting to a world diverted by new industrial developments.

Linguists recognize many predictable routes by which meanings change, among them widening, narrowing, semantic shift, and semantic drift. An example of widening is the word *citizen*, which used to mean a city dweller and now means the inhabitant of a state or nation, and an example of narrowing is the word *meat*, which originally meant any solid food and now means a particular type. An example of semantic shift is the word *bureau*, which originally referred to a coarse woolen cloth over a desk, then to the desk itself (and by association other chests with drawers) and then to the organization that uses desks—as in the National Bureau of Standards. *Silly, foolish,* and *vegetate* are all examples of semantic drift. In *Origins* we focus on the stories that underlie such changes: the shift in power from the city-states of Greece to the empire of Rome that underlies the widening of the meaning of *citizen*, the growing diversity of foods available for eating that underlies the narrowing of the meaning of *meat*. We do not emphasize the linguistic terminology for these changes.

Exploring Popular Speech and Cross-Cultural Metaphors

Popular speech and cross-cultural metaphors provide opportunities for affirming a student's own language, whatever that may be. All word meanings grow out of experience in ways similar to those presented in the word family chapters of Volume 2. Students can discover how their home or street language also grows out of experience. Consider having students make a list of expressions from their own slang or street talk and then speculate about their sources. (We conducted a similar session with a group of teachers in a summer workshop, the results of which are presented at the end of the "Linguistic Background" chapter. You can get a sense of the possibilities by looking at this material.)

As you and your students speculate on the origins of a particular expression, keep in mind that such origins are sometimes elusive. For instance, Frederic Cassidy and his colleagues, who are compiling the *Dictionary of American Regional English*, were trying to trace the expression "There's a dead cat on the line." They found that twenty people had cited the expression as meaning "Someone is trying to deceive you" or "Something fishy is going on," but no one knew its source. Only after many months did they find an old man in Louisiana who was able to explain that it came from an experience connected with catfishing in the bayou. Fishermen would leave trot lines in the bayou and come to check them every day. If someone checked a neighbor's line and found a dead catfish, he knew something was wrong, something was "fishy"—and he'd better check on his neighbor. "Something fishy is going on here" was generalized to a sense of "Someone is trying to deceive you"—a sense that wasn't present in the original experience. The researchers still aren't sure if this is the true history of "There's a dead cat on the line"; they were never able to confirm it through other sources. You can tell this story to your students as an example of how the source of an expression may be elusive.

More often, however, probable sources will suggest themselves fairly readily, as in the following: *crib* meaning "your house"; *chill* meaning "to cold shoulder"; *lunchin'* meaning "out of it"; *biting* meaning "copying"; and *jonesing* meaning "wanting something really badly." *Lunchin'* and *jonesing* seem to be interesting plays on the older expressions "out to lunch" and "keeping up with the Joneses" (acquiring what the neighbors have). *Biting* adds an aggressive thrust to the act of copying, opening up possibilities for boastful swagger in talking about something usually thought of in more furtive terms. *Chill* takes the image of coldness in a different direction from that of *chill out* (discussed above) and fits with numerous other images of coldness and warmth used to describe emotional states, as in: a warm friendship, a hot romance, a relationship that blows hot and cold, a lukewarm greeting, a cold look, a cool reception, an icy stare. These expressions reflect an intuitive understanding of the physics of excitement: molecules that are stirred to motion produce heat; as they subside toward stillness, things cool off. (Excitement can be positive, as in a *hot prospect*, or negative, as in *hot and bothered* or *boiling mad*. Likewise, lack of excitement can be positive, as in *keeping your cool* during an emergency, or negative, as in treating someone *coldly*.)

If you have students who speak languages other than English, you can explore whether there are similar metaphors based on heat and cold in their languages. Such metaphors seem to be widespread: we have found them in Spanish, Tagalog, Thai, and Hungarian. You can also explore metaphors based on the body. No matter how climate, geography, and custom may vary from one culture to another, we all experience the world through our bodies. That fundamental experience is reflected in all languages. Sometimes the metaphors are similar to ones we have in English, sometimes they are quite different. In Thai the metaphor that expresses what we mean when we say heartbroken is "chestbroken." In Tagalog a generous person is described as having an "open palm"—an image similar to the English *open-handed*. In Hungarian a clever person is an "eye-eared" person—not an expression with a close parallel in English but an image we can readily picture. In Temne a restless person, one who cannot settle down, is described by an expression that means "the foot keeps going."

A good way to begin exploring body metaphors in other languages is to brainstorm a list of such metaphors in English. You can use the "Body Metaphors in English" list at the end of the "Linguistic Background" chapter to generate ideas. Once you have made a list of English expressions, you can bring in expressions from other languages (those cited above, those in the "Bringing Words to Life" chapter, and any others from your own experience).

The combination will give students an idea of what to search for in their own language. Have them talk with their parents about the list of body metaphors, then tell the rest of the class what new ones they came up with.

You might want to see if metaphors in some of the word families are found in other languages, as well. For example, do other languages express the idea of happiness through images of light, as in *glad* (from GHEL, "to shine")? Are images of "up" and "down" used in other languages to express emotional states—as in the image of "falling" that underlies *dreary* in the DHREU family?

Sound and Meaning

"Sound cousins" alert students to a particular connection between sound and meaning—a connection between certain alliterative clusters and the imagery that becomes associated with them. You can play further with this association between sound and meaning by exploring the "sound families" listed in the "Linguistic Background" chapter. Most of these sound families have a core of words that come from a particular Indo-European root, but the most significant link among them is an initial consonant cluster that has an imitative quality. Such play with links between sound and meaning can, of course, be extended to other imitative words—*crunch, hiss, crackle, buzz, meow, thump, screech, whiz, rustle,* etc.

The following exercise can provide further insight into how the sounds of words influence our sense of their meaning. Use the pairs of "nonsense" words listed below and pose the following questions: Which is larger/smaller? Which is heavier/lighter? Which is quicker/slower?*

> dobe   dabe
> meeg   mog
> scozzle   scuzzle
> spant   spint
> gleep   gloop

Provide students with a list of the nonsense words and read each pair aloud. Students usually have little hesitation about choosing a *dobe*, a *mog*, a *scozzle*, a *spant*, and a *gloop* as the larger, heavier, and slower members of their pairs. When asked to choose whether a *dobe* or a *dabe* is bigger, they usually have an immediate response and *know* which creature is bigger. (You might have your students imagine these nonsense names as creatures and then draw them.) It should be emphasized, however, that there are no right or wrong answers in this exercise.

The tendency to associate sound and meaning can readily be undercut and overridden by other associations. Although students usually associate the

---

*The concept of this exercise and some of the examples are drawn from *Origins of the English Language: A Social and Linguistic History* by Joseph M. Williams (New York: Macmillan, 1975).

"larger" sound with the larger creature, some students will find that the name *spant*, for example, evokes personal associations (the name of a pet mouse, a creature they saw in a cartoon) that lead them to decide that a *spant* is smaller than a *spint*—though the tendency of most students is to make the opposite choice. Links between sound and meaning operate in just this way. The sounds of a word nudge our sense of its meaning in certain directions—toward a sense of openness or a sense of constriction, toward a sense of sharpness or a sense of softness, toward a sense of liquid movement or a sense of movement blocked and cut short. (Students can have fun investigating such connections by making up their own pairs of nonsense names. Which is softer, a *mig* or a *mish*? Which moves more smoothly, a *smallow* or a *smatt*?) Such links between sound and meaning are real, but not definitive. Other associations can override them and move the meaning in another direction. Language can be particularly powerful, however, when both sound and meaning move in the same direction—as good poets have always known.

Sound and Spelling

In *Origins* we do not treat spelling systematically, but we do discuss certain spelling patterns, in the word family chapters of Volume 2, in the "Linguistic Background" chapter, and in the "Mixed Heritage of English" section of the "Brief History of English" chapter. One teacher commented that after her students had been immersed in *Origins* for a year, they shifted from considering English spelling an unreasonable burden to seeing it as an interesting story, though still a challenge. The value of the *Origins* materials that bear on spelling—information about vowel-*r* inversions and consonant shifts, about silent letters and varying patterns of pronunciation, about spelling patterns inherited from Anglo-Saxon, French, Latin, and Greek origins—lies in awakening such interest. Although none of the information provides a magic formula for remembering the spelling of particular words, making spelling an interesting story, not merely a rote task, can have practical results as well as intrinsic appeal.

A Brief History of the English Language

Why is the *k* of *know* not pronounced? Why is it there at all? What is the story behind the *-ture* of *nature*, the *-tion* of *station*, and the *ph-* of *photograph*? Behind the irregularities of English spelling lies a story of invasions—both military and cultural. As a result of those invasions, English vocabulary is a composite: Anglo-Saxon, or Old English*, the Germanic base; French, the language of the conquering Normans; and Latin, the language of scholars during the Renaissance. Words of Greek origin entered the language through Latin and later borrowings. The English we speak today echoes with the voices of diverse peoples and cultures. It has remained open to adopting new words whenever it rubs elbows with another language or dialect. American English has constantly enriched itself by drawing on the vocabularies and idioms of its many national and cultural groups.

In this chapter we look at the historical events that underlie the mixed heritage of English: the Anglo-Saxon invasions and settlement of Britain, the Viking incursions, the Norman Conquest, and the Renaissance. We then explain how the common ancestry of Anglo-Saxon (Old English), French, and Latin was discovered—and how that discovery provides resources for vocabulary study. Finally, we look at how various groups of Americans have contributed, and continue to contribute, to the growth of American English. It should be emphasized that we focus on only one part of the story of how English has developed—vocabulary. We do not describe the development of grammar. It should be emphasized, as well, that we sketch the history in broad outlines rather than in fine detail. Those who want to study the story of English in greater detail should see the annotated bibliography at the end of this chapter.

---

* Although "Old English" is the linguistically preferred term for English from A.D. 400 to the time of the Norman Conquest, we also use the term "Anglo-Saxon." "Old English" is confusing to students. As far as they're concerned, "Old English" might be the language their grandparents spoke. For students, the term "Anglo-Saxon" ties the language more clearly to the historical period in which it was current.

The Anglo-Saxon Invasions: The Beginnings of English

Many of the common, everyday words in our language are Germanic in origin because, over a two-hundred-year period, England was invaded and settled by tribes from the area known today as Germany and Denmark. In the mid-400s Germanic tribes known as the Angles and the Saxons began leaving their homeland in northern Europe to seize the fertile and poorly defended coastal lands of southeast England. England had been part of the Roman Empire—a land inhabited by Celts, but ruled by the Romans who had conquered them. In the early fifth century, however, the Roman troops were called back to defend the heart of the Empire against the wave of barbarian invasions flooding across Europe. The Celts were left without a strong defense.

Anglo-Saxon Invasion and Settlement of England
ca. 450-600

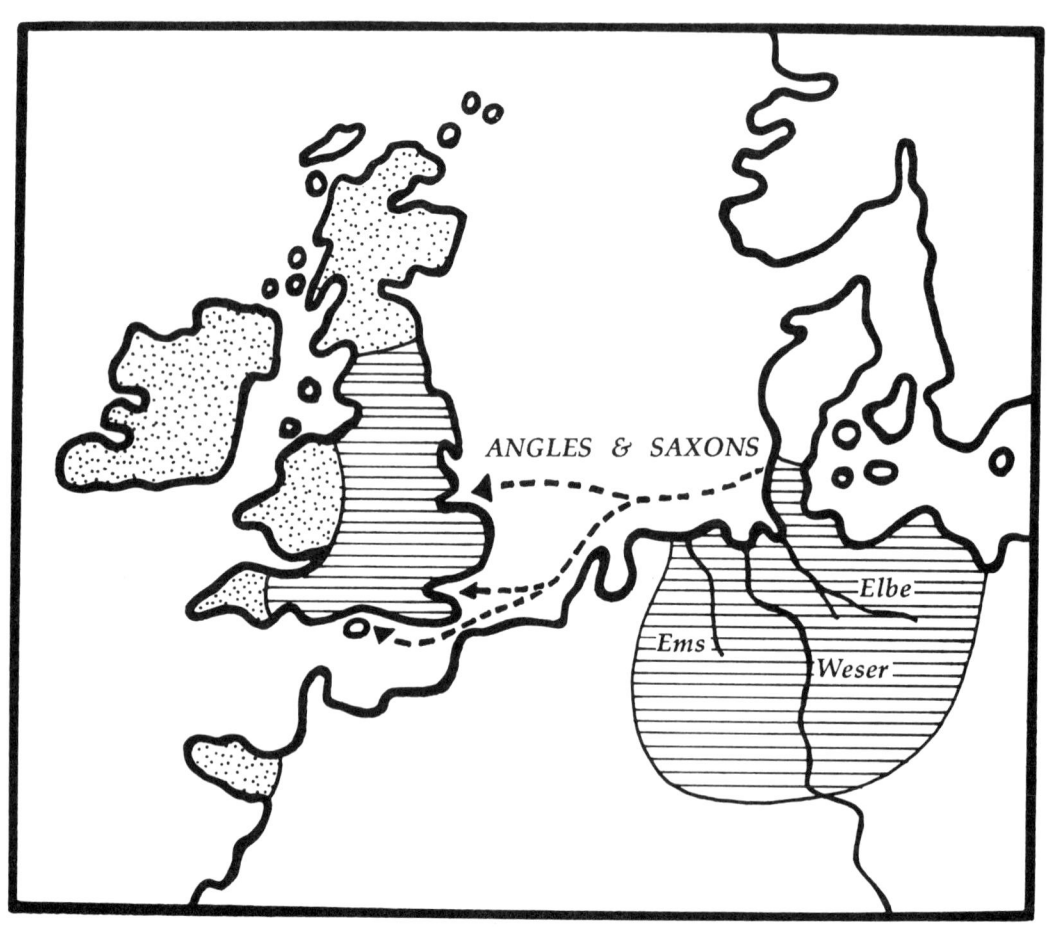

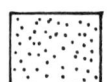 CELTS

 ANGLES & SAXONS

Other Germanic tribes—probably Jutes, Frisians, and Franks—accompanied the Angles and the Saxons in relatively small numbers, but the invaders came to be generally known as Saxons, or Anglo-Saxons, because these were the dominant tribes. The invaders got a toehold in the southeast corner of Britain and then began pushing outward in all directions, settling and tilling the land as they won it. The spreading conquest was brought to a temporary halt by one last great Celtic victory. Unified and rallied by a leader, who was probably the legendary King Arthur, the Celts defeated the Saxons at Mount Badon, a strategic height somewhere in south-central Britain.

The victory gave the Celts two generations of peace. Then the Anglo-Saxons began advancing once again. Most Celts began their final retreat into the far corners of the island—areas today known as Scotland, Wales, and Cornwall. Some migrated even further. One tribe, the Britons, from whom we get the name Britain, resettled in the northwest corner of France now known as Brittany. Breton minstrels preserved the old Celtic tale of King Arthur and later, as minstrels in the courts of the Norman conquerors, brought the tale back to England.

By the end of the sixth century, then, most of England (from Angleland, or land of the Angles) was in Anglo-Saxon hands. The Celts who remained in the conquered territory began to speak the languages of their Saxon overlords. Like the language of the Indians in America, the language of the Celts in England left its trace primarily in the form of place names such as Avon, the Welsh word for "river."

Although the Germanic tribes who settled England spoke a variety of dialects, they could understand one another. The Germanic language of the island came to be known as Anglo-Saxon, later as Angle-ish or Engle-ish (language of the Angles) and, finally, as English. From this "language of the Angles" come our words for the basics of life: *eat, sleep, bread, drink, meat, love, hate, sun, father, rain, earth, mother, birth, death, speak, walk, sing, child, friend, flesh, bone, foot, hand, head, heart, soul, seed, crop, tree, stone, sea, fish, bird, fire, ash, ask, give, bless, curse, heal, rise, fall, float, deep, high, strong, weak, weave, knit, churn, plow, bake, brew, bubble, breathe.*

Old Norse: Some Closely Related Germanic Words Are Added to Anglo-Saxon Vocabulary

A new invasion brought a new influx of words. During the latter part of the Viking Age (850-1050), Anglo-Saxon was enriched by words from Old Norse, the Germanic language of the Danish Vikings who invaded and settled parts of England. Where speakers of Anglo-Saxon and Old Norse lived side by side, many became bilingual, especially those who intermarried. When both languages were spoken in the same communities and the same houses, they influenced each other. Many Old Norse words flowed into Anglo-Saxon, or Old English. Because Old Norse and Old English both came from the same Germanic ancestor, words from both sources are often very much of the same mold.

Like the words of Old English, the Danish words inherited by English tend to be associated with everyday life: *bark, blunder, cozy, dawn, egg, flake, gale, gift, happy, knife, kindle, law, loan, loose, loom, mistake, muggy, outlaw, rake, raise, rot, spray, stack, swirl, tangle, thrift, tight, want, wing, window.* Many *sk-* and *sc-* words in the language come from Old Norse: *scalp, scare, scold, scorch, scout, scowl, scrape, scream, scuffle, skate, ski, skid, skill, skin, skip, skirt, skit, sky.*

The Norman Conquest: French Becomes the Language of the Ruling Class in England

In the eleventh century the Anglo-Saxons were driven from all important positions of power by French-speaking conquerors, the Normans. The Normans (the name derives from *Norsemen*) were of Viking ancestry, but had adopted French language and culture after forming an alliance with the French king and settling in northern France in what we now call Normandy. The Norman conquest of England was an unlikely one that succeeded through many turns of luck.

In 1066 William, Duke of Normandy, who came to be known as William the Conqueror, gathered troops and ships in the estuary of the River Dives in northwest France. He was related to the English royal family and had laid claim to the English throne. The English had ignored his claim, and now he set forth to seize the throne by force.

The Norman Invasion of England, 1066

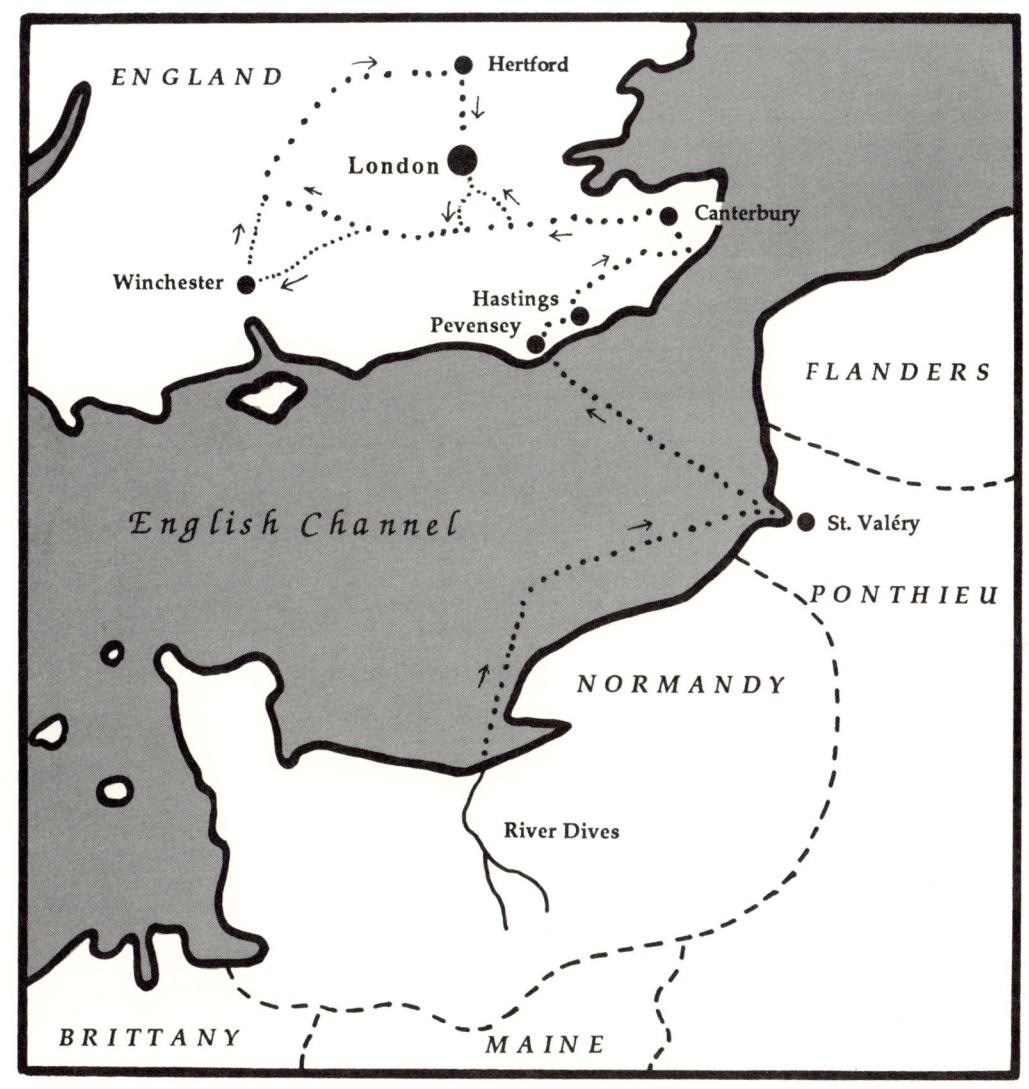

Few Normans expected William to succeed. His plan of invasion was considered foolhardy. It depended on luck—a wind to blow his ships straight for a good English harbor. Weather prediction, hardly reliable now, was wholly unreliable then. The Norman fleet was neither equipped to row nor to tack; the ships could only sail before the wind, and any shift of wind could scatter the invaders. Because the Normans had forgotten the seafaring arts of their Viking ancestors and had settled into a feudal life on land, they were not skilled sailors. In addition, the feudal nobles had adopted the French style of fighting on horseback. William's plan of invasion, then, called for unskilled sailors to transport both troops and horses in unwieldy boats.

The risky nature of his plan shaped the army he gathered. The Norman barons owed William approximately forty days of military service a year, but they were quick to decide that feudal duty did not include a reckless overseas adventure. William raised only part of his army from among his barons. The rest were paid soldiers lured by the hope of pillaging England.

As it happened, luck rode with the Normans, though few would have recognized their first run of luck as good. On September 12, the Norman ships ran the ebb tide out of the Dives estuary and sailed before a south wind toward England. Then disaster struck, or so it seemed. The wind shifted, a gale rose, the fleet scattered. Storm winds blew ships eastward along the rocky Norman coast, where some foundered on the rocks. Survivors edged into the first safe harbor they came to, St. Valéry.

Refusing to heed common wisdom—autumn storms had begun, the sailing season was at an end—William held his army on the beaches of St. Valéry for two weeks, waiting for the next favorable wind.

During those weeks, the English army, which had been guarding the coast against probable invasion, went home. The English had known of William's plan for some time, but considered the autumn storms a sure defense against further threat that year.

As the army dispersed, King Harold of England was called north to quell a Viking invasion led by King Harald of Norway. Raising his army as he went, the English king marched north in record time, took the Viking king by surprise, and defeated the invaders decisively. Legend has it that the English were celebrating at a victory feast when word came that William had landed on the English coast. Against all odds, when the equinox had passed and winter gales were to be expected, William had gotten a favorable wind that held steady for the whole of his crossing. Nine hundred years have passed since the Norman invasion, and no invader has copied its success.

King Harold came south by a forced march. At the Battle of Hastings, he was killed (by an arrow through the eye, we are told) and the English were defeated. Harold was to be the last English-speaking king for three hundred years. The Norman Conquest was rapid. Within five years of the Battle of Hastings, William had dispossessed nearly all important English landholders and granted their land to his followers.

The Normans who seized the estates of the Saxon nobles changed the landscape of England. Where the rambling wooden halls of the Saxon nobles had stood open to the peasants of the countryside, the Normans now built castles to dominate subjects hostile to their new lords. Built with forced Saxon labor, castles rose above the surrounding countryside on huge mounds of dirt surrounded by defensive earth walls and ringed by moats. The first castles were thrown up in haste and built of wood. In time the Normans cemented their hold on the country quite literally: they built castles of stone and mortar. These castles, so durable that many survive today, became the fixed points of power throughout England. By the end of the eleventh century, French-speaking Normans held all the important positions of power in England.

The Anglo-Saxons were reduced to the status of a servant people. They did the hard and underpaid work of the land: growing crops, grinding grain, spinning flax, shoeing horses, and hauling wood and stone to build the increasingly elaborate castles and estates of the Normans. Robin Hood, an actual person as well as a figure of lore, robbed the rich Norman overlords to share the wealth with the oppressed Saxons.

The Conquest Reshapes the Language: From Bilingual to the Blending of French and English Vocabulary

The Normans spoke French, and the Latin roots of French were quite different from the Germanic roots of Anglo-Saxon. The Norse of the Danish Vikings had been a language some Anglo-Saxons could understand; the French of the Normans was not.

For two hundred years following the Norman conquest, two languages were spoken in England. The language of the ruling class was French; the language of the underclass was Anglo-Saxon, or English. That structure of power and class is reflected in the language we speak today. During the 1300s, English re-emerged as the primary language of England, but it was a changed English: it had lost many Anglo-Saxon words and gained many French ones. The new blend of vocabulary reflected the history that followed the Conquest. In the word lists below, notice that words of French origin are grouped by areas of life where the Normans were dominant following the conquest: military power, law and government, art, fashion, dining. Words of the Germanic origin reflect the life of the Anglo-Saxons as a peasant and laboring people: the seasons, the landscape, the marking of time, domestic animals, basic foods, family relationships, the world of the fisherman, the tools and materials of the worker.

Words of French origin

army	captain	government	defendant
navy	combat	state	judge
battle	beseige	royal	attorney
enemy	fortress	authority	jury
peace	dungeon	tax	evidence
defense	moat	revenue	verdict
soldier	tower	crime	fine
art	fashion	dinner	herb
painting	robe	feast	boil
sculpture	lace	beef	stew
beauty	jewel	veal	platter
color	satin	cream	table
music	fur	sugar	fruit
poem	diamond	salad	peach

Words of Anglo-Saxon origin

stars	storm	morning	cow
moon	hail	evening	sheep
sun	dew	day	goat
field	mist	night	bee
tree	snow	week	lamb
leaf	winter	month	calf
stone	summer	year	swine
meat	man	whale	rope
milk	wife	fish	hammer
salt	mother	boat	bench
water	father	sail	nail
wheat	child	sea	wheel
butter	brother	water	leather
honey	folk	ship	copper

The picture presented by these lists is oversimplified, of course. The influx of French vocabulary was a disorderly, human process and didn't always fit neatly into these categories.

Though French vocabulary replaced Anglo-Saxon vocabulary in many areas of the language, French did not replace it. Why? Why did the language of the peasants, rather than the language of the rulers, emerge as the common language of England? The reasons are many. The first is sheer numbers. Though the Normans held political power, they were a minority. Only one person out of ten in England was Norman. Norman lords had to learn the English of the peasants and servants in order to run their estates. Merchants who migrated from Normandy to England following the Conquest found they needed to learn the language if they wanted their business to thrive. When Normans intermarried with the English, as many did, the predominance of French was further undercut.

In addition, a series of historical events contributed to the decline of French and the revival of English. A major blow to the dominance of French occurred when King John of England lost Normandy to King Louis VII of France in 1204. Normans who held estates in both England and Normandy were forced to abandon one or the other. They had to choose which king they would serve and decide whether to be French or English. No longer could they shuttle back and forth as they pleased. The nobles who chose allegiance to England were cut off from the mainstream of French language and culture. They lost the closeties to the continent that kept a sense of French identity alive among them.

A further blow to the survival of French came when France and England fell into the prolonged period of fighting (1337-1453) known as the Hundred Years' War. Though many in the upper classes still spoke French, they had known no home but England for over a hundred years and considered themselves English. France was now the enemy. Thus the prestige of French declined and a sense of English nationalism grew.

Another major event of the 1300s, the Plague, contributed indirectly to the growing importance of English. The Plague struck England in 1349, killing forty percent of the population. In the resulting upheaval, social and economic barriers diminished. For Anglo-Saxons who survived the Plague, there were new opportunities. Because of the serious labor shortage, wages rose sharply. In the confusion of the times, many were able to break free of their legal bondage to one man's land and travel about, seeking the highest wage. Others migrated to the towns where the growth of trade and crafts supported a growing middle class, many of whom rose to positions of considerable wealth. Those who spoke English had increasing influence and power.

The revival of English was accompanied by a flowering of English literature, most notably the tales and poetry of Geoffrey Chaucer. Chaucer's language reflected the English that was becoming the language of the land—an English greatly enlarged by French vocabulary. Part of Chaucer's genius was to use the full range of the language that swirled around him—from its earthy Germanic core to the often musical and multisyllabic French words that had now given English a new look.

The Renaissance:
English Receives an Influx of Latin Words

Latin entered the English language through an invasion that was peaceful—the Renaissance of the 1500s. Latin had been the language of learning ever since the crumbling of the Roman Empire during the fifth century because Latin was the language of Christianity. Only under the protection of church monasteries did the arts of reading and writing survive the violence and upheaval that spread through Europe after the fall of the Roman Empire. For centuries, the only schools were church schools. When universities began to develop independently, Latin continued to be the language of learning.

Starting with the adoption of Christianity in England in 597, Latin words had trickled into the language through the church, its schools, and its influence on daily life: *altar, angel, candle, chalice, mass, priest, school, verse, meter, grammar, notary, lentil, millet, pear, radish, savory, lily, cap*. During the Renaissance, the trickle became a flood. Latin, accompanied by a comparatively smaller number of Greek words, flowed into English as the vocabulary of intellectual thought. A revival of learning led to the rediscovery of the classical writings of Greece and Rome. The Greek classics were first translated into Latin, then both were translated into English because of popular demand, demand created by the printing press. William Caxton had introduced the printing press to England in 1476 and by the mid-1500s books, pamphlets and single-sheet "broadsides" poured from the presses. The wealth of reading material inspired increasing numbers of people to learn to read. The literate public grew rapidly, further fueling the productivity of the publishers. A growing number of the works were by English authors and written in English. Authors who wrote in Latin might get rejection notices, such as the one received by Thomas Drant in 1567: "Though, sir, your book be wise and full of learning, yet peradventure it will not be so saleable." Classics previously published in Latin for a small band of Latin-speaking scholars were now translated into English for more profitable sales to the general public. One challenge in translating Latin into English was finding adequate vocabulary. Because Latin had been the language of scholarship, English lacked a vocabulary for expressing scholarly ideas. Many translators responded to the challenge by simply anglicizing Latin words—words intimately familiar to *them* because Latin was their second language. Because English already contained many French words, which are derived from Latin, the new vocabulary did not seem entirely strange to the general public either. Many of the new words passed quickly from books, where they first appeared, into general speech.

The invasion of Latin and Greek vocabulary was not entirely peaceful, however. Major arguments broke out over whether the new words enriched English or ruined it. Some writers got so carried away with using Latin words that their writing became overblown and difficult to understand. The growing number of "erudite" words brought into the language created barriers for those who knew no Latin. The following exchange between Groucho and Chico Marx might have come from this period:

> GROUCHO: If we're successful in disposing of these lots, I'll see that you get a nice commission.
>
> CHICO:　　What about some money?

Loud voices were raised against those who used "inkhorn terms," as many of the new words were called. Champions of "pure" English, in their attempt to purge the language of the growing Latin influence, proposed substitutes for the non-English impostors: *mooned* for *lunatic, gainrising* for *resurrection* and even *ungothroughsome* for *impenetrable*. Other writers eased Latin words into the language by pairing them with familiar synonyms, as did Sir Thomas Elyot: "*animate* or give courage," "*devulgate* or set forth," "*obfuscate* or hid," "*explicating* or unfolding." Shakespeare, of course, seized all the resources of the burgeoning language, celebrating both the earthy energy of "pure" English and the rolling syllables of Latin imports, sometimes setting "native" words beside the Latin to interpret them:

> Will all great Neptune's ocean wash this blood
> Clean from my hand? No; this my hand will rather
> The multitudinous seas incarnadine,
> Making the green one red.
> *(Macbeth)*

New words flooding into English during the Renaissance rose to a volume of 10,000-12,000, the great majority of them Latin. About 5,000 of those words remain in use today. Translations of classics were not the only source of new vocabulary. Activity in many fields spurred the growth of the language. Explorers set sail on voyages of discovery, centers of trade and commerce flourished and grew, new arts and technologies blossomed. Galileo explored mathematical and physical laws, as well as astronomy, William Harvey discovered circulation of the blood and William Gilbert was a pioneer in discovering magnetism. Latin and Greek provided *navigation, mathematics, circulation, skeleton, commerce, physics, gravity,* and *magnetism* (possible alternatives using non-classical sources would have been *course-charting, number-lore, blood-movement, bone-parts,* etc.). Here is a sampling of other Latin and Greek words that entered the language during that period: *scientific, thermometer, atmosphere, chronology, system, antithesis, heterodox, conjecture, expectation, conclusion, method, function, capacity, dexterity, democracy, politician, jurisprudence, audacious, egregious, malignant, compatible, conspicuous, appropriate, necessary, incredible, rational, intellect, genius, history, moderate, magnify, prosecute, indict, testify, notary, hereditary, popular, individual, habitual, private, solitary, spacious.*

English after the Renaissance

During the years that followed the Renaissance, the pace of change slowed. Publication of the first substantial English dictionary, Samuel Johnson's *Dictionary* (1775), was one reflection of a widespread impulse toward settling in to define "correct" English after the upheaval of the Renaissance. English continued to change, of course. New events generated new vocabulary and people continued to coin new words. However, the resources people used for creating new words did not change much after the Renaissance. The basic word stock we draw on today, as we combine and re-combine elements, was in place by then: a Germanic base joined with major strands of French and Latin vocabulary, as well as a small but significant strand of Greek vocabulary. For new scientific and scholarly terms, we still draw on Latin and Greek. Although English has continued to absorb foreign words—from British sailors and settlers who brought words home from all around the world, and from immigrants who have contributed words to American English—these borrowings have added threads of color to the language rather than giving it a look as radically new as those created first by the Norman Conquest and then by the Renaissance.

The Mixed Heritage of English: Variety and Diversity in One Language

The mixed heritage of English provides great variety within one language. We have a vocabulary based on two sets of roots—a Germanic set familiar through the common names of things around us, and a Latin and Greek set often used for expressing abstract ideas. We have a language rich in synonyms and distinctly varied in its levels of formality. We also have a spelling system that gives many people a headache because it contains the different spelling patterns of several languages.

Two Sets of Roots: Familiar and Unfamiliar

Children learn the familiar names of things as a natural part of growing up, but learning names based on Greek and Latin roots often requires special effort. What is the *solar* system? A system that revolves around the sun. What is an *arboretum*? A *dormitory*? Young children know the words *sun*, *tree*, and *sleep*, but few know that the Latin roots *sol-*, *arbor-*, and *dorm-* also mean "sun," "tree," and "sleep." By contrast, a Spanish child is likely to know that the *systema solar* has something to do with the sun because the word for sun in Spanish is *sol*. In Spanish, complex vocabulary tends to be built on the words that children learn as they are growing up. In English, however, complex vocabulary is often built on roots that are different from those that underlie our everyday words. The adjective that describes "things having to do with dogs" is *canine*. The adjective that describes "things having to do with horses" is *equine*. The Latinate adjectives must be learned, not as extensions of the familiar names of the animals, but as separate vocabulary words.

English then is based on two sets of roots—familiar and unfamiliar. The familiar roots tend to be those of Germanic origin because, as we have seen, the Anglo-Saxon vocabulary that survived the Norman Conquest was the vocabulary of down-to-earth reality: *eat, sleep, wake, walk, run, come, go, bed, bowl, knife, roof, floor, room, rake, plow, seed, grain*. The words that survived in the speech of peasants living close to the land not only are familar, they often have an earthy liveliness as well: *creep, wriggle, sway, droop, slouch, crumple, shatter, flutter, rustle, ramble, hustle, fetch, fling, swoop, glide, glitter, blaze, dazzle, flash, flicker, dawdle, drift, ripple, splash, spray*. Our Germanic words are often the vivid words of the language.

The unfamiliar roots of the language are those of Latin and Greek origin. These roots underlie both the French words that came into the language following the Norman Conquest (French started off as "bad Latin," a provincial dialect of the Roman Empire) and the Latin and Greek vocabulary that entered English in the Renaissance. Words based on these roots are often less vivid for us because they are a step removed from our everyday names for things. Thus, *cordial*, based on the Latin *cor*, which means "heart," does not have the immediacy of the word *hearty*. (We do not always want a familiar immediacy, and at times prefer the more distant *cordial*.) Words based on the Greek *photo-* and *tele-* do not suggest images of light and distance as readily as vocabulary based on Germanic words of the same meaning, *light* and *far*. The word *retain*, based on the French form of the Latin *ten*, "to hold," does not have the same immediacy as the Germanic phrase "hold back."

To describe English as based on two sets of roots, familiar and unfamiliar, is, of course, to oversimplify. Many words of Latin origin, especially those that entered the language through French, became so integrated into daily speech that they are as familiar as any words in the language. The words *cry, touch, clear, mean, rude, cruel, calm*, and *safe*—all of French origin—have the same immediacy for us as words of Germanic origin. What remains true, however, is that many of the "big" words of the language are based on unfamiliar roots. The word *geography* is based on the Greek for "earth" (*ge*), not on the familiar word *earth*. In German, by contrast, the word for "geography" (*Erdkunde*) is built on the common word for "earth" (*Erde*). In German, as in the Romance languages, there often is continuity between common names and complex vocabulary. In English there seldom is.

Synonyms and Levels of Formality

Having a vocabulary drawn from several languages can create difficulties, but the mixed heritage of English also gives us a word stock rich in synonyms. Look at the following word pairs:

eat / dine
climb / ascend
teach / instruct
smart / intelligent
dawdle / procrastinate
scold / reprimand

begin / commence
rot / decay
speed / velocity
grow / develop
need / require
handle / manage

deadly / mortal
fix / repair
hurt / injure
end / terminate

spit / expectorate
deep / profound
hard / obdurate
light / illuminate

In each pair of synonyms the first word is of Germanic origin, the second of French or Latin origin. Each synonym covers a slightly different range of meaning, allowing us to draw fine distinctions that are not always possible in other languages. Sometimes the distinctions are connected to the degree of formality we associate with a word. The Latinate words usually have a more formal tone than their Germanic synonyms. We *eat* at McDonald's; we *dine* at an elegant restaurant. The government prefers the formality (and cushioning obscurity) of *terminating* a program to the informality (and frankness) of *ending* it. You and I may want to throw a little *light* on a subject; a philosopher might seek to *illuminate* it. English is full of synonyms that allow us to choose the tone and level of formality that best suit our purpose. It is the mixed heritage of English that gives us an abundance of synonyms and a vocabulary larger than that of any other Western language.

Phrases: Another Source of Synonyms

Synonyms can be phrases as well as words. We can *talk over* the day's events or *discuss* them, *come to* a conclusion or *arrive at* it. We can *let go* or *release*, *put off* or *postpone*, *set up* or *establish*, *try out* or *audition*, *give up* or *relinquish*, *put up with* or *tolerate*, *rise above* or *transcend*, *breathe in* or *inhale*, *run into* or *encounter*, *speak up for* or *advocate*. We coin phrases as readily as we coin words, and popular speech is full of them: *clam up, buzz off, space out, rip off, chill out*. The words in these phrases are assembled the way affixed words are assembled, but in a phrase the elements of meaning are left freestanding and in an affixed word they are "glued" together.

The use of phrases as alternatives to affixed words became prevalent in English because of changes in its Germanic vocabulary. If you look at the Lord's Prayer in Anglo-Saxon (below), you will see unfamiliar affixes attached to otherwise reasonably familiar words: the *-um* of *heofunum* (heaven), the *-a* of *willa* (will), the *ge-* of *gelaed*. Prior to the Norman Conquest, the Germanic vocabulary of English had many more affixes than are in active use today. Many affixes began to "fade," as linguists say, and fall out of use. The process began before the Conquest and continued for several hundred years. Some

Fæder ūre,
þū þe eart on heofonum,
sī þīn nama gehālgod.
Tōbecume þīn rīce
Gewurþe ðīn willa on eorðan swā swā on heofonum.
Ūrne gedæghwāmlīcan hlāf syle ūs tō dæg.
And forgyf ūs ūre gyltas, swā swā wē forgyfað ūrum gyltendum.
And ne gelæd þū ūs on costnunge,
ac ālȳs ūs of yfele.   Sōþlīce.

(The Lord's Prayer in Anglo-Saxon)

affixes disappeared altogether: no words today begin or end with *ge-*, *-um*, or *-a*. Other affixes remain embedded in our vocabulary, but are no longer used to form new words: the *be-* of *behold, between, become,* and *because*; the *for-* of *forgive, forsake, forbid,* and *forget*; the *with-* of *withhold, withstand, without,* and *withdraw*.

As affixes were lost, the meaning was carried instead by freestanding words. For example, our tendency today is to put *hold* and *up* together in a phrase (*hold up*) rather than to combine them in an affixed word like *uphold*—a word that predates the Norman conquest. *Uphold, behold, withhold, withstand, understand, outstanding,* and *bystander* all reflect the earlier period when verbs were usually modified to express new meaning through affixing. Today, our tendency is to build a family of phrases on *hold* or *stand*, instead of a family of words: *hold up, hold off, hold down, hold onto, hold back, on hold*, and *stand by, stand for, stand up to, stand up for*, etc.

The "imported" Latinate words of the language did not undergo the same changes as the "native" Germanic words and remain highly affixed. Having both strands of vocabulary in the language often allows us a choice between a Germanic phrase and an affixed Latin word: we can *obtain* something or *get hold of* it, we can be *detained* on our way to a meeting or *held up*, we can *substitute* for others or *stand in* for them. The rhythm and feel of the phrase is different from the rhythm and feel of the affixed word. The choices we make as we use one or the other shape the style of our speaking and writing.

The Different Spelling Patterns of Several Languages Thrown Together

For a child who can sound out words, Spanish spelling is easy. It is almost always true that each sound can be represented by one, and only one, letter. The child who tries to spell English words by sounding them out, however, quickly runs into difficulties. If you rely solely on your ear when spelling *nation*, you are likely to spell it n-a-s-h-u-n. If you rely solely on your ear when spelling *school* and *night*, you are likely to spell them *s-k-o-o-l* and *n-i-t-e*. In English, any one sound may be represented by any of several letters, in part because the language includes spelling patterns from Anglo-Saxon, French, Latin, and Greek. Often, the spelling of a word is a clue to its identity. Here are a few of the clues.

Anglo-Saxon

Words of one and two syllables that begin with silent letters are usually of Anglo-Saxon origin. The letters were not always silent. In Anglo-Saxon times (known to linguists as the period of Old English) both of the beginning consonants in the following words were pronounced.

knee	gnaw	wrist
knob	gnarl	wrinkle
knuckle	gnat	wrench
knight	gnash	wrong

Words with *gh* are also of Anglo-Saxon origin. Though now silent, the *gh* was pronounced in Old English and Middle English (the English spoken in the Middle Ages following the Norman Conquest) with a guttural, throat-clearing sound similar to that given the *ch* in the German *nacht*.

fight	bought	caught
sight	thought	taught
high	ought	haughty
sigh	fought	naughty

A good way to help students remember these silent letters is to have them experiment with pronouncing the words as they were originally pronounced.

French

We can be fairly certain that a word entered the language via French when we encounter the following:

- Two-syllable words that end in *-ain*:

mountain	bargain	maintain
fountain	refrain	contain
certain	complain	obtain

- Words that end in *-ue*:

blue	hue	virtue
due	continue	statue
sue	value	revenue
glue	construe	retinue

- Words in which *ci* is pronounced like *sh*:

gracious	spacious	magician
delicious	special	suspicious
precious	musician	pernicious

Latin or French

Words ending in *-ture* or *-tion* are of French or Latin origin.

pasture	structure	nation	fraction
nature	armature	station	addition
capture	aperture	caption	subtraction
adventure	agriculture	election	selection
fracture	horticulture	mention	traction
culture	ligature	invention	eruption

Sometimes a Latin root, in passing through French, has acquired a distinctive French spelling. The French form of the Latin *cor-*, for example, is *cour-*, as in the word *courage*. The French form of the Latin *ten-* is *tain-*. The French form appears in the words *contain* and *retain*; the Latin form appears in the words *content* and *retention*. During the Renaissance the French spelling of many words was "corrected" to a Latin spelling by scholars who considered the classical languages to be the truest and purest form of language. Thus *parfait*, the French form of *perfect* found in the English of Chaucer's day, was "corrected" to *perfect*. Therefore, it is often difficult to tell whether a word originally came into English through French or through Latin.

Greek

You know a word is of Greek origin if it has a *ph* or if it has a *ch* that is pronounced with a *k* sound.

photograph	autograph	school	ache
phonograph	symphony	character	echo
physics	hyphen	Christmas	chaos
philosophy	atrophy	chorus	chrome
phobia	physical	chord	chlorine
phrase	telephone	choir	chronological

Words that begin with a silent *p* are of Greek origin. In Greek the *p* is still pronounced.

| pneumonia | pterodactyl | ptolemy | psoriasis |
| pneumatic | ptomaine | pseudonym | psychology |

Words with the consonant cluster *rh-* come from Greek:

rhetoric	rheumatism	rheostat
rhythm	hemorrhage	rhinoceros
rhubarb	rhapsody	

The story behind such "tricky" patterns—the story of the invasions that shaped English—can make some of the challenges of English spelling both interesting and understandable.

The Indo-European Family of Languages

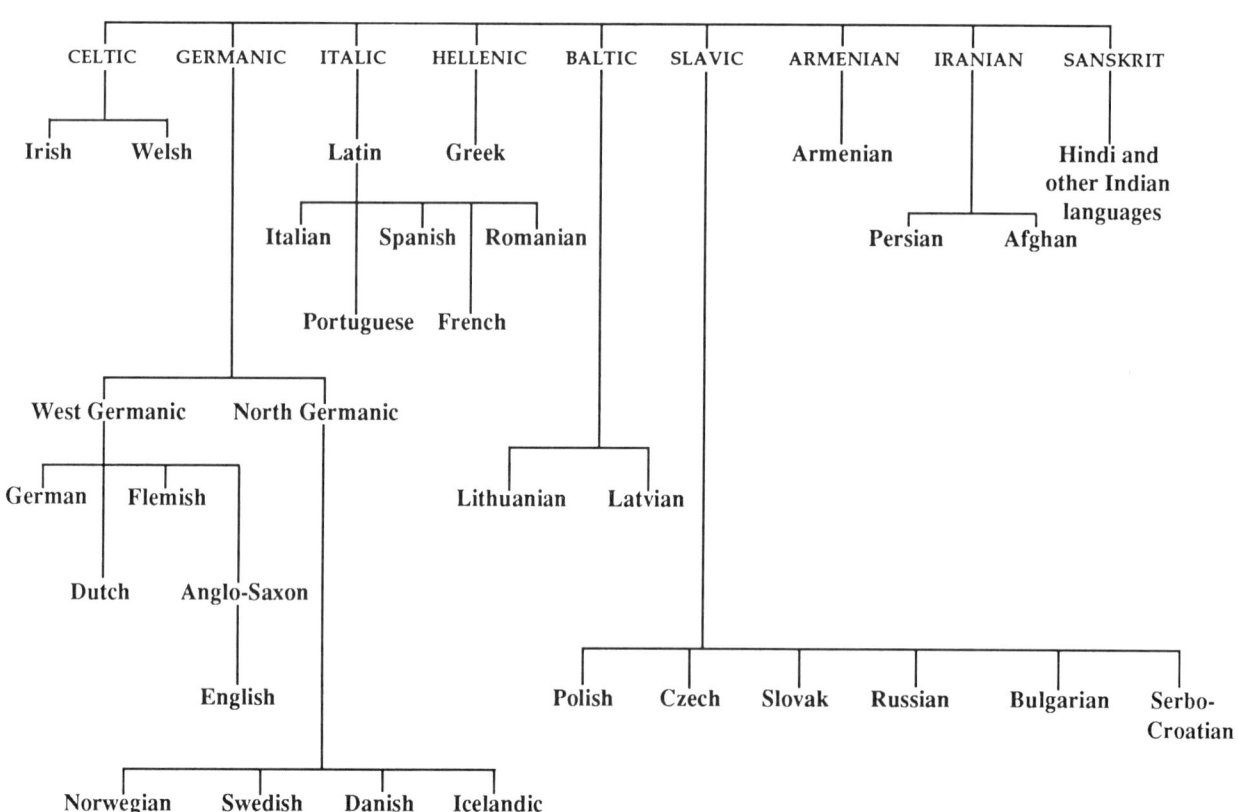

This is an abbreviated chart. A more complete chart can be found on the inside back cover of the 1969 edition of *The American Heritage Dictionary* and on pp. 112-113 of *The American Heritage Dictionary of Indo-European Roots* (1985).

Indo-European Origins:
The Languages That Contributed to English
Are Ultimately Related

The roots of words brought to England by the Normans reached back to Latin. The roots of words spoken by the Anglo-Saxons were of Germanic origin. Differences between these separate strands of language are many, but in the early nineteenth century linguists began tracing the separate strands back to a common source. Using word clues and clues of grammar, they discovered that, like most European languages, French and Anglo-Saxon share a common ancestor. Linguists named the ancestor Indo-European and pieced together clues that suggest that Indo-European was spoken about six or seven thousand years ago by tribes living in the area today known as southern Siberia. These tribes eventually began heading outward in all directions—some branching out across Europe, others migrating around the eastern edge of the Mediterranean and down into India. As the Indo-European tribes became isolated from one another, each followed its own separate path of change. From one common language, many separate languages evolved—all the languages pictured on the Indo-European chart.

The chart shows that some members of the Indo-European family are more closely related than others. You might say that Anglo-Saxon and German are siblings, but that Anglo-Saxon and French are cousins. English and Sanskrit are very distant cousins. Speaking of family connections, it should be noted that Indo-European is just one of many language families: Chinese belongs to the Sino-Tibetan family; the Cree language belongs to the Algonquin family; Arabic belongs to the Semitic family; Swahili belongs to the Bantu family.

Below are some of the word clues linguists used as they traced the Indo-European family tree and reconstructed its roots. Can you guess what English words belong in the blanks at the head of each column?

ENGLISH			
GERMAN	mutter	nacht	schnee
DUTCH	moeder	nacht	sneeuw
SWEDISH	mor	natt	sno
LATIN	mater	noct-	niv-
FRENCH	mère	nuit	neige
SPANISH	madre	noche	nieve
ITALIAN	madre	notte	neve
GREEK	meter	nukt-	nipha
RUSSIAN	mat	noch	sneg
SANSKRIT	mataram	naktam	snehas

Similarities can be seen fairly easily when these cognates (word relatives) of *mother, night,* and *snow* are assembled in one chart, but many other patterns of connections were not clear until linguists pieced them together. Through the common ancestry of Indo-European, then, the languages that contributed to English—Anglo-Saxon, Old Norse, French, Latin, and Greek—are all ultimately related. The few tribes who spoke the "parent" Indo-European tongue would be astonished to glance through history and see how their language has evolved.

American English: The Story Continues

The story of English continues to be one of change. In his book *Word Play*, Peter Farb tells of a young English woman who entered a convent in 1914 and remained in total seclusion for twenty-eight years. When she emerged, social customs and the map and politics of Europe were radically different, but what confused her most was the language people spoke. Words familiar to her had fallen out of use and many new expressions had come into being. Any person isolated for thirty years would have a similar problem of re-entry. Language is always changing. New experiences produce new vocabulary. The space age generated *astronaut, blast-off, lift-off, splashdown, boil-off, skylab.* Existing words took on new meaning: *docking, satellite, thrust, capsule, shuttle. In orbit* and *spaced out* became descriptions of psychological states. The term *spaceship earth* engendered a new perspective on the planet.

From the first days of settlement on the Atlantic coast, the American experience has shaped American English. Early settlers coined names for the features of the territory they pioneered: *foothill, bluff, hollow, water gap, backwoods, underbrush, watershed.* From contact with French and Spanish settlers came *prairie, bayou,* and *butte,* and *canyon, mesa,* and *arroyo.* As the country expanded into French and Spanish territories, local place names remained to remind us of their history: Baton Rouge, Louisiana, St. Louis, Sault Sainte Marie, Fond-du-Lac, Des Moines, Grand Teton; Nevada, Colorado, Rio Grande, San Antonio, El Paso, Orlando, Florida, California, San Diego, San Francisco. Names of New World plants and animals were adopted from Native American languages: *woodchuck, chipmunk, skunk, moose, opossum, hickory, pecan, persimmon, catalpa, hominy, squash.* Many place names are, of course, similarly drawn from American Indian languages: *Massachusetts, Connecticut, Minnesota, Mississippi, Tallahassee, Tuscaloosa, Roanoke, Potomac, Chesapeake, Susquehanna, Rappahannock, Passaic, Raritan, Penobscot, Kennebec, Merrimac.*

As farmers moved west, the challenge of putting new land to the plow produced the word *sodbusters*. From *cowboys* came *roundup* and *to bite the dust.* As rails were laid for a new form of transportation, the words *railroad, boxcar, switchyard,* and *cow catcher* (the front fender of the engine) were coined and *sidetrack, backtrack, make the grade, be in the clear,* and *reach the end of the line* quickly moved beyond the confines of the rails to express more general ideas. The Gold Rush gave us several metaphors that are still in the language: *pan out, stake a claim, strike it rich, hit pay dirt*. Clearing the land generated *bobsled* (usually two short, or "bobbed," sleds hitched together for carrying logs), *lumberjack*, and *fly off the handle*—as ax heads did with sometimes deadly results and as lumberjacks often did in the isolation of logging camps. Encounters with the weather inspired *blizzard* (probably of onomatopoeic origin), *cold-snap*, and *cloud-burst*. High spirits and a love of rolling sounds on the tongue gave birth to *rambunctious, scalawag, hornswoggle,* and *skedaddle*. One lure of the frontier was *lighting out* and leaving your troubles behind you. If you needed to leave town quickly, you could not only *scoot* or *skedaddle*, you could also *high tail it, hot foot it, pull stakes, make tracks, fly the coop*, or *hit the trail*.

If you were in the Ozarks you might *cut mud*, leave *lickety-whoop*, and *skin your eyes* (be alert) to make sure no one was following you. Many regions spawned their own turns of speech, which did not necessarily make it beyond the borders of the region. In the Ozarks you might also *raise sand* (create a disturbance), *cut your own weeds* (mind your own business), or *touch hands* with your neighbors (cooperate with them, stick together), while keeping your eye on the clouds to see if the coming rain is going to be a *drizzle-drozzle*, a *gully-washer*, a *fence-lifter*, a *goose-drowner*, or a *toad-strangler*. Along the Maine coast you might have to bring a sailboat to port by *ash breeze* (using oars) or you might be a *shorehugger* who never ventures far on a boat—or any other enterprise. You might feel that everything is *bung up and bilge free* (in good order, like casks properly stored on a boat) if you *get your bait back* (break even on a deal). If you do so well as to have a few dollars *salted down* (set aside for the future the way salted meats were stored on boats and in lumber camps), you might get *all rigged out* (dressed up) to celebrate. In the West you might encounter an *Arizona cloudburst* (sandstorm), take the *ankle express* (go by foot), or feel *cold-footed* (cowardly) when tangling with a *barb wire deal* (tough situation to handle) or with someone who is *all horns and rattles* (in a fit of temper—like a cow aiming its horns and a snake shaking its rattles.)

Just as regional speech often reflected regional particularities, activities shared by people across the country created a shared vocabulary. American politics, springing from new experiments in government, had a flavor and a vocabulary all its own. In the late 1800s the use of barns for performances by itinerant actors came to be known as *barnstorming*, a word soon borrowed by equally itinerant politicians—as was the *bandwagon* of the circus parade. *Grandstanding* (borrowed from baseball) politicians often seized the attention of voters with lively turns of speech: *landslide, gag rule, dark horse, gerrymander, lobbyist, pork barrel, lame duck, fat cat.* Sports and games contributed many figures of speech to the language: *out in left field, off base, play hardball, back a winner, on the ropes, saved by the bell, cut a deal, ante up, in the chips, cash in, par for the course.* With the advent of electricity we could get a *charge* out of things and with the advent of cars we could *step on it* or be *out of gas.* Aviation gave us *on the beam, flying blind, tailspin, nose dive,* and *bail out.* American coinages have often been graphic and lively: *fork over, cave in, go-getter, ripsnorter, roughneck, back talk, scofflaw, has-been, do-gooder, down and out, flat-footed, roughhouse, comeback, get a move on, make good, no slouch, backbone, start off, show up, stay put, cut and run, sit up and take notice.*

Immigrants brought words of diverse origins into American English. From French settlers in the Louisiana territory came *levee, depot, bureau,* and *picayune* (derived from the name of a small French coin.) From Spanish-speaking immigrants came the words *mustang, lasso, lariat, bronco, pinto, corral, stampede, rodeo, ranch, adobe, siesta, patio, bonanza, tornado, tortilla, tacos, tamale, chili,* and *cafeteria.* From German settlers came *cookbook, delicatessen, kindergarten,* and *hoodlum,* and the expressions *and how, no way, will do* (direct translations from German). Speakers of Yiddish have given us *kibbitzer, klutz, chutzpah, mensch, schlep, schmaltz,* and *schmooze.* The vocabulary of many nations is especially evident in the foods that immigrant groups have contributed to the American diet: *sauerkraut, pumpernickel, hamburger, frankfurter, liverwurst,* and *schnitzel* (German); *blintzes, borscht, matzoh, bagels,* and *lox* (Yiddish); *kielbasa* (Polish); *parmesan, pasta, spaghetti, macaroni, salami, ravioli, minestrone, pizza, zucchini,* and *broccoli* (Italian); *lutefisk* and *smorgasbord* (Scandinavian); *chop suey, chow mein, dim sum, soy* sauce, and *ketchup* (Chinese); *pita, humus,* and *tahini* (Middle Eastern); *goulash* and *paprika* (Hungarian); *yam, gumbo,* and *okra* (African).

African-Americans have made numerous contributions to American speech, contributions that go beyond individual words of African origin, such as *tote, juke* (in jukebox), *jazz*, and *banjo*. Jazz, that unique contribution of African-Americans to American and world culture, was but one territory where they defined the vocabulary: *jam, riff, in the groove, cat, mellow, bop, hip*. Improvisation, which lies at the heart of jazz, is central not only to African musical tradition, but also to the spoken traditions of the griots, or African bards.[1] Forbidden to learn to read and write well after their arrival in the United States, African-Americans preserved elements of their oral traditions in various forms. Rap songs, hip-hop, playing the dozens, and pulpit oratory, diverse though they be, all share roots in African tradition through their emphasis on verbal agility and on the ability to compose during performance. It is interesting to note that Martin Luther King improvised the famous lines of his "I Have a Dream" speech. Reared in the African-American preaching tradition, King was a master of improvisation in rhythms and cadences familiar to African-American congregations but new to most of the nationwide audience who first heard them during the 1963 March on Washington. King had prepared a restrained, low-key speech for that occasion, but as he neared the end of it, he abandoned his text. As one author put it, he achieved permanent status as an American orator and statesman by "setting aside his text to cut loose and jam, as he did regularly from two hundred podiums a year."[2] In wholly different settings and often serving very different ends, rap artists and other street-corner poets in the inner city still practice a similar art of improvising.

The verbal inventiveness of such traditions has infused American popular speech with new terms, especially in recent years. The expressions *hang-up*,

---

[1] The bardic tradition, with its emphasis on spoken art and composition during performance, is of course a part of Western tradition as well. Both Homer and the Beowulf poet embody this tradition. Their bardic performances were written down—and thus preserved for us—as their civilizations were turning toward literacy. Alfred Lord's *The Singer of Tales* (Cambridge, Massachusetts: Harvard University Press, 1960) analyzes the elements of bardic performance using recorded interviews done in the 1930s (by Bela Bartok, among others) with Serbo–Croatian bards in Yugoslavia. These bards were still reciting epics as long as *The Iliad*—but they were the last generation to keep the art alive. Isidore Okpewho makes a similar analysis of bardic tradition in Africa in *The Epic in Africa: Toward a Poetics of Oral Performance* (New York: Columbia University Press, 1979). Because in the West emphasis on oral performance was displaced so long ago by emphasis on literary composition (the Yugoslavian bards were part of an Islamic tradition unfamiliar to most Westerners), our most direct link to that tradition runs through African-American heritage. Oral performance remained alive in Ireland much longer than it did in England or continental Europe and the rhythms of that tradition have influenced English literature. (Listen to Yeats "sing" his poetry.)

[2] Taylor Branch, *Parting the Waters* (New York: Simon and Schuster, 1988), p. 887.

rip off, uptight, make it, drop out, get it together, cool it, and *chill out* have, at various times, gained fairly wide currency. Current expressions coined by young African-Americans often spread worldwide, thanks to the popularity of their music and to global telecommunications. A production assistant for the PBS television series *The Story of English* was amazed to discover, as she watched the rough cut for the program on black English, that the latest expressions from Philadelphia's inner city were already on the tongue of her ten-year-old son in London.

Today English is spoken throughout the world. Movies, television, tapes, and other forms of technology create a pool of common experience among the various "Englishes"—British, American, Canadian, Indian, Australian, West Indian—but speakers in each setting adapt the language to their own situations. In India, many daily newspapers are published in English, but native words mix with English vocabulary in journalists' reports. In the West Indies, African patterns of pronunciation and grammar have shaped the native Creole and are influencing the "standard" English spoken in the islands, as well. Wherever English takes root, it comes to reflect the lives of those who speak it. In the words of Ralph Waldo Emerson, "Language is a city, to the building of which every human being [brings] a stone."

Linguistic Background

As you explore each word family, you will find that some changes in sounds and letters took place as the family developed. The brief explanations of such changes given in the word family chapters are sufficient for your students, but for those of you who would like further background, we include here a discussion of the following: why several of the Indo-European roots have unfamiliar consonant-*h* patterns; why knowing the history of silent letters can be helpful; why the vowels change from one word to another in a family; why *r* often shifts its position in a word; and why certain consonant shifts have been common in English and its parent languages. To bring some of this seemingly esoteric information down to earth, listen to some toddlers who are learning to speak. Does the toddler's version of a word have the same vowels as the version used by older members of the family? Do you hear *t*'s that are pronounced as *d*'s or *p*'s that are pronounced as *b*'s? Vowel shifts and consonant shifts are part of our personal history, as well as part of the history of the language.

Unfamiliar Consonant-*h* Patterns of Indo-European Roots

Why do the roots BHEL, DHREU, GHEIS, MEDHYO, and GHEL have consonant-*h* patterns that no longer exist in the English derivatives? The *h* in these roots represented a puff of breath following the consonants—a pronunciation unfamiliar to speakers of English. Just as people stopped pronouncing the sound represented by the *k* of *knee* and the *w* of *wrong*, they also stopped pronouncing the sound represented by the *h* in BHEL, DHREU, GHEIS, MEDHYO, and GHEL. Don't worry about how to pronounce these roots. You can pronounce them as though the *h* were silent, or you can make up your own version of a breathy sound. No one knows for sure how the *h* was pronounced.

We considered converting BHEL, DHREU, MEDHYO, and GHEL to Germanic forms that would eliminate the *h*, but decided against it because we found that students enjoy the air of mystery—the sense of connection with something ancient and different—of these exotic patterns. You may want to point out the Indo-European languages where such patterns still persist: Afghani, Hindu, and other Indian languages. The name Afghanistan, of course, is one example, and a map of Afghanistan provides others: Ghazni, Ghurian, Balkh, and Andkhvoy. Bhaktapur, Dhankuta, Junagadh, Mhow, Khandwa, Jhunjhunu, and Dharmsala are examples from India. The languages of Pakistan and Iran are also Indo-European in origin. In Pakistan you will find Jhal, Musa Khel, Bhera, and Dera Ghazi Khan, and in Iran Khorramabad, Sarakhs, Maragheh, and Abhar. In Greece, as well, you will find Khania, Khios, Dhomokos, Edhessa, and Khranidhion. If you know native speakers of any of these languages, you might ask them how the patterns are pronounced in their language. Names in the news and words imported from these regions (Khomeini, Bhutto, ghee, dharma, Buddha) can also point up the linguistic kinship of these other languages with Indo-European roots.

Silent Letters

When sounds fall silent, the letters that represent them are not always dropped. We no longer pronounce the *g* of *gnaw*, the *b* of *thumb*, the *l* of *walk*, the *t* of *fasten*, the *n* of *autumn*, or the *p* of *psychology*. The letters remain as clues to sounds that were once a part of the word—as the *h* of BHEL reminds us of a sound from the ancestry of English. The WER family (*wrap, wrestle, wriggle,* etc.), the GHEIS family (*ghost, ghastly, aghast*) and the GHEL, DHREU, MEDHYO, and GHEL roots all provide opportunities for alerting students to the idea that history lurks in silent letters. No letters started off as silent. Experimenting with sounding silent letters gives students an amusing way of remembering them.

Regional and cultural variations in pronunciation show that sounds that are enunciated in one area may be dropped in another. In Appalachian English, the *g* of the *ing* suffix is regularly dropped, and *lovin'* rhymes with *oven*. In Black English, final blends are regularly simplified, with only one of the letters pronounced: *child* becomes *chile, first* becomes *firs, send* becomes *sen*. In songs, *wild* is rhymed with *smile, when* rhymed with *friend*. Poetry and songs are always good clues to pronunciation. For instance, you can learn a lot about Elizabethan pronunciation by examining Shakespeare's rhymes. Be alert to patterns of pronunciation in your own classroom. If students have difficulty with spelling, they may find it helpful to know what letters are silent for them and need extra attention.

Vowel changes

Try the following exercise: run through the sounds represented by consonants, then pronounce sounds represented by vowels. Remember, you are pronouncing the sound represented by a letter, not the name of the letter.

Consonants

Notice that all of the consonant sounds involve cutting or filtering the flow of air that you exhale as you speak. When you pronounce the sounds represented by *d* or *t*, the air is cut by the tongue hitting the roof of the mouth. The air is filtered through closed teeth when you pronounce the sound represented by *s*. Linguists call such filtered sounds *fricatives* (a term related to the word *friction*). A fricative is formed when air is forced into a channel so narrow that hissing or buzzing results. Observe how you form other consonant sounds. Where in your mouth and with what (lips, tongue, teeth) do you form other consonant sounds?

Vowels

Notice the openness of vowel sounds. In pronouncing them you shape the air, but you do not cut or filter it. Because vowel sounds are more open (less clearly tied to a particular point of articulation—lips, tongue, teeth), they change form more readily. Listen to people whose accent is different than yours. How does it differ? Primarily in the vowel sounds. A northerner pronounces the number following nine as *ten*, but many southerners pronounce it as *tin*. Some New Englanders pronounce *ate* as though it were *et*. In these variations the consonant sounds remain the same and the vowel sound changes. Consonant sounds do change, but not as readily.

R as a Semi-vowel

Moving from the root WER to its derivatives *wrap, wreath,* etc., the pattern changes from *w*-vowel-*r* to *w-r*-vowel. This inversion of *r* and the vowel is common, both in the historical development of words and in some children's spelling. You may have taught children who, in spite of genuine attempts to learn the correct spelling, persist in spelling *birth* as *brith* or *scratch* as *scartch*. Such inversions occur relatively often because *r* is a semi-vowel.

Try pronouncing *birth* and *scratch.* Notice how you shape the sound represented by *r.* You "squeeze" the flow of air more tightly than you do when shaping vowel sounds, but you don't cut or filter the flow as you do when shaping sounds represented by such consonants as *b* or *f.* The *r* sound is not open enough to substitute for a vowel, but it is open enough to share with vowels a tendency toward shifting about.

It is not unusual, then, to find inversion represented by the shift from the vowel-*r* pattern of WER to the *r*-vowel pattern of *wrestle.* Children who have difficulty pinning an *r* to its proper position in a word will find comfort in knowing that people have been inverting *r*'s and vowels for centuries. Sometimes the knowledge cheers them enough so they are ready to tackle this spelling problem with renewed energy.

In spoken English, *r* sometimes slides out of the picture altogether. In some regions an *r* that follows a vowel tends to be lost and replaced by an *uh*-like vowel. Listen to politicians who have a Boston accent. They speak, not about the *future* of the country, but about its *fuchuh*. In some southern areas, *storage* is pronounced as *sto'age* and *barrel* as *b'al*. Listen to the various patterns of pronunciation in your classroom. Children who come from areas where *r* is not always pronounced may find it useful to recognize that, for them, *r* is sometimes a silent letter and may need extra attention when it crops up in the spelling of a word.

Consonant Shifts

Although consonant sounds are more stable than vowel sounds, they do sometimes change. Certain shifts are common in English and its parent languages. In the DWO and DERU families, the *d*-sound of the root and its Latin derivatives has shifted to the *t*-sound of the Germanic words of the family. The Latinate words of the DWO family are *double, duplicate, duplicity, deuce,* and *duet;* the Germanic words are *two, twelve, twenty, twice, twin, twine, twig, between,* and *twilight.* The Latinate words of the DERU family are *endure, obdurate,* and *duress;* the Germanic words are *trust, true, truce, tryst, tree, tray,* and *trough.*

How did the shift from *d* to *t* take place? Experimenting with how we make the sounds reveals that we form both of them with the same "mouth action": the tip of the tongue hits the roof of the mouth just behind the teeth. The difference between the two is that the sound represented by *d* (/d/) is voiced and the sound represented by *t* (/t/) is unvoiced. Try making both sounds (be sure not to add a vowel sound after the /t/) while holding your throat. You will feel your vocal chords vibrate as you sound /d/, but not as you say /t/. A speech sound that involves vibrating the vocal chords is *voiced*; one that is made simply by cutting the flow of air, with no vibration of the vocal chords, is *unvoiced*. In English there are several pairs of consonant sounds in which one is a voiced or unvoiced version of the other: /b/ is a voiced /p/, /g/ is a voiced /k/, /v/ is a voiced /f/, and /z/ is a voiced /s/. The *th-* sound can either be unvoiced, as in *bath*, or voiced, as in *bathe*. All of these pairs have the same "mouth action" and differ only in terms of being voiced or unvoiced. We sometimes slip from one member of a pair to the other without realizing it. Shifting between /d/ and /t/ is particularly common. *Little* is often pronounced as though it were spelled *liddle*. *Walked, helped,* and *laughed* are regularly pronounced as though they were spelled *walkt, helpt*, and *laught*. Pronunciation is influenced by the sounds surrounding the /d/ or /t/ and by what feels "natural."

Both the KER and KEL families reflect a similar shift from the voiced /g/ to the unvoiced /k/. The original Indo-European form of KER is GER and the original Indo-European form of KEL is GEL. In this book, we have adapted the roots to their Germanic form to simplify exploration of vocabulary that had only the Germanic *k*-sound.

Some consonant shifts involve changes other than moving from a voiced to an unvoiced speech sound. The shift from /k/ to /h/ in the KERD/HEART and KAPUT/HEAD families is a shift from one unvoiced consonant to another. In this shift it is the "mouth action" that changes. Try making both sounds. You will notice that, as you make the *k*-sound, the back of your tongue hits the back of the roof of your mouth. When you make the *h*-sound the "mouth action" is focused in the same area, but the tongue drops down to squeeze—rather than to cut—the flow of air. (The relatively "open" sound represented by *h* makes it, like *r*, a semi-vowel. This is why, historically, it has been considered correct to use *an* rather than *a* before words beginning with *h*.) As in the shift from /k/ to /h/, most consonant shifts take place in the same region of the mouth, and it is relatively easy to imagine people moving from one point of articulation to the other.

A Word of Explanation about the Roots Used in *Origins*

The roots listed as the sources of word families in *Origins* have been drawn from *The American Heritage Dictionary of Indo-European Roots*. In the word family chapters, we do not identify the roots as Indo-European because we choose to focus on how they were used to create new words, not on labeling them.

For those of you who want to look up the roots in the *Dictionary*, a word of explanation is in order: these roots are not all presented in exactly the same form as they appear in the *Dictionary* (or the *Appendix* of the 1969 edition of *The American Heritage Dictionary*). In consultation with Calvert Watkins, the editor of the *Dictionary*, we made a few changes designed to make the material more accessible to students. In three cases roots are given in Germanic, rather than Indo-European form: FLEU is the Germanic form of the Indo-European PLEU; KEL is the Germanic form of the Indo-European GEL; and KER is the Germanic form of GER. In addition, we have given the root meanings of FLEU and KER in terms that are easier for elementary students to understand than those used in the *Dictionary*.

In the *Dictionary* you will often find roots that are spelled the same but have different meanings (as in bear, "to carry," and bear, the animal) and these are differentiated by numbers: BHEL[1], BHEL[2], etc. For the sake of simplicity, we do not use these numbers in *Origins*, but here are identifying numbers in case you are interested: BHEL[2], GER[3] (KER), GHEL[2], GEL[1] (KEL), WER[3].

Additional Word Families Based on Indo-European Roots

Here are some additional word families based on Indo-European roots. Many are small and are fun to share informally during a spare moment or as a word or image of the family may arise. Others merit more attention. See the "Developing Your Own Word Families" section of the "Using *Origins*" chapter for ideas on exploring the larger families.

Like the word families of Volume 2, the following word families have been drawn from *The American Heritage Dictionary of Indo-European Roots* edited by Calvert Watkins (Boston: Houghton Mifflin, 1985). In some cases, roots that have different meanings are spelled the same, just as *mail* (armor) and *mail* (letters) have the same spelling but are unrelated. When this happens, roots are identified by numbers (as in BHEL³ or MEL⁸).

Abbreviations indicating origins of words are as follows: *G* for Germanic, *L* for Latin, *F* for French, *Gk* for Greek, *It* for Italian, *R* for Russian, and *C* for Celtic.

ANGH. Tight, painfully constructed

    G. anger   L. anxiety, anxious
       angst   anguish

ANK. To bend

    G. ankle   Gk. anchor
    L. angle

BABA. (A root that imitates indistinct or unarticulated speech.)

    G. baby, babe   It. bambino   F. baboon
       babble   R. babushka   Gk. barbarian, barbaric

BHEL.³ To thrive, bloom

G.	blow (to flower)	L.	flower		florist
	bloom		flour		foliage
	blossom		flourish		defoliate
	blade		floral		portfolio

The transformation of the *b* of the Indo-European root to the *f* of its Latin derivatives is common, exemplified in this family and the following two families, as well as in the related words *brother* and *fraternal*, which both come from the Indo-European BHRATER. You may want to have students experiment with pronouncing both consonants to see how the "mouth action" involved takes place in the same area.

Blade originally referred to a blade of grass or similar plant and later by analogy of shape to part of a knife or sword. *Flour* was not originally distinguished from *flower* in its spelling. It originated in the phrases *flower of wheat, flower of barley, flower of meal*—meaning the finest portion of the grain—and only later came to have its own spelling and identity. The *folio* of *portfolio* is the Latin word for "leaf"—as in *leafing* through a book.

BHREG. To break

G.	break	L.	fracture
	breach		fraction
			fragment
			fragile
			refract

BHREU. To boil, bubble, effervesce

The unifying idea is that of coming to life through bubbling, expanding, warming.

G.	brew	F.	ferment
	broth		fervent
	bread		effervescent
	breath		
	brood, breed		

DEL. Long   Later form: DHLON-GO

    G. long   L. longitude
        length   longevity
        linger   prolong
        Lent   elongate

Lent comes from an Old English word for spring, which in turn comes from a Germanic word meaning "lengthening day."

DHER. To make muddy; darkness

    G. dark
        dregs
        dross

DHWER. Doorway—originally designating the entrance to the enclosure surrounding the house proper

    G. door   L. foreign
                          forest
                          forum

Foreign and *forest* both originally meant "outside or beyond the doors." A *forum* was originally the enclosed place around a home—a place "within the doors" or gates—and later a marketplace.

DRAGH. To draw (pull), drag on the ground

    G. draw   L. trail   detract
        drawer   train   distract
        drawback   tractor   extract
        withdraw   tractable   retract
        drawl   traction   subtract
        drag   abstract
        dragnet   attract
        bedraggle   contract
        draft
        drink
        drench

If you present this family to students, it might be better to give the root meaning as *pull*, since most students think of *draw* in terms of "drawing a picture" rather than in terms of its primary meaning of "pull" or "drag." *Drink* and *drench* may seem like odd members of the family. They are based on the imagery of drawing water in.

ED. To eat

    G. eat   L. edible
        etch

GEL. Cold; to freeze

    G. chill   L. gelatin
        cool   jelly
        cold   congeal
                    glacier

GEN. To compress into a ball

    G. knapsack   knoll   knead
        knob   knot   knock
        knuckle   knit   knell

Knit comes from origins meaning "to tie into a knot" and *knell* from origins meaning "to strike, as with a knobby object." All the *k*'s were once pronounced, of course. *Knife* is also a member of this family. A *knife* might have originally been a blunt instrument.

GENE. To give birth, beget

    G. kin   L. generate   ingenious   gentleman
        kind   generation   engine   gentle
        kindred   engender   genes   generous
        kinship   progeny   genus   degenerate
        king   genesis   generic   genial
                 genius   gentry   congenial

GHER. To enclose

        G. gird   L. orchard
           girdle   horticulture
           girth
           garden
           yard
           kindergarten

GHRE. To grow, become green

        G. green   grass
           grow   graze

GNO. To know

        G. know   L. notice   F. connoisseur
           can   notify
           canny   notorious   Gk. prognosis
           uncanny   notion   diagnosis
           cunning   noble   gnostic
           ken   ignoble
                         cognitive
                         cognizant
                         ignore
                         ignorant
                         recognize

KAN. To sing

        G. hen   L. chant   incantation
                    enchant   cantor
                    canticle   charm

KEL. To cover, conceal

        G. hall   L. color
           hull   cell

  hole   conceal
  hell
  hollow
  holster
  helmet

Color comes from "that which covers" and *cell* from a word that meant storeroom or chamber.

KERS. To run

  L. car   L. corridor F. course
   carry   current
   cargo   excursion
   career   occur
         recur
         cursory

LEIS. Track, furrow

  G. last (endure) L. delirium
    last (re: shoe)
    learn
    lore

The metaphors here are intriguing. *Last* (to endure) comes from a word meaning "to follow a track"—and obviously comes from a time when following a track through the wilds was no easy matter. *Learning*, likewise, originates in the idea of following a track or course. *Lore* is the result of following such a path. *Delirium* comes from intermediate roots meaning "to go out of the furrow"—a metaphor from an agricultural society. *Last* (as in the *last* of a shoe) is the one obvious connection with the idea of a track or footprint.

LENTO. Flexible

  G. lithe L. relent
    linden   lenient

LUFTUZ. Sky

    G. loft
       lift
       aloft

MEL¹. Soft

G. melt	L. mollify	F. enamel
mild	emollient	
smelt	mollusk	

MEL⁸. To crush, grind

G. meal (coarsely ground grain)	L. mallet
mill, miller	malleable
millet	molar

The *meal* of this family is the *meal* of *cornmeal* or *oatmeal*. *Meal* (breakfast, lunch, etc.) comes from a root that means "a measure, mark or an appointed time".

MORI. Body of water

G. mere	L. marine	F. morass
marsh	submarine	
mermaid	marina	
	mariner	
	marinate	

MUS. A mouse, muscle (because of the resemblance of a flexing muscle to the movement of a mouse)

    G. mouse   L. muscle

PED. Foot

    G. foot   L. pedal
       fetter   pedestrian
       fetch   piedmont
       fetlock   podium
                    expedite
                    impede
                    centipede

REUD. Red, ruddy

    G. red   L. rouge
       ruddy   ruby
       rust   russet

SED. To sit

    G. sit   L. sedentary
       set   sedate
       seat   sediment
       settle   assiduous
       saddle   dissident
       soot   reside
                    subside

SKEI. To gleam

    G. shine   L. scintillate
       shimmer   stencil
                   tinsel

SKER. To cut

G. sharp	skirt	L. scrutiny	scribe
shear, shears	skirmish	inscrutable	scribble
shred	scrap	curt	script
shrub	scrape	curtail	describe
shirt	scrub		inscribe

short	scroll		prescribe
share			subscribe
shard			transcribe
shrew			manuscript
shrewd			

The *scribe* and *script* words have their origins in a root that means "to cut" because writing was first done by cutting into a surface with a sharp tool. There are also many words and phrases built on *cut*: *shortcut, undercut, cutback, cut in, cut off, cut out, cut loose, cut to the bone*, etc.

STA. To stand

G.	stand	L.	stable	standard	establish
	stay		stage	stamen	restore
	stem		statue	stamina	obstacle
	stool		stature	staunch	substitute
	steady		status	stanch	constant
	steadfast		station	obstinate	destitute
	homestead				circumstance
	stalwart				

There are also many words and phrases built on *stand*: *bystander, outstanding, understand, stand for, stand up for, standby, stand-off, standoffish, stand-in, stand in for, stand up, stand up to, standpoint, standstill*.

STER. Stiff

G. stare
stark
starch
stern
stork
strut
startle

A *stare* is stiffer than a gaze, no?

TWER. To turn, whirl

      G. storm   L. turbine   F. trouble
         stir   disturb
                    perturb

WE. To blow

      G. weather   L. vent, ventilate
         wind
         window
         wing

A *window* was originally the "wind's eye."

WEBH. To weave

      G. weave
         web
         waffle
         woof, weft
         wobble
         wave (of the hand)
         wave (of water)
         waver

Body Metaphors in English

Head

headstrong
head of (a company, a country)
head up (a committee, etc.)
heading
headline
hard-headed
cool-headed

clear-headed
soft-headed
level-headed
muddle-headed
over one's head
to hold one's head high (to be proud)

Heart

hearty
heartless
open-hearted
heavy-hearted

heart-broken
warm-hearted
light-hearted
at the heart of (a city, etc.)

Face

two-faced
to save face

Nose

nosy
to look down one's nose at (someone, etc.)
to turn up one's nose

Eyes

to see eye to eye
to turn a blind eye to (something, etc.)
to shut your eyes to (something)

Ears

to turn a deaf ear to (someone, etc.)
to lend an ear
to be all ears

Shoulder

to shoulder a burden
shoulder to shoulder (united)

Back

to turn one's back on
behind one's back
off one's back

Arm

to keep at arm's length
to twist one's arm
to strong-arm

Hand

to handle
to have a hand in
to sit on one's hands
to dirty one's hands
(to be or to have) on hand
to set one's hand to; to turn one's hand to (something)
to hand over
to keep hands off

Knuckle

to knuckle under
to knuckle down

Foot

to put one's foot down
to get cold feet
to drag one's feet
to get one's feet wet
to keep one's feet on the ground
to stand on one's own two feet

Exploring Popular Speech

The material presented here came from a group of Washington, D.C., teachers during a workshop. The meanings given are approximate, since many of the terms can be fully understood only in context.

Term	Meaning	Probable Image
Solid	Expression of confirmation that can range from "okay" to "terrific"	Doesn't fall apart, holds together; can be relied on
Split	Leave	Image of separation
Out of it	Not in touch with what's going on	Spatial image—you're out on the periphery, not at the center
Spaced	Not at all in touch with what's going on	Into outer space. Compare the contrasting imagery of "down to earth."
Out to lunch Lunch box He's with the lunch bunch. He's lunchin'.	Not in touch with what's going on	Absence from the scene where business is being conducted
Laid back	Relaxed about things	The body at rest

Term	Meaning	Probable Image
Bent out of shape	In some kind of emotional pain or discomfort. Alternatively, being off balance psychologically, not having your act together.	Contorted body. If your body is bent out of its natural shape, you may be in pain or discomfort. Alternatively, if your body is bent out of shape, you're not in a position to perform smoothly.
Don't get your hips on your shoulders. Don't get hipped.	Same as above	Same as above
Nose out of joint	In a bad temper—with a sense of being put upon	A face reflecting unhappiness. Most adults have lost the facial mobility necessary for demonstrating the expression well—children are best at it.
The hawk is out.	It's freezing cold.	Image of being gripped, seized by the cold. Compare "The cold held them in its grip" or "It's biting cold."
The eagle flies today.	It's payday.	From the image of the eagle on the dollar bill
Foxy	Beautiful, moves with elegance, sometimes sly	The animal and its characteristics

Some of the terms listed by the workshop group fell in a special category: the use of negative words to denote positive qualities, a use common in several West African languages and in African-American idiom. Thus, mean and bad denote "fine, super, excellent," and rags means "fancy clothes."

Sound Families

The following word clusters are linked through shared imagery and sound patterns. It should be emphasized here, as it was earlier, that the connection between the sound pattern—the initial consonant cluster—and the imagery is not an absolute one. Other sounds in a word or a definition that move a word clearly in another direction can override our tendency to associate a given sound pattern with particular imagery, experience, or feeling. Nevertheless, as the following word clusters or "sound families" demonstrate, the psychological tendency to associate sound and meaning has a firm base in reality. The sound families listed below are not, of course, definitive. We list the most obvious candidates for inclusion. You may find, as we do, that once you become alert to the link between *SW-* and the imagery of bending and turning, for example, you begin to see elements of these curvilinear movements in *SW-* words other than those listed below.

SW-. Associated with turning, bending

sweep	swing	sway	swirl
swoop	swerve	swivel	

Swoop and *swivel* actually come from an Indo-European root SWEI, which means to bend or turn. Two other words, *swift* and *swap*, come from the same root. The way they share in the imagery of bending and turning is not as immediately obvious, but can be fun to explore (compare the idea of *swapping* with the idea of "your turn"). Students often propose the words *swish*, *swoop*, and *swipe* as members of the sound family, as well. Although bending and turning movements are not explicit in the definitions of these words, the actions they describe often include elements of bending and turning.

SP-. Associated with movement outward—often a quick burst of movement

spit	spatter	spigot	sprinkle
spew	spurt	spray	spring
spout	spurn	sprawl	sprout
sputter	spume	spread	splash
			splatter

Spit, spew, spout, and *sputter* come from the Indo-European SPYEU, an expressive root meaning "to spew, to spit." The other words share in the expressive force that is grounded in the physical spitting forth of the *sp-* sound.

FL-. Associated with free, often quick, movement

flash	flicker	flap	flail
flare	flick	flip-flop	fling
flame	flip	flounce	

These words are in addition to all the members of the FLEU family.

A few other words participate in the sense of free movement associated with these words: *flamboyant, flag* (as in a flag waving in the breeze), and *flourish* (as in to pull something forth with a *flourish*).

SN-. Associated with the nose

snore	sneeze	sneer	snooty
sniff	snooze	snob	snotty
sniffle	snorkel	snicker	snout
snarl	snoot	snuff	
snort	snoopy	snuffle	

Snout, snuffle, snivel, sniff, snoop, and *snub* are all presented in *The Dictionary of Indo-European Roots* as coming from SNU, described as the "imitative beginning of Germanic words connected with the nose." The other words of the group participate in the connection between the *sn-* sound and the nose. Some of the words that describe attitudes are associated with facial expressions that involve "wrinkling the nose at" or "looking down the nose at."

An Annotated Bibliographical Note

For those who would like further information about the evolution of English, the essay "Language, Culture and the American Heritage" by Lee Pederson in *The American Heritage Dictionary* (Boston: Houghton Mifflin, 1982) and the essay "Indo-European and the Indo-Europeans" by Calvert Watkins in *The American Heritage Dictionary of Indo-European Roots* (Boston: Houghton Mifflin, 1985) provide excellent summaries of scholarship in the field, as does the essay "The Indo-European Origin of English" by Calvert Watkins in the 1969 edition of *The American Heritage Dictionary*. Two fine books on the subject are *Our Marvelous Native Tongue: The Life and Times of the English Language* by Robert Claiborne (New York: Times Books, 1983) and *The Story of English* by Robert McCrum, William Cran, and Robert MacNeil (New York: Viking, 1986). Both books are written with wit and grace and an appreciation both for the treasures of the past buried in the language and for the delights of the newly coined words that constantly enrich the language. *Our Marvelous Native Tongue* follows a straightforward chronology, whereas *The Story of English*, a companion to a PBS television series, pays particular attention to the development of English around the world, ranging from Scotland and Ireland to Australia, Jamaica, West Africa, and India, as well as the United States. Both books provide good and provocative discussions of black English. The two books are complementary.

Classic books in the field are Albert Baugh's *A History of the English Language* (New York: Appleton-Century Crofts, 1957); Otto Jesperson's *Growth and Structure of the English Language* (New York: The Free Press, 1968); and Thomas Pyle's *The Origins and Development of the English Language* (New York: Harcourt, Brace & World, 1964). Two highly readable overviews of the subject, written for teachers and students, are J.N. Hook's *The Story of British English* (Oakland, N.J.: Scott, Foresman, 1974) and Marshall Brown's *Language: The Origins of English* (Columbus, Ohio: Charles E. Merrill Publishing Co., 1971). Unfortunately these books are out of print, but you may be able to find them in the library. Two gracefully written books that give particular attention to the way historical experience is reflected in etymology are Logan Pearsall Smith's *The English Language* (New York: Henry Holt and Company, 1912) and Owen Barfield's *History in English Words* (first published in 1925 and reprinted by Lindisfarne Press, Great Barrington, Massachusetts, 1985). *The English Language* has been reprinted only in a library edition, though it can be special-ordered through bookstores. Another book by Robert Claiborne, *The Roots of English: A Reader's Handbook of Word Origins* (New York: Times Books, 1989) discusses word families revealed by Indo-European roots.

Books that cover grammar, phonology, and social aspects of English, as well as its history, are *The Gift of Language* by Margaret Schlauch (New York: Dover, 1955) and *Origins of the English Language: A Social and Linguistic History* by Joseph Williams (New York: Macmillan, 1975). Peter Farb's *Word Play: What Happens When People Talk* (New York: Knopf, 1973) pays particular attention to how social rules shape the way we speak—and how these rules differ in different cultures.

A book that stands in a class by itself is *1066: The Year of the Conquest* by David Howarth (New York: Viking, 1977). Howarth, a wonderful storyteller, describes the Norman Conquest in vivid detail, taking us intimately into the lives of the English and the Normans, as well as the Norsemen, whose attack in northern Britain was a proximate cause of King Harold's defeat by the Normans at the Battle of Hastings on the southern coast. Since all of these peoples were important to the development of English, the book can be read as more than just a tale of battle.

For those interested in exploring American popular speech and its role in the historical development of English, we recommend (in addition to *Our Marvelous Native Tongue* and *The Story of English*) the lively and irreverent *American Tongue and Cheek* by Jim Quinn (New York: Pantheon Books, 1980) as well as H.L. Mencken's classic work in a similarly irreverent vein, *The American Language* (New York: Alfred A. Knopf, 1937). Mencken's book and its Supplements I and II were abridged and updated by Reven McDavid in 1963. *Our Own Words* (New York: Alfred A. Knopf, 1974) by Mary Helen Dohan explores the interplay of history and language as it is reflected in the development of American vocabulary. *Chin Music, Tall Talk and Other Talk* (New York: J.B. Lippincott, 1979) reports on American folk speech collected by Alvin Schwartz, and *Down in the Holler: A Gallery of Ozark Folk-Speech* by Vance

Randolph and George P. Wilson (Norman, Oklahoma: Oklahoma University Press, 1953) is a classic. *American Talk: The Words and Ways of American Dialects* by Robert Hendrickson (New York: Viking, 1986) provides an appreciative look at the life and origins of American regional speech, and *A Dictionary of American Idioms*, edited by Adam Makka (New York: Barron's, 1987), is a treasure trove of informal American speech. The *Dictionary of American Regional English,* edited by Frederic G. Cassidy (Cambridge, Massachusetts: Harvard University Press), is an ambitious and continuing survey of American folk and regional speech. Volume I, which includes the Introduction and entries under A-C, was published in 1985. The introductory essays provide a good overview of American regional speech. The research for the *Dictionary* is being done by the American Dialect Society at the University of Wisconsin in Madison, and researchers are very kind about answering written inquiries.

We highly recommend Geneva Smitherman's *Talkin and Testifyin* (Boston: Houghton Mifflin, 1975), which both analyzes and reflects the vitality of black vernacular English. In the course of her wide-ranging analysis of black speech, she explores both the influence of African languages and the influence of African oral tradition. Edith Folb's *runnin down some lines* (Cambridge, Massachusetts: Harvard University Press, 1980) pays homage to the linguistic creativity of African-American teenagers as exemplified by the language of young people in the Watts and South Central area of Los Angeles. Lawrence Levine's *Black Culture and Black Consciousness* (New York: Oxford University Press, 1977) and Thomas Kochman's *Black and White Styles in Conflict* (Chicago: University of Chicago Press, 1981) are excellent books that give special emphasis to the creativity of African-American cultural tradition.

Rudolph Arnheim looks at the way language is grounded in experience from a slightly different perspective—that of a philosopher of the arts. Against a background of exploring the role of perception and abstraction in the arts and in all thought, he observes that "the histories of languages show that words which do not seem now to refer to direct perceptual experience did so originally." His observations on language are found in the chapter "Words in Their Place" in his *Visual Thinking* (London: Faber and Faber Ltd., 1969). In *Functions of Language in the Classroom* (New York: Teachers College Press, 1972), edited by Courtney Cazden, Vera John, and Dell Hymes, Eleanor

Leacock's "Abstract Versus Concrete Speech: A False Dichotomy" describes the ways in which both popular and erudite language are metaphorical. She analyzes the abstract thinking reflected in both and considers the implications of this analysis for those who teach. *Metaphors We Live By* by George Lakoff and Mark Johnson (Chicago: University of Chicago Press, 1980) looks at how metaphor operates as a fundamental vehicle of thought, both shaping and expressing our view of the world. Mark Johnson's *The Body in the Mind: The Bodily Basis of Meaning, Imagination, and Reason* (Chicago: University of Chicago Press, 1987) expands on the work of *Metaphors We Live By*.

For a discussion of dictionaries we have used in exploring word histories, see the "Sources and Materials" section of the "Introduction" and the "Developing Your Own Word Families" section of the "Using Origins" chapter.

For those interested in student activities that bear specifically on the history of English, Good Apple Press (Box 299, Carthage, IL 62321) publishes two workbooks for students in grades 4-8: *What's in a Word: Word History Activity Sheets* by David Zaslow and *Slanguage: Activities and Ideas on the History and Nature of Language* by John Artman.

Appendix

The Words Project

Origins is at the center of a larger venture, the Words Project. Below are descriptions of various Words Project experiments, along with opportunities for you to take part.

Using *Origins* as a Base for a Literacy Program

We used the materials of *Origins* as a base for a literacy program when we ran a pilot program for the Job Corps for twelve students, ages 19 to 21, who were reading at second- and third-grade levels. Celia Alvaraz, a linguist who now teaches at Columbia University, worked in partnership with me to plan and run the program.

We devised a weekly cycle of activities that included introducing a word family, generating and decoding other words based on spelling patterns of words in the family, playing card games to review and study these word groups and words of the families, and reading poetry (mostly by African-American poets, since the students were African-American) that used the imagery of the family. Finally, drawing on all the vocabulary that had become familiar during the week, students did their own writing. The cycle of the following week began as students read each other's writing, which we had typed up and copied over the weekend.

Despite initial resistance, the students got genuinely involved with the material. Exploring items of their own speech seized their attention and gave them a sense of connection with those who had coined the vocabulary of the word families. We started with the BHEL family. *Bold* vaulted them into competitive posing, and laughter and play-acting replaced their indifference. The playful spirit carried over into the more mundane activity of decoding words that shared spelling patterns with words of the family, and was reinforced by reviewing the patterns through card games, which students infused with their own sense of drama and panache. The poetry (such as Langston Hughes' "The Negro Speaks of Rivers") evoked a strong sense of connection; virtually every student wanted to struggle through what for them was the challenging vocabulary—which we reviewed ahead of time—to do his or her own reading of the poem. At every turn we praised success, helped out where needed, and ignored errors. Students picked up on our attitude and played by the ground rules of respecting and not criticizing each other—an attitude especially important when it came to their own writing. We presented writing as an opportunity, provided any help requested, and expressed confidence in their abilities. If a student simply copied a few lines of the poem—which was posted on the wall along with all the other vocabulary of the week—we said, "That's great. Can you add a few lines of your own?" Each week we added new vocabulary without taking down the old, so that students gradually became surrounded by a huge quantity of familiar vocabulary. Though students' first attempts were extremely rudimentary, we typed them all (correcting spelling but leaving the grammar natural to students' own speech), copied them, and invited students to read their own writing aloud for each other. The typed copies were greeted with "This looks like re*al* writing." Every student wanted to read—and they all continued to share their work each week as their efforts were greeted with appreciation.

The program lasted five weeks, and subsequent funding cuts eliminated any opportunity to try a longer program. In five weeks there were no significant changes in test results. We saw many significant changes in the students, however, which we felt would translate into test results over a longer span. One student, whose first efforts at writing produced "The ball is on the hill," wrote a story half a page long during the last week of the program—for him a real triumph. We saw a young woman who had produced a few modest and uninspired lines each week suddenly blossom into writing a jazz poem, which she read aloud with verve and rhythm. Students were playful with the words of the families, tossing them back and forth as they chatted around the edges of the class, and they made steady progress in mastering increasing numbers of words for spelling tests. Most important, they became serious about their own work, taking pride in what they produced. Their regular reading teacher, whose class they continued to attend, reported that the students' motivation and commitment to learning increased markedly in her class. We would be happy to send a copy of our full report on the project to anyone who is interested. Write to us at: The Words Project, 6404 Ridge Drive, Brookmont, MD 20816.

Inventing Stone Age Languages

At the Sidwell Friends School in Washington, D.C., Priscilla Alfandre has used *Origins* as a resource for having her third- and fourth-grade students invent their own primitive languages in conjunction with studying Neanderthal people. The challenge of giving a voice and a vocabulary to these ancient ancestors excited students and prompted them to think clearly and precisely about the experiences of Stone Age hunters and gatherers. Priscilla responded to the excitement by carrying the project through to a highly elaborated conclusion. After initial brainstorming as a group, students were divided into three "tribes," and each tribe invented and recorded the basic nouns and verbs they would need for everyday activities and communication. Each group had an adult working with it. In preparation for writing dialogues and stories in their tribal languages, students then went on to devise other words that were still needed. This was difficult and challenging work, requiring a clear understanding of language and history, an understanding Priscilla helped engender as she guided her students. Her vivid account tells how she and her students progressed toward making dictionaries and writing stories and a Neanderthal burial ceremony in their invented languages. We will be glad to send you a copy of her report.

Using *Origins* in French Class

At the Capitol Hill Day School in Washington, D.C., Ann Craig, a French teacher, has used the history of English as a resource for having seventh and eighth graders introduce fifth and sixth graders to French. Starting with the announcement, "This story is going to tell you what a difference was made in the English language by the victory of William the Conqueror," her seventh and eighth graders staged a replay of the Norman Conquest for their fifth/sixth grade audience. The actors had researched and developed the drama themselves. At the end of the play, an announcer brought out a list of French words that had almost identical counterparts in English, and the fifth and sixth graders enthusiastically identified the English counterparts. After this lively (and often humorous) introduction, the fifth/sixth grade classroom teacher continued to point out connections between French and English vocabulary as she prepared students for beginning a formal study of French. We will be glad to send you a report on this project.

Exploring Cross-Cultural Metaphors

Exploring cross-cultural metaphors is relatively new territory for us. So far, we have had time for initial research (conducted through interviews with native speakers), but not enough time for collecting an abundance of examples. We are continuing the research. We would be interested in hearing about work you have done with students in this area. For an update on our research and for information about participating, write to us.

A Final Word

Origins is in a state of continual evolution. Every time we assimilate new ideas and sketch new possibilities for using the material, we begin to see further possiblities for its use. We are interested to know how you are using the material and what questions and ideas you might have. We have done preliminary work on a future volume that would include the DRAGH- (to pull), GENE- (to give birth), PED- (foot), SED- (to sit), SKER- (to cut), and STA- (to stand) families listed in the "Additional Word Families Based on Indo-European Roots" section of the "Linguistic Background" chapter. In that future volume we would like to focus on the multitude of metaphors that spring from certain basic images— in the form of Latin words, in the form of Germanic words and phrases, and in metaphors drawn from other languages around the world. For example, there are many words and phrases built on the Germanic word for *stand* as well as many words (both Latinate and Germanic) built on the root STA (to stand). Are there also metaphors based on images of *standing* in languages wholly unrelated to English? Seems likely. We would like to explore such metaphors and imagery in poetry as well as in individual words, and we hope to draw the poetry from as many languages and cultures as possible. We would like to explore further the stylistic choices created by the many synonymous pairings of Latinate words and Germanic words or phrases that are found in English.

The volume would be geared toward junior high and high school levels and designed to be used as a resource in teaching literature and writing.

We would be interested in any suggestions, questions, samples of poetry, etc. that you might have. Write us at:

    The Words Project
    6404 Ridge Drive
    Brookmont, MD 20816.

(Sound cousins)